Spiritual Ark:

THE ENCHANTED JOURNEY
OF TIMELESS QUOTATIONS

To the Little Free Library
Enjoy reading!
With love,
Ann Marie Ruby

Ann Marie Ruby

DEDICATION

Dedication is an inspiration of the inspired. My life journey has been filled with blessings from the unknown, unseen strangers of life whom I call Angels in disguise. I had started to write as history leaves us with the gift of the past through words of wisdom. Even when all is but lost, words remain in the books of wisdom. I have woven my life and all my inspiration through words of wisdom.

I have collected a journal of enchanted words throughout history. History teaches us what is but in the pages of life. Throughout time, even when all is but lost, words remain forever through the blessed souls of humanity. Humans have created a bond with each other through the wonders of words written throughout history.

A person, a historian has had an impression, a positive imprint in my life from a faraway land. A teacher, a world leader, a very modest person has taught me to live my life to the fullest even without his knowledge.

My inspiration is a direct spiritual inspiration from a person I have never seen, known, or even knew about. He has been my inspiration through his dedication to serve this world in his own way. Sometimes, people inspire you for even the simplest things like riding a bicycle to work to save our Mother Earth. These small thoughts live on even past time and tide, as they have made a permanent house within my soul. I believe all humans carry humanity within themselves. I believe complete strangers, are but Angels in disguise. I believe within all there is good and all we have to do to find virtue within everyone is be good first. I believe to be in peace you must spread peace first. I have seen another person who lives across the globe from me who believes in all of these virtues. Like me, he too believes in one basic rule that unites all race, color, and religion, which is known as basic moral values.

I am honored once again to say this person was the sole reason and inspiration for my first book and so as I have gathered all my quotations into one soul, I again dedicate my woven book, my *Spiritual Ark: The Enchanted Journey Of Timeless Quotations*, to His Excellency, The Honorable Prime Minister Mark Rutte.

INTRODUCTION

Words throughout history have kept eternity in a bond through love, joy, and harmony. Words are the blessings of wisdom. Powerful words travel throughout time and make a place in history for themselves.

Throughout this blessed book, I have gathered words in my basket and woven them into blessed spiritual and inspirational quotations. Life is a journey filled with obstacles and blessings, but within life, we are blessed to have as our companion, the holy sounds we call words. I believe words can create and break a heart and the path she travels upon is made up by we the humans. Each and every day, we leave behind words from our soul. Some we throw out in anger and some we keep within the memories of love and peace. Always, as we leave them behind, we create history.

Today, I have created one book in which I have kept all of my original inspirational quotations from my previously published books. I have added some extra prayers, but I the dedicant have kept the original dedicatees for each individual book. I have taken out individual introductions and have made one introduction for this complete book of all my original, spiritual, and inspirational quotations. I have made this for all of you whom have wanted one complete collection within your hands. Yet, original, individual books still remain for all of you whom wish to pick up the individual ones. Spiritual inspiration has awakened all my love for all the creation of The Creator. May all my books be a bridge of union for all the creation of The Creator. Today within this love, from this love, and for this love, I am but uniting my four books of original inspirational quotations. I leave upon your door with all my blessings my, *Spiritual Ark: The Enchanted Journey Of Timeless Quotations.*

MESSAGE FROM THE AUTHOR

Come upon this ark and journey through these spiritual quotations. Now, they too have traveled throughout time and united upon this spiritual ark. From four different corners, traveled four books and today, they have come upon one path as one passenger throughout time.

May these inspirational quotations find solace within your spiritual soul as they travel throughout time. Open the doors to all of your spiritual souls and accept this friend who travels for peace and harmony.

Words travel throughout time and become words of wisdom. These spiritual quotations have taken birth to unite all humans with humanity, the basic moral value we the humans but live with and for.

Today, hand in hand, let us the travelers take this journey through time. I give you my complete collection of inspirational quotations, *Spiritual Ark: The Enchanted Journey Of Timeless Quotations*.

INVISIBLE HOLY ARK

My Lord, my Creator,

Within Your world, Your oceans, The Ark but is.

The Ark for the devotees

Invisibly swims the oceans all around the world.

She searches with her light and sound,

Searching for devotees.

She carries all the devotees one by one.

My Lord, my Creator,

May I, Your true devotee,

Be amongst one of the blessed to board upon this

INVISIBLE HOLY ARK.

*From my prayer book, *Spiritual Songs: Letters From My Chest*.

BOOK ONE

SPIRITUAL TRAVELERS

Life's Journey From The Past To The Present For The Future

Ann Marie Ruby

DEDICATION

With the windmills blowing in the air retelling stories from the past to the present awaiting the future generation, tulips blooming from beneath the Earth, Holland stands in my eyes as a holy land. As She brews race, religion, and color into one, She calls Herself Holland.

Dreams haunted me as they landed upon my door. There was a fisherman's village where I kept finding myself. I knew there was a flood somewhere and everything was flooded. Again, I saw myself at a different place, this time near a castle, which had a moat and a bridge. Never in my life had I heard of these stories nor had I wanted to look into them out of fear. What if my dreams came to reality? All these dreams stayed with me for years until one night a strange dream haunted again. This time, a person knocked on my door.

I asked him, *"Who are you?"*

He said, *"Oh I am Mark, Mark Rutte."*

I asked, *"I never met you?"*

He said, *"No."*

I asked, *"You are a president?"*

He said, *"Yes, you can call me that. I am a Prime Minister."*

I said, *"Oh you are Tony Blair, Prime Minister Tony Blair?"*

He laughed and said, *"No. That was a few years ago. I am Mark Rutte and I work for the..."*

I stopped him and said, "*You work for the Queen.*"

He said, "*I used to, but now I work for the King. Prime Minister Mark Rutte.*"

As I woke up from this dream, I knew it was a knock on my door. For the first time without fear, I looked into my dreams and did the research. I got the biggest shock. I felt feverish as in front of me on the computer there was Prime Minister Mark Rutte from the Netherlands. History showed me there were floods in the Netherlands. There is a place called the fisherman's village. There is a port in Rotterdam which was a shock because I saw in another dream I live in the sister port city of the country that haunts me in my dreams. I live in Seattle, and the sister port city is Rotterdam in the Netherlands. I don't know how I ended up here, but I know I was there in my dreams.

Maybe one day, life will tell me how. In the meantime, I found this leader whom I have never met. Through my research, I was inspired by his quotes and the remarkable way he lives his life. Don't fear the past. Don't let fear knock you out. He teaches as he is a teacher and a historian. Without him knowing, he has taught me a lot.

I had always thought life is a circle. But, I learned he believes life is not a circle. He believes you complete the circle. As I kept reading about him, I understood what an honorable man he is. He believes in history as a lesson and guidance, but you create your own path. You create your own history. He teaches all humans should have equal rights. This historian goes and sits with Muslims, walks with Hindu and Jewish leaders, visits the Pope, and still believes all people regardless of their faith, religion, or race, deserve the right. All this time, I realized despite living in this century, I am an old soul and my dreams guided me to another who lives like an old soul.

Life is simple. Give the gift of kindness. Try to give and even though your gift might not be appreciated, in time, the future generation will be guided through your gift. I live not to be appreciated, but my soul wants to see the future generation being guided through my words.

Words are my soul and the wisdom I live for. Mahatma Gandhi inspired me from the past and Prime Minister Mark Rutte inspires me from the present. I know with time, all of this shall again be the past, but I wanted to frame my thoughts, my words of inspiration into a book. I began writing my thoughts for others who have been knocked out or those who need just a word or line to get back up and complete the journey they were born to take, for each one of us has a reason to be born.

Sometimes, we feel we have no reason to be here or get up in the morning, see the sun rising, or the sun setting for we let our depression take over. But, word of advice from one who has been there, there is tomorrow. For me, there is always today. Until today is over, I keep on living for one day I shall be history. But, I want my words to be there for you as a great man's word started my journey and gave me hope to continue the journey of my life.

My life journey is a wagon filled with struggles from all aspects of life. I take all of these as a traveler's journey of endurance. Life brings along this path inspiration from all different corners. My corner was an amazing grace from The Holy Spirit. Through my dreams, I was guided by The Holy Spirit and that path brought me to a stranger, a leader of a small European country known very well for his own journey and simple ways of life.

Sometimes in life, a person leaves a great imprint on one's soul, even though you may have never met. In my life, this person was Prime Minister Mark Rutte, who without knowing inspired this old soul.

From his inspiration, I find inspiration for all of you. I never met him personally, but I feel I know him through simplicity and his wisdom. From a faraway land, he has inspired this unknown person and may I an unknown person inspire you.

I call this book, *Spiritual Travelers: Life's Journey From The Past To The Present For The Future.*

Mark Rutte, The Historian, The Teacher, was my inspiration and for this, I dedicate this book to His Excellency Mark Rutte, Prime Minister of the Netherlands.

THE TRAVELERS

I the traveler walk upon my journey.

The heated sun burns, blazing my skin.

The cold shivering chills of the freezing nights

Blister my skin.

I still am glad for I know this pain is nothing

For I have the glad tidings of my Lord

On This Path.

This Path, The Path to Heaven is all I want.

I see many travelers on the journey

Whom I bump into along the way.

Busy they are with the pleasures of life.

Women and men find comfort in each other,

Hiding from the cold nights as a one night stand.

People missing work for

They want to escape the blazing sun.

Escape you may today from the fire and cold,

But tomorrow at The Lord's House,

You shall burn and freeze eternally.

I teach them my Lord along the way,

Give glad tidings to your Lord and walk upon

His Road even though hard it may seem.

For this hardworking Road

Will take you to The Eternal Peace.

On The Road of The Lord,

You will find your true blessings.

These blessings may come hard,

But will take us to our Final Destiny.

The traveler I am, seeking to please my Lord.

Sacrifice I commit is but all my love for my Lord.

No sacrifice is but a sacrifice

For my Lord has a House ready upon my arrival,

Where no fire shall burn me,

Nor cold shall touch me,

Nor any misery shall befall.

For my Lord has The House ready

For those of us whom make the journey,

THE TRAVELERS.

*From my prayer book, *Spiritual Songs: Letters From My Chest*.

A DAY IN MY LIFE:
Ann Marie
Back From Heaven

Seattle is a city full of life where strangers say, "Hello," walk, and smile as if we are the best of friends, helping hands all around, never a dull moment. I had a strange encounter with a stranger, who had stopped and just said, "So Ann Marie, how does it feel to be back from Heaven?" I was shocked how he knew my name, not in his question.

I walked past him without uttering a word, but the words stayed with me. I believe in reincarnation and that life is a circle, but also believe this life has been given so we complete the circle, not let the circle complete us. Change what has been wronged and not be wronged. Some words linger on and just stay with you forever, for me these words of a stranger.

Words said are gone like the winds of time and tide. May we not throw out whatever comes to our mind, but always be of a helping hand, through our words and actions. Words are the prayers I live for. Words are the most powerful tool we were gifted with. Use them wisely as even with time, life becomes history, but words remain forever.

So, I give you words from my heart to yours, my inspirational quotations.

SEVEN DAYS OF INSPIRATION

Monday brings all creation back to reality, after all, life goes on.

Tuesday is for you and me as we all complete this journal of life.

Wednesday is hope giving day for all humans to stay involved with positivity.

Thursday is for all of whom are seeking the knowledge of guidance.

Friday the nights are always darker, but dawn is around the corner.

Saturday on this day let us give back to nature what she gives us without being asked.

Sunday even for one day and one night, may we the creation remember The Lord, as The Lord watches over us for eternity.

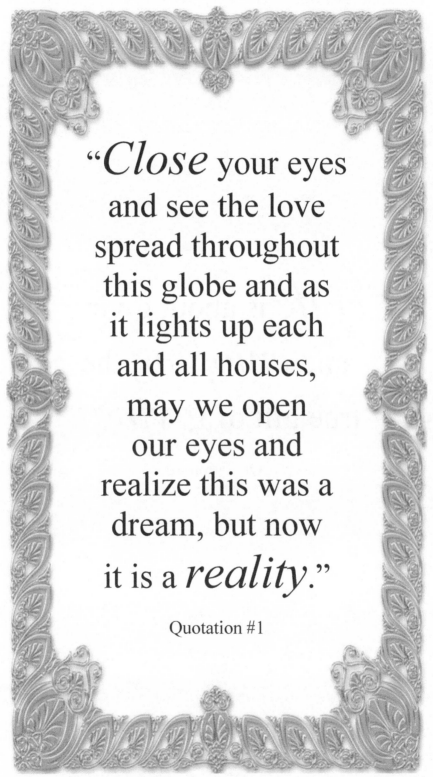

"*Close* your eyes and see the love spread throughout this globe and as it lights up each and all houses, may we open our eyes and realize this was a dream, but now it is a *reality*."

Quotation #1

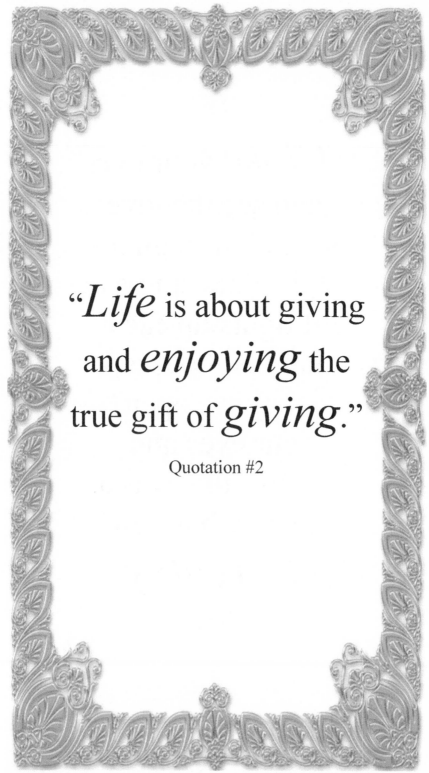

"*Life* is about giving
and *enjoying* the
true gift of *giving*."

Quotation #2

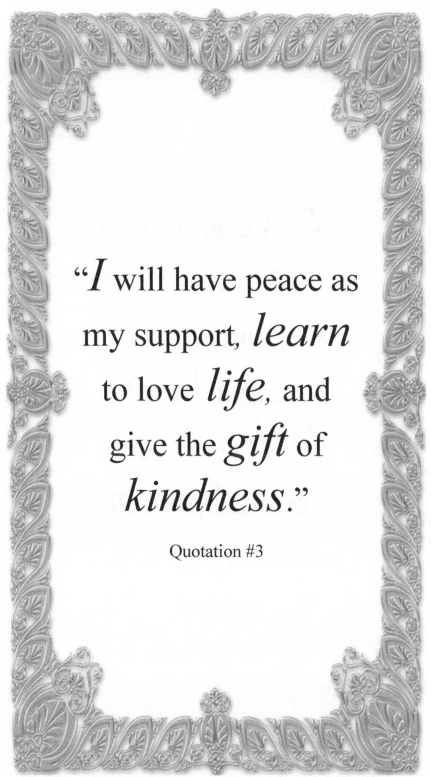

"*I* will have peace as my support, *learn* to love *life*, and give the *gift* of *kindness*."

Quotation #3

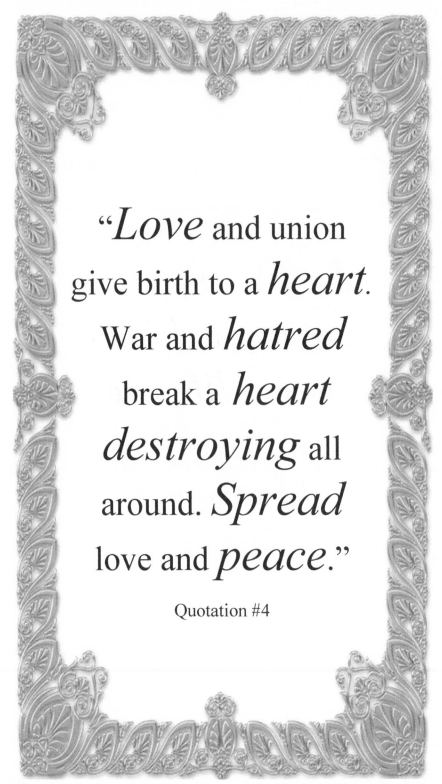

"*Love* and union give birth to a *heart*. War and *hatred* break a *heart destroying* all around. *Spread* love and *peace*."

Quotation #4

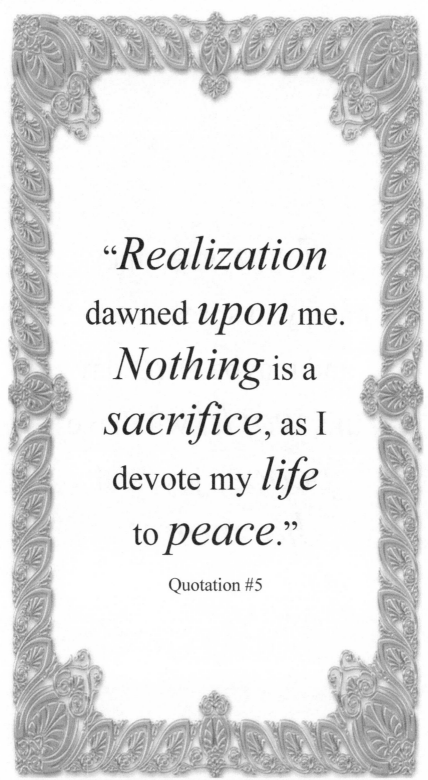

"*Realization* dawned *upon* me. *Nothing* is a *sacrifice*, as I devote my *life* to *peace*."

Quotation #5

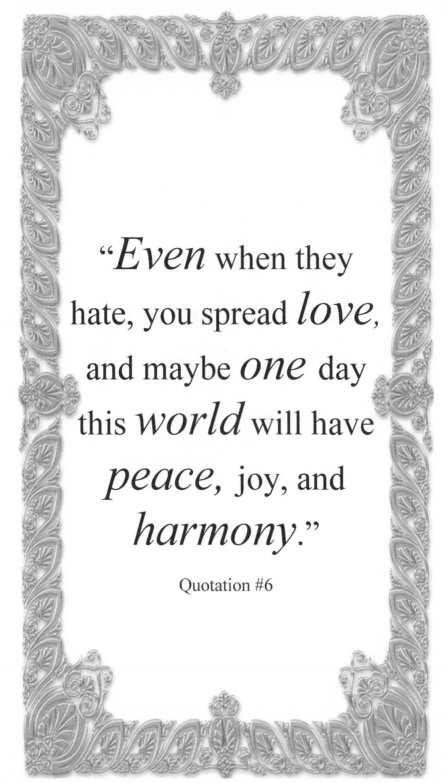

"*Even* when they hate, you spread *love*, and maybe *one* day this *world* will have *peace*, joy, and *harmony*."

Quotation #6

"*I* struggled to stand up for *myself* first, *for* I know it is *then* I can stand up for *you*. Each blessed day I learn to *be* there for *myself* first as that is the *only* way I *can* be there for you *too*."

Quotation #7

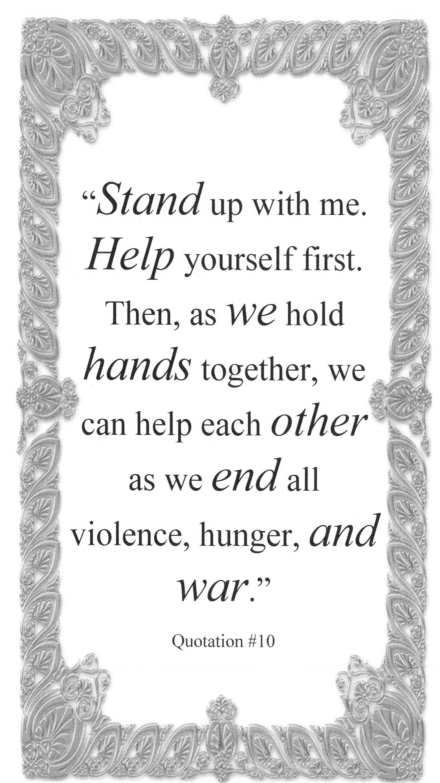

"*Stand* up with me. *Help* yourself first. Then, as *we* hold *hands* together, we can help each *other* as we *end* all violence, hunger, *and* *war*."

Quotation #10

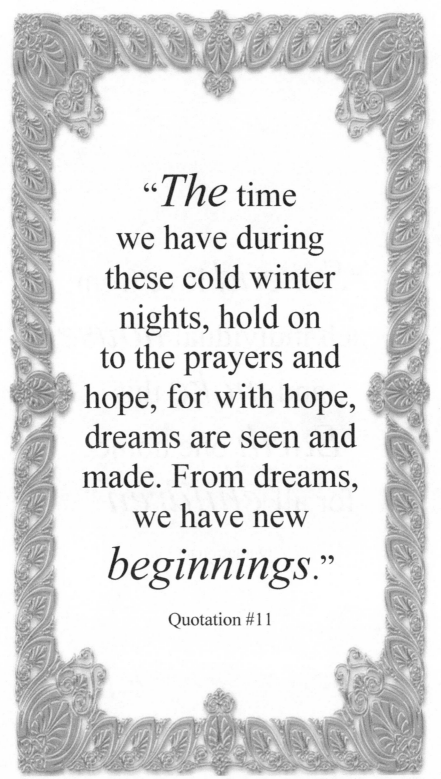

"*The* time
we have during
these cold winter
nights, hold on
to the prayers and
hope, for with hope,
dreams are seen and
made. From dreams,
we have new
beginnings."

Quotation #11

"*Spread* love from each individual *house* and *make* this *Earth* one home for all *children.*"

Quotation #12

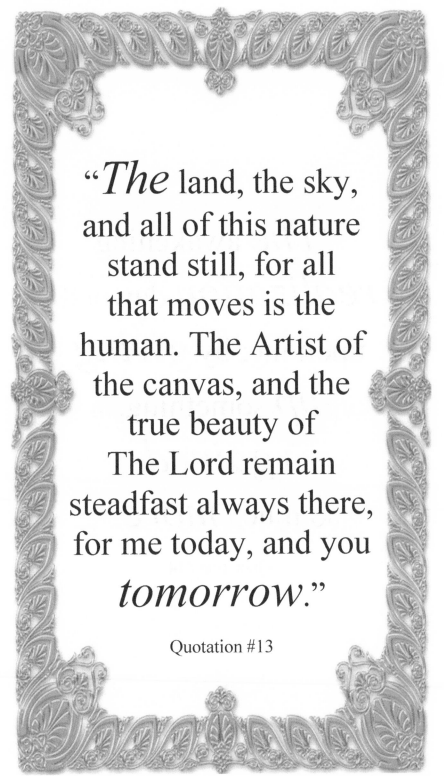

"*The* land, the sky, and all of this nature stand still, for all that moves is the human. The Artist of the canvas, and the true beauty of The Lord remain steadfast always there, for me today, and you *tomorrow*."

Quotation #13

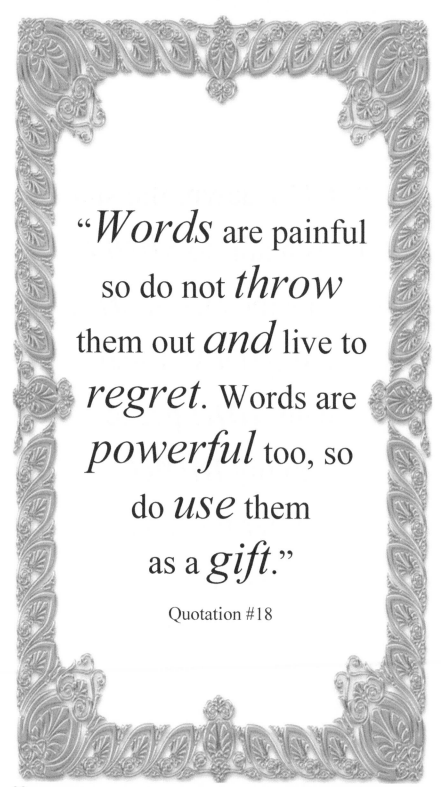

"*Words* are painful
so do not *throw*
them out *and* live to
regret. Words are
powerful too, so
do *use* them
as a *gift*."

Quotation #18

"*It* is true storms come,
but it is also *true* that
they *disappear*
as *well*."

Quotation #19

"*Racism* is an *infectious* disease that *spreads* throughout the *lands*. These *days*, it is *infecting* even those of whom *we* *thought* to be *immune*."

Quotation #24

34

"*Dreams* are a form of *guidance* from The *Lord*."

Quotation #25

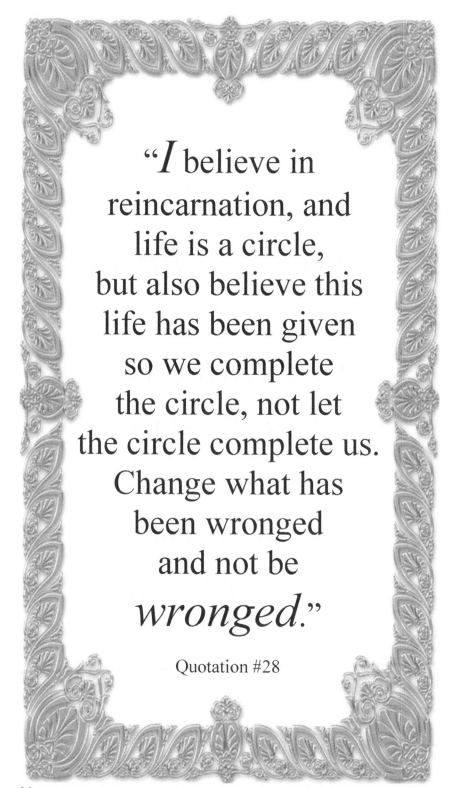

"*I* believe in
reincarnation, and
life is a circle,
but also believe this
life has been given
so we complete
the circle, not let
the circle complete us.
Change what has
been wronged
and not be
wronged."

Quotation #28

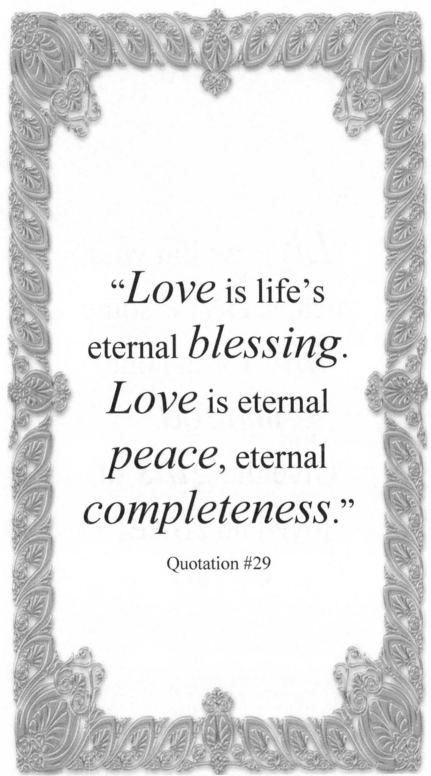

"*Love* is life's
eternal *blessing*.
Love is eternal
peace, eternal
completeness."

Quotation #29

"*Live* within your
means. *Save* some
time for the ones
in *need*.
Give the *gifts* of
love and *time*."

Quotation #30

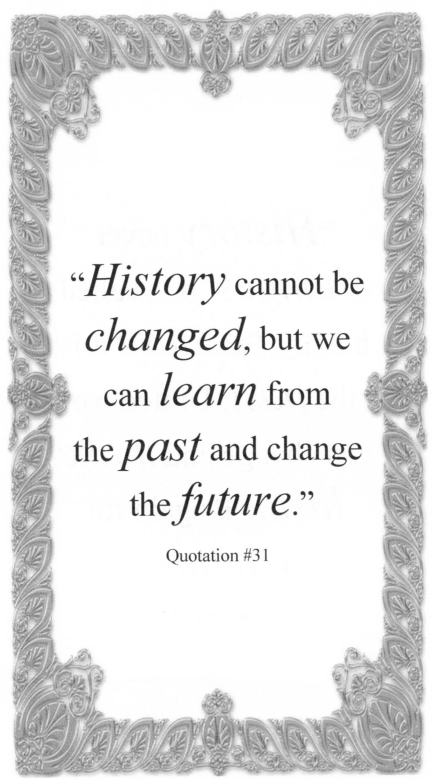

"*History* cannot be *changed*, but we can *learn* from the *past* and change the *future*."

Quotation #31

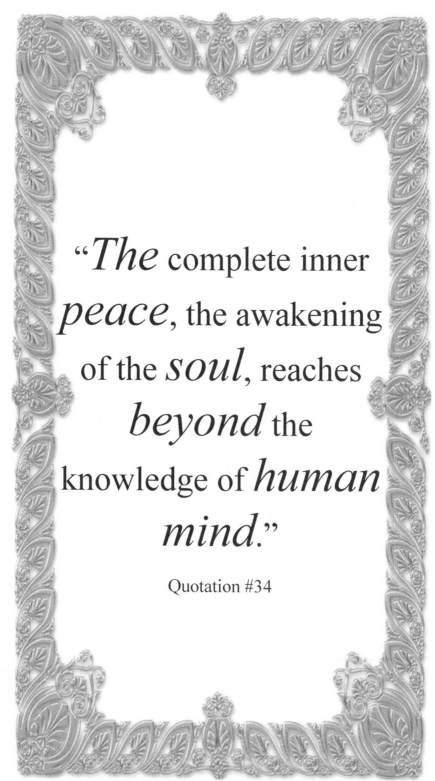

"*The* complete inner *peace*, the awakening of the *soul*, reaches *beyond* the knowledge of *human mind*."

Quotation #34

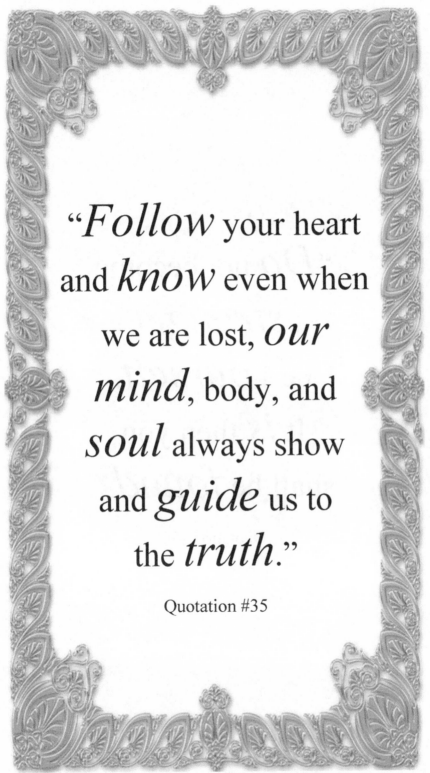

"*Follow* your heart and *know* even when we are lost, *our mind*, body, and *soul* always show and *guide* us to the *truth*."

Quotation #35

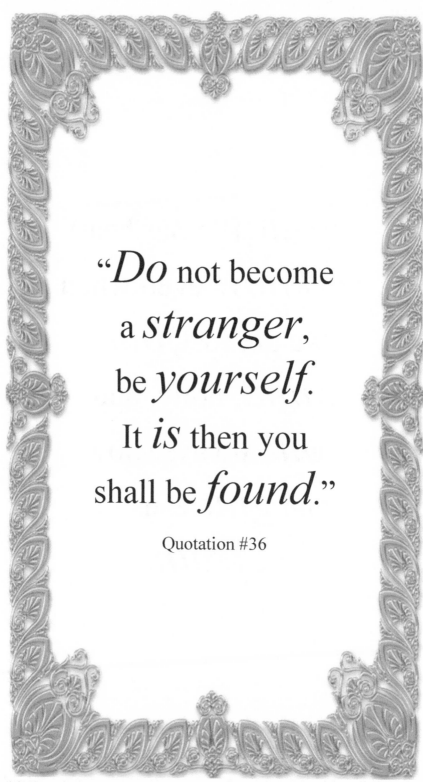

"*Do* not become
a *stranger*,
be *yourself.*
It *is* then you
shall be *found.*"

Quotation #36

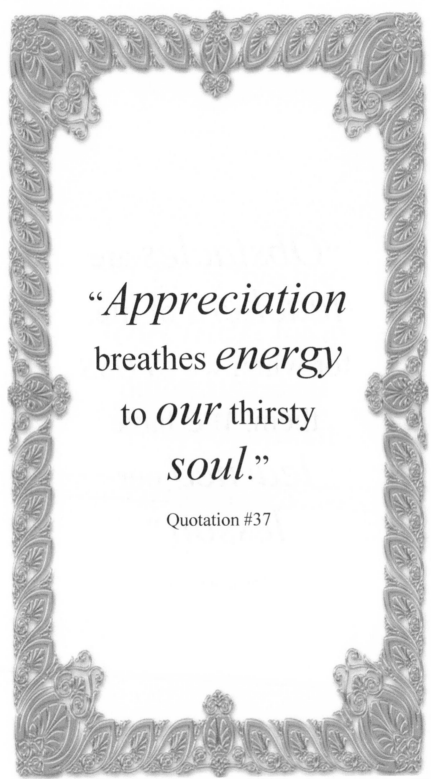

"*Appreciation* breathes *energy* to *our* thirsty *soul*."

Quotation #37

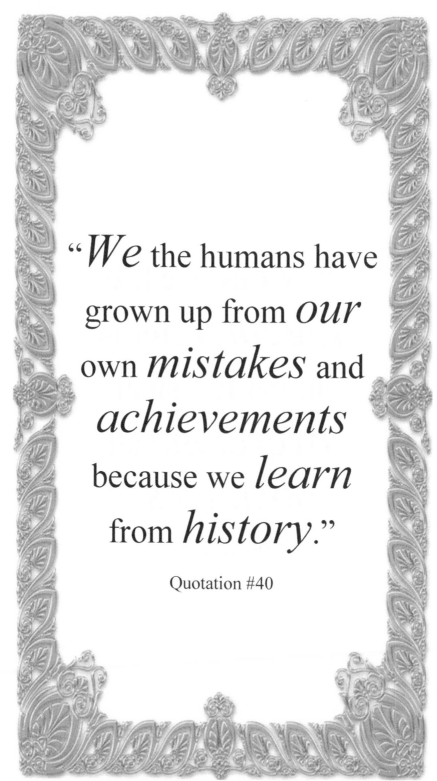

"*We* the humans have grown up from *our* own *mistakes* and *achievements* because we *learn* from *history.*"

Quotation #40

"*Remember* in every corner we *have* a *friend*, a *helping* hand whom *we* call *strangers*. I call them my *Angels*."

Quotation #41

"*A* mother sees all *children* with the same *love*. A father *welcomes* all *children* with the same *heart*. I *love* all *humans* with my *soul*."

Quotation #42

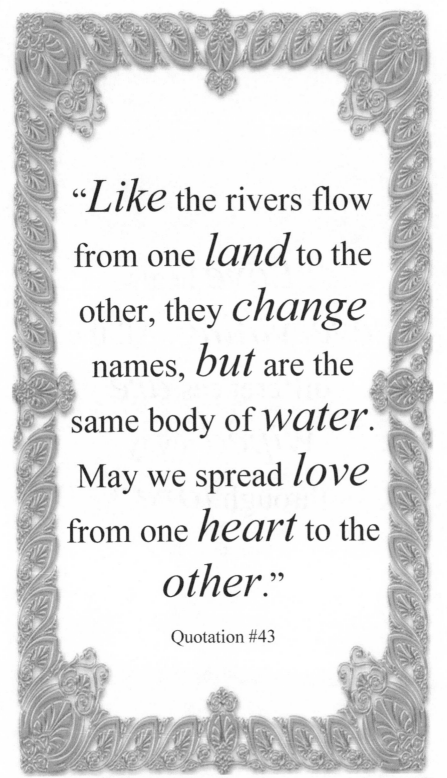

"*Like* the rivers flow from one *land* to the other, they *change* names, *but* are the same body of *water*. May we spread *love* from one *heart* to the *other*."

Quotation #43

"*Love* heals
everything. All the
differences *are*
wiped away
through *love*."

Quotation #44

"*As* the days pass by, we know we *can* never *stop* time or tide, but we have *this* day, this *time*, so *today* *love* all of this around *us*."

Quotation #45

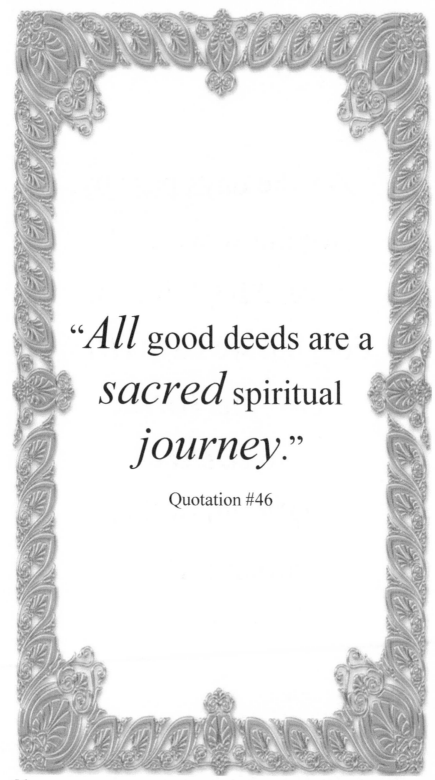

"*All* good deeds are a *sacred* spiritual *journey.*"

Quotation #46

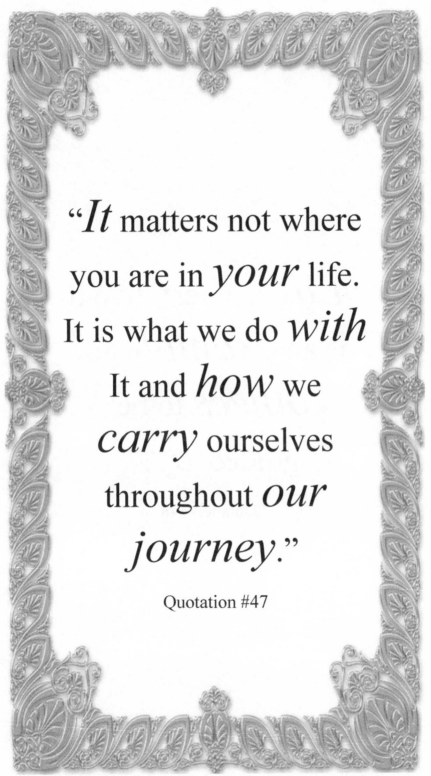

"*It* matters not where you are in *your* life. It is what we do *with* It and *how* we *carry* ourselves throughout *our* *journey*."

Quotation #47

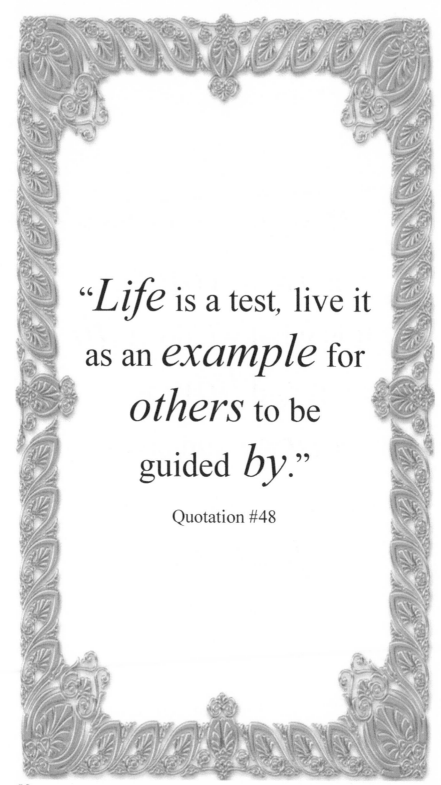

"*Life* is a test, live it as an *example* for *others* to be guided *by*."

Quotation #48

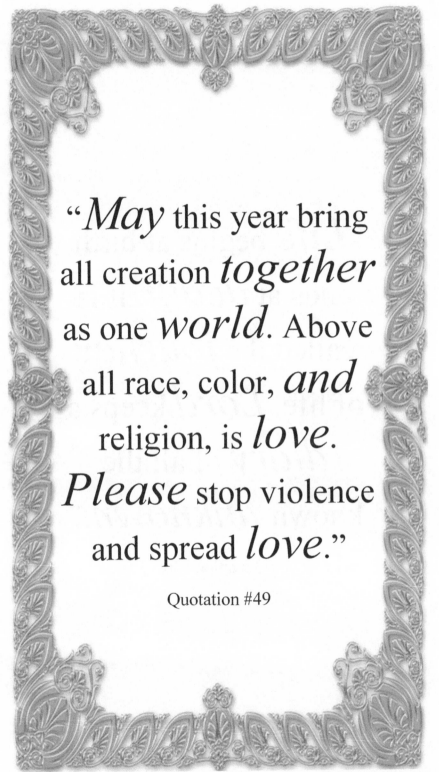

"*May* this year bring all creation *together* as one *world*. Above all race, color, *and* religion, is *love*. *Please* stop violence and spread *love*."

Quotation #49

"*Life* begins at birth, ends at *death*. It is called the *journey* of life. *Lord* keeps a *diary* of all the known *unknown*."

Quotation #50

"*Where* is the love?
In our *soul* is the
love. We spread it
one by *one.*"

Quotation #51

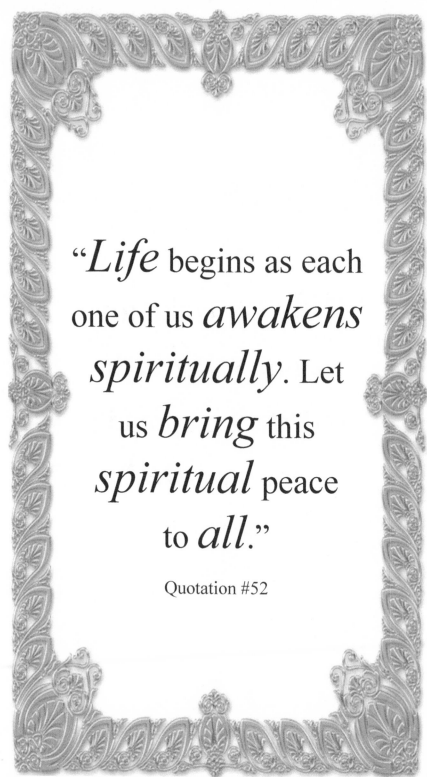

"*Life* begins as each
one of us *awakens*
spiritually. Let
us *bring* this
spiritual peace
to *all*."

Quotation #52

"*May* the children create a *merciful bridge* of rainbow across all *lands* and unite all *humans*."

Quotation #53

"*Mother* Earth holds
on to *all* the memories
as they are *lost*
and *found*
throughout *time*."

Quotation #54

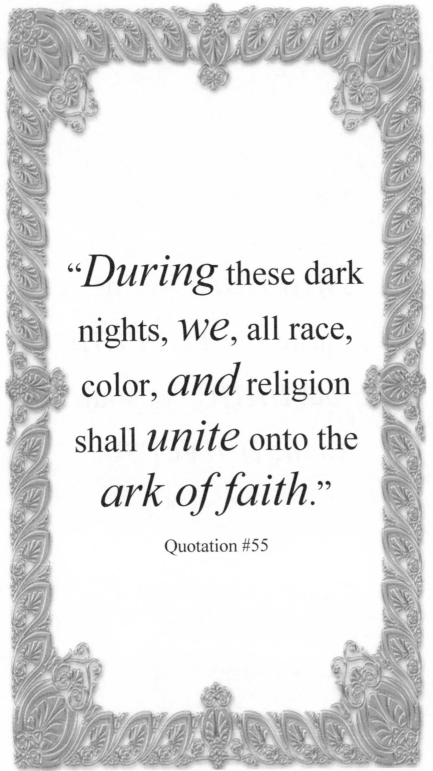

"*During* these dark nights, *we*, all race, color, *and* religion shall *unite* onto the *ark of faith.*"

Quotation #55

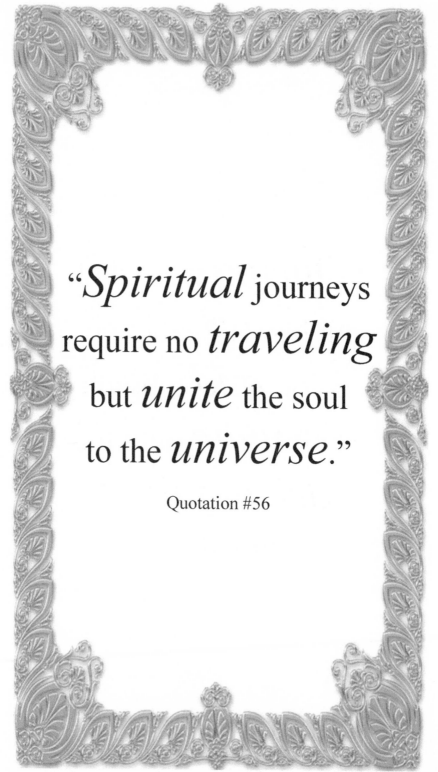

"*Spiritual* journeys
require no *traveling*
but *unite* the soul
to the *universe*."

Quotation #56

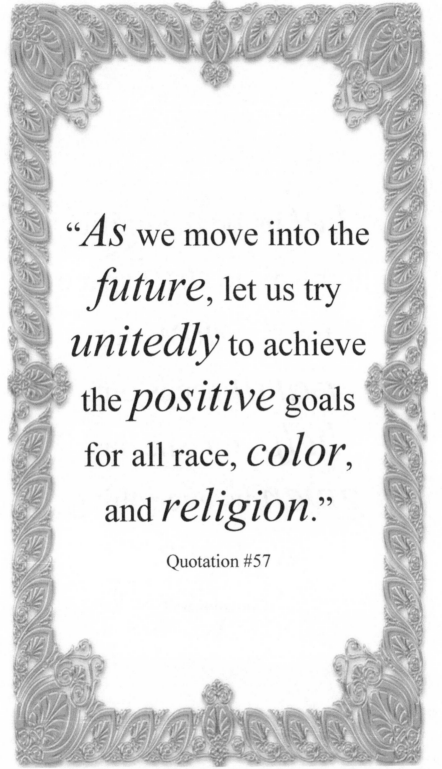

"*As* we move into the *future*, let us try *unitedly* to achieve the *positive* goals for all race, *color*, and *religion*."

Quotation #57

"*Let* us be the unifier in this time *and* space for it is *now* our *Earth* needs our *help*, for She has *given* us everything we *have*."

Quotation #58

"*We* have this
day. As it has arrived
at our door, it may
leave joy, sorrow, or
pain at our doorstep.
We know tomorrow
is peeking through
the dark night's sky.
As dawn breaks
through, we shall
have daylight
again."

Quotation #59

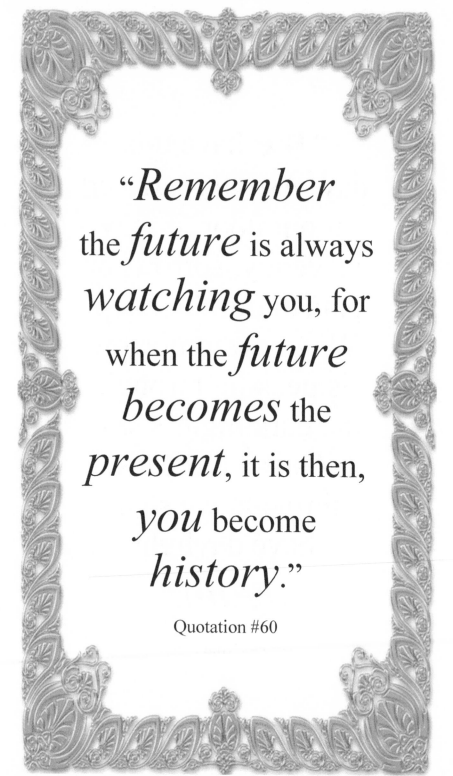

"*Remember* the *future* is always *watching* you, for when the *future* *becomes* the *present*, it is then, *you* become *history*."

Quotation #60

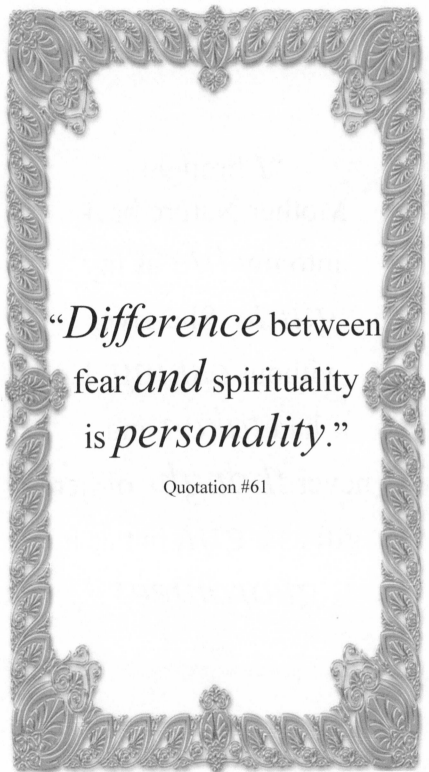

"*Difference* between fear *and* spirituality is *personality*."

Quotation #61

"*I* brought Mother Nature back into my *life* as my *guide*. She gives without *asking*. I had *taken* and never *thought* of her gift as a *gift*, but as a *guarantee*."

Quotation #62

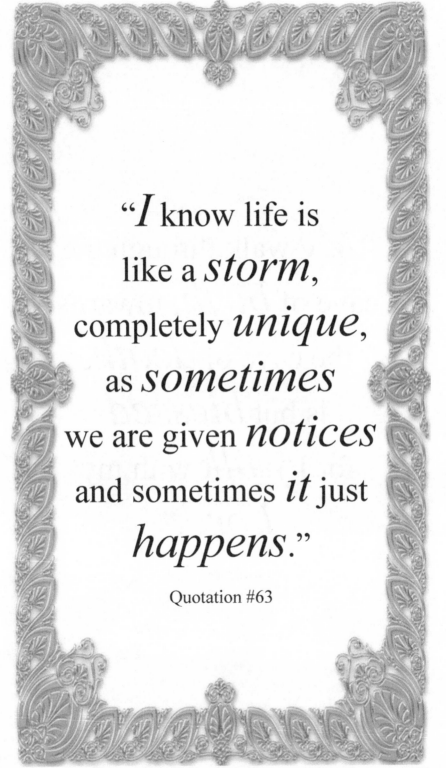

"*I* know life is
like a *storm*,
completely *unique*,
as *sometimes*
we are given *notices*
and sometimes *it* just
happens."

Quotation #63

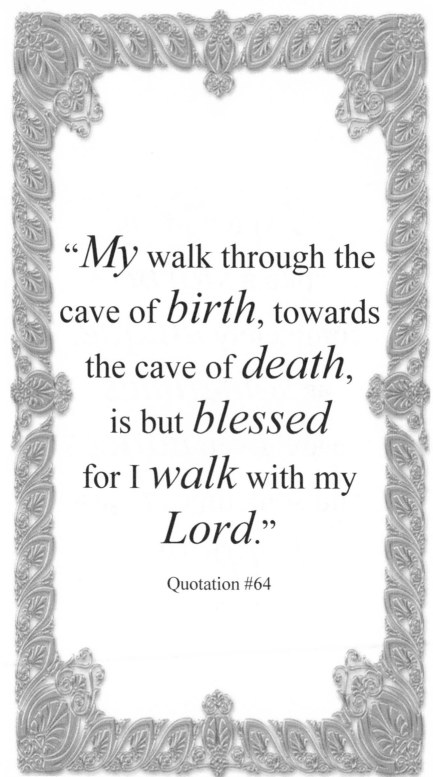

"*My* walk through the cave of *birth*, towards the cave of *death*, is but *blessed* for I *walk* with my *Lord*."

Quotation #64

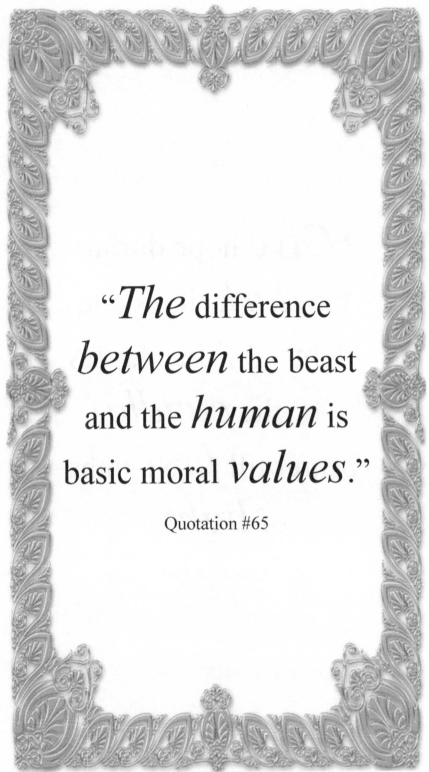

"*The* difference
between the beast
and the *human* is
basic moral *values*."

Quotation #65

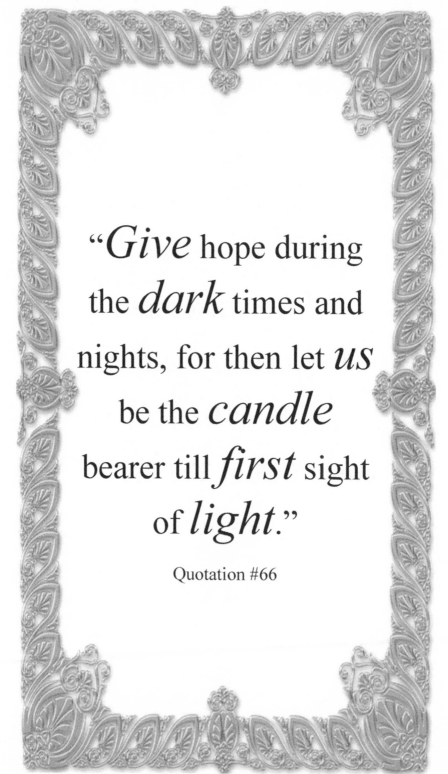

"*Give* hope during the *dark* times and nights, for then let *us* be the *candle* bearer till *first* sight of *light*."

Quotation #66

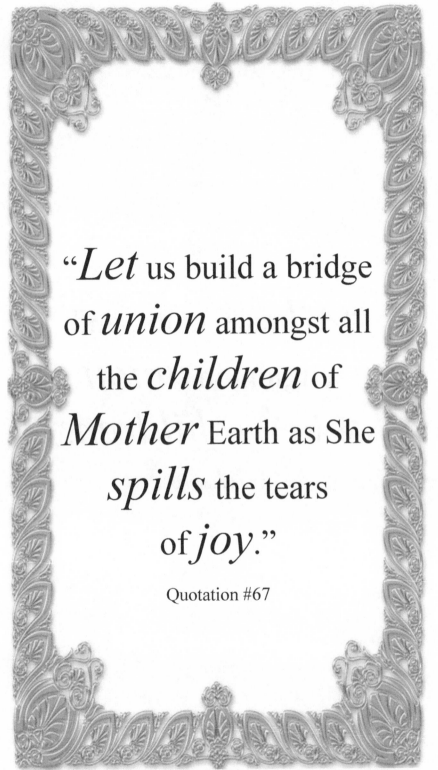

"*Let* us build a bridge
of *union* amongst all
the *children* of
Mother Earth as She
spills the tears
of *joy*."

Quotation #67

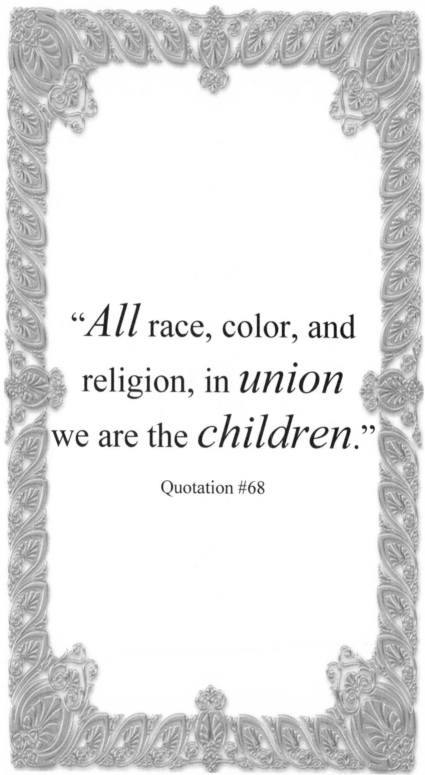

"*All* race, color, and religion, in *union* we are the *children*."

Quotation #68

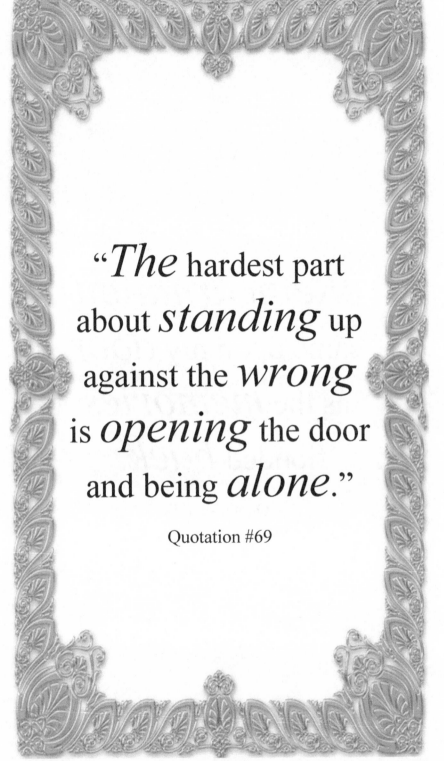

"*The* hardest part about *standing* up against the *wrong* is *opening* the door and being *alone*."

Quotation #69

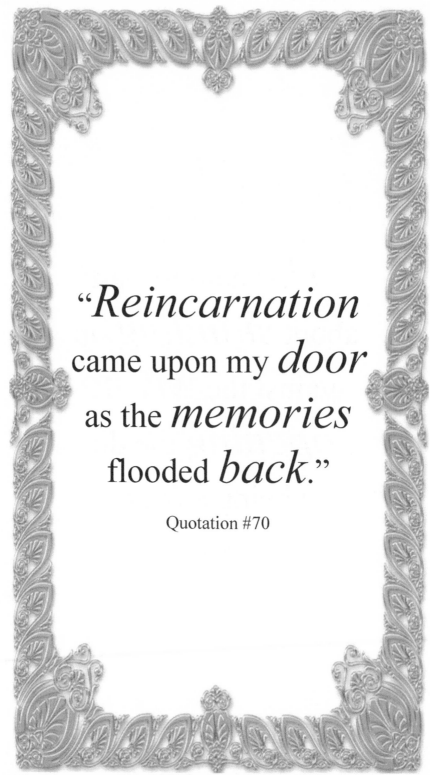

"*Reincarnation*
came upon my *door*
as the *memories*
flooded *back*."

Quotation #70

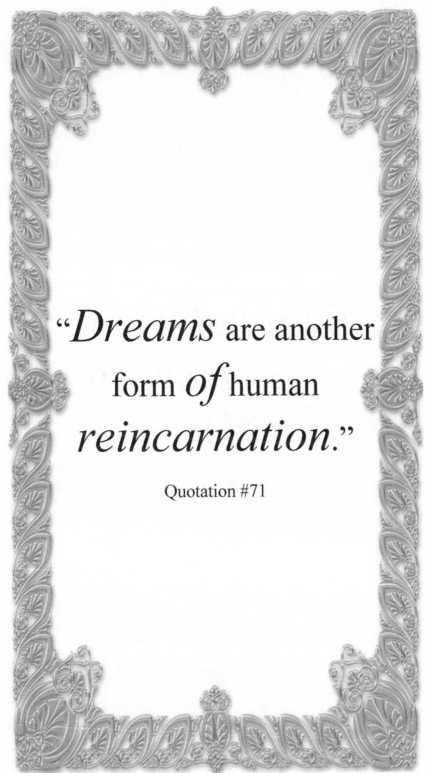

"*Dreams* are another form *of* human *reincarnation.*"

Quotation #71

"*Through* dreams,
we get *Heavenly*
guidance."

Quotation #72

"*The* Angels of The *Lord* pick us up as we *fall* and place us back on *track*."

Quotation #73

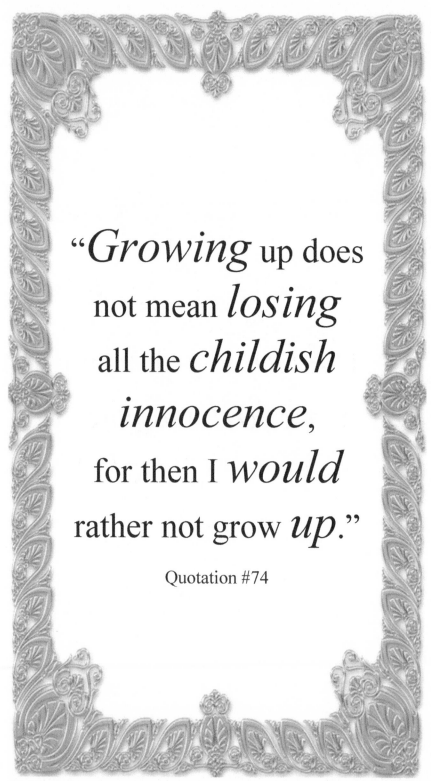

"*Growing* up does not mean *losing* all the *childish innocence*, for then I *would* rather not grow *up*."

Quotation #74

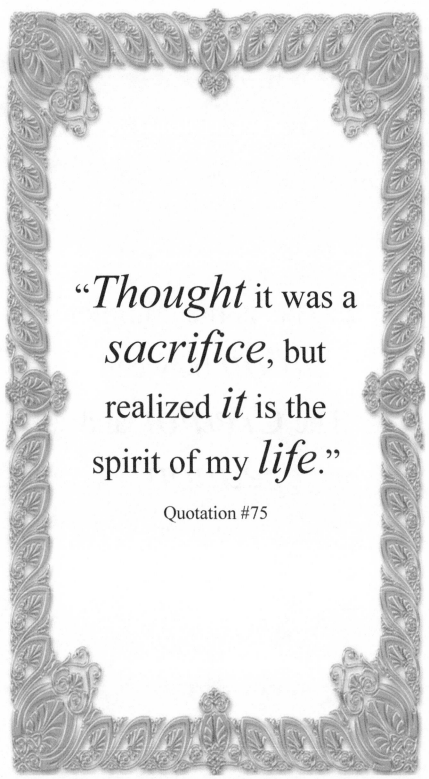

"*Thought* it was a *sacrifice*, but realized *it* is the spirit of my *life*."

Quotation #75

"*Love* is the complete *union* between The *Creator* and *creation*."

Quotation #76

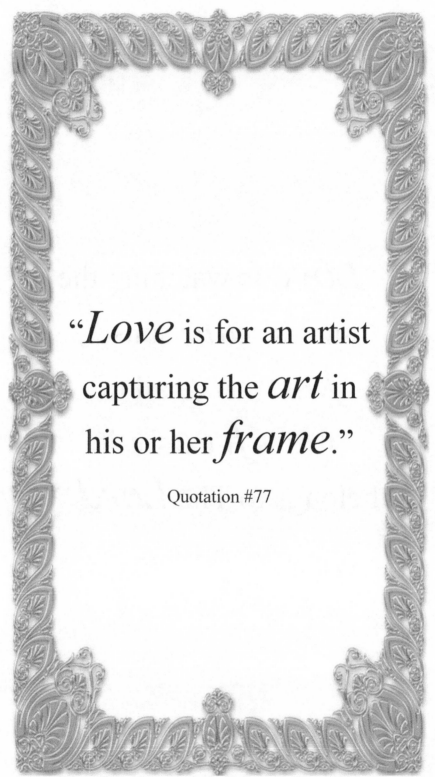

"*Love* is for an artist capturing the *art* in his or her *frame*."

Quotation #77

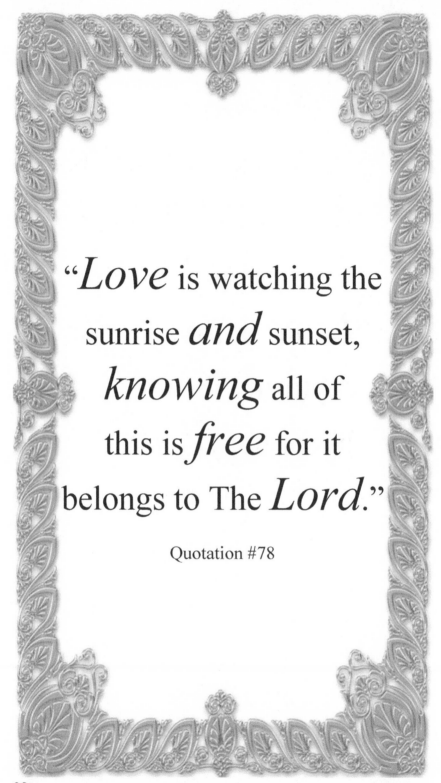

"*Love* is watching the
sunrise *and* sunset,
knowing all of
this is *free* for it
belongs to The *Lord*."

Quotation #78

"*Life* is a gift from God. Let us *share* this *gift* with all through *kindness*, love, and *joy*."

Quotation #79

"*Please* say a prayer, *asked* an elderly *mother*, a newlywed, and a *new* mother, as *I* went for a short morning *walk*."

Quotation #80

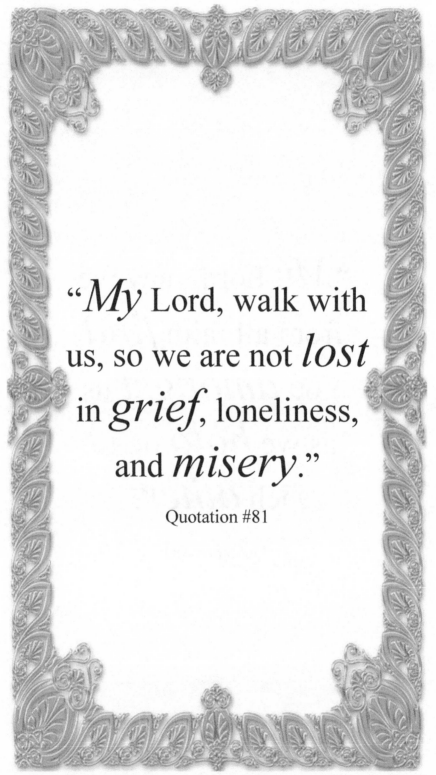

"*My* Lord, walk with us, so we are not *lost* in *grief*, loneliness, and *misery*."

Quotation #81

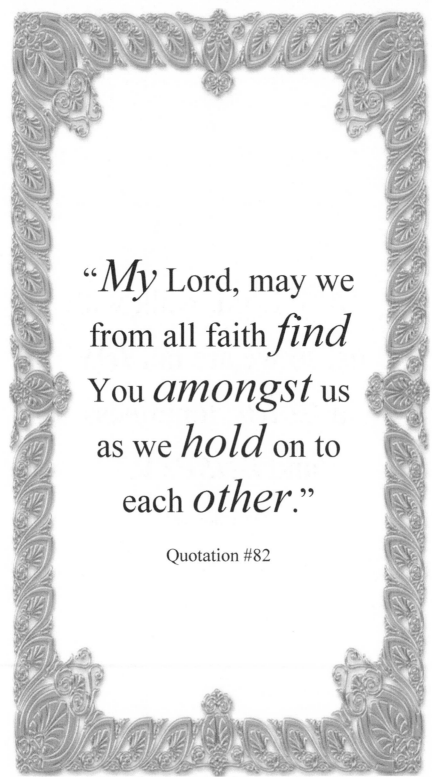

"*My* Lord, may we from all faith *find* You *amongst* us as we *hold* on to each *other*."

Quotation #82

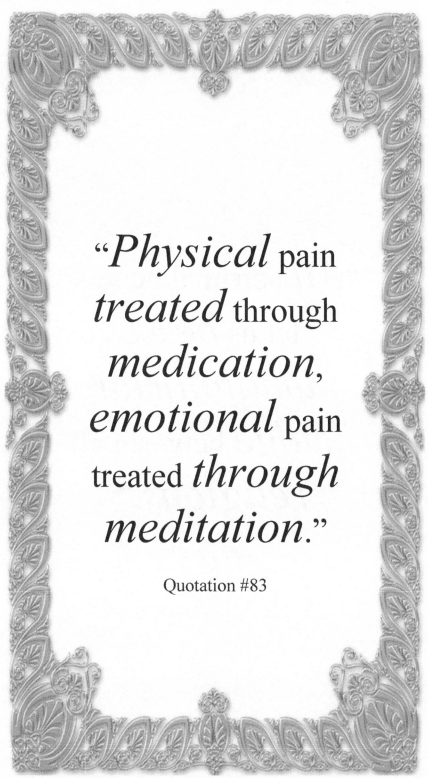

"*Physical* pain *treated* through *medication,* *emotional* pain treated *through meditation.*"

Quotation #83

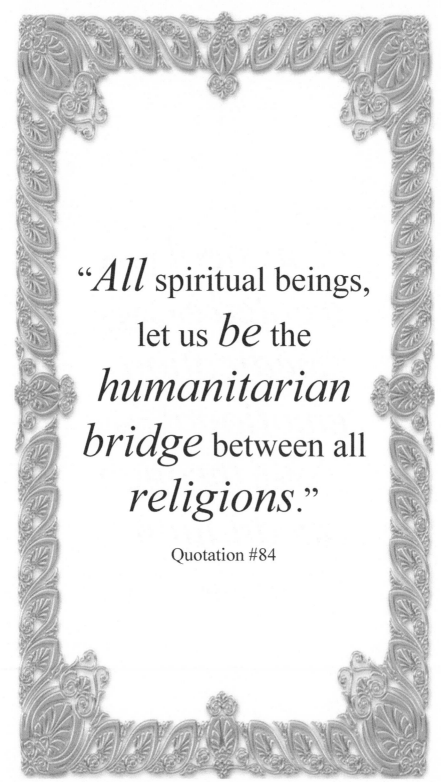

"*All* spiritual beings, let us *be* the *humanitarian bridge* between all *religions.*"

Quotation #84

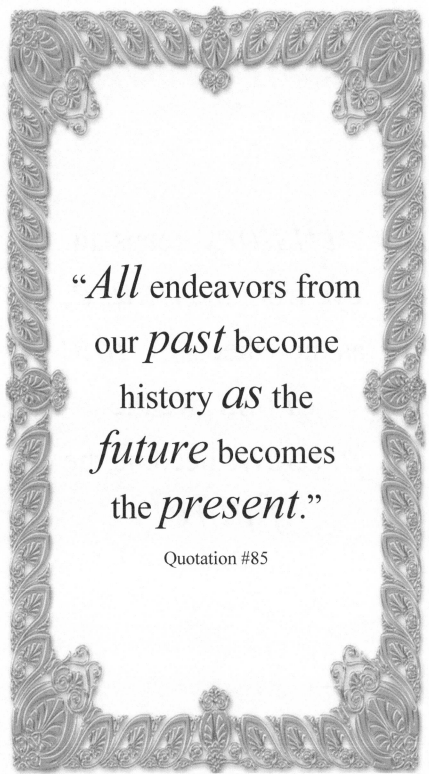

"*All* endeavors from our *past* become history *as* the *future* becomes the *present*."

Quotation #85

"*History* keeps an eye from the *future,* as the wheels of *time cross*, we the *present* become the *future*."

Quotation #86

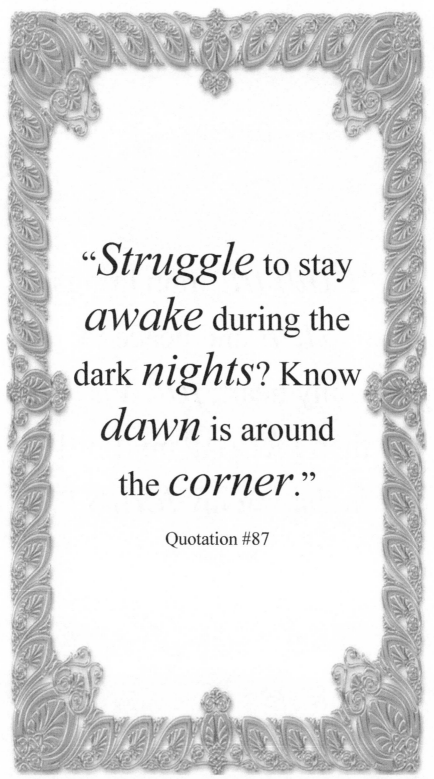

"*Struggle* to stay *awake* during the dark *nights*? Know *dawn* is around the *corner*."

Quotation #87

"*Pouring* rain brings *calm* and peace to my heart, *for* it is then I *know* my Lord is sharing my *tears*."

Quotation #88

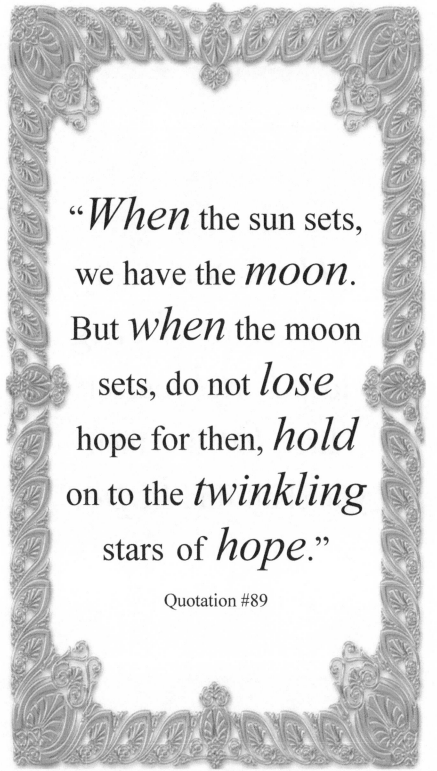

"*When* the sun sets, we have the *moon*. But *when* the moon sets, do not *lose* hope for then, *hold* on to the *twinkling* stars of *hope*."

Quotation #89

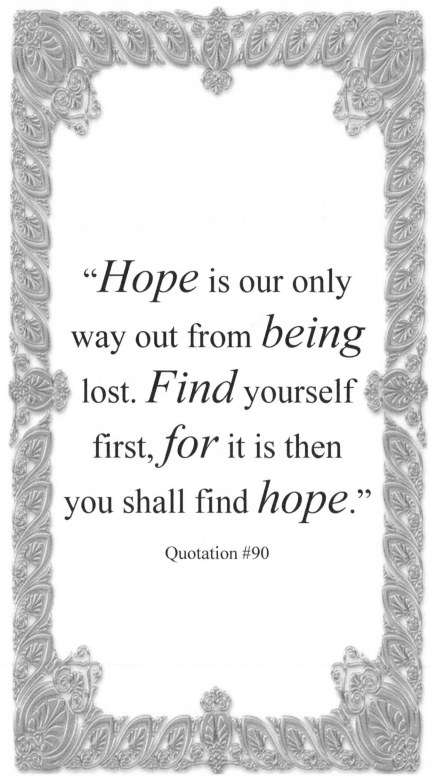

"*Hope* is our only way out from *being* lost. *Find* yourself first, *for* it is then you shall find *hope*."

Quotation #90

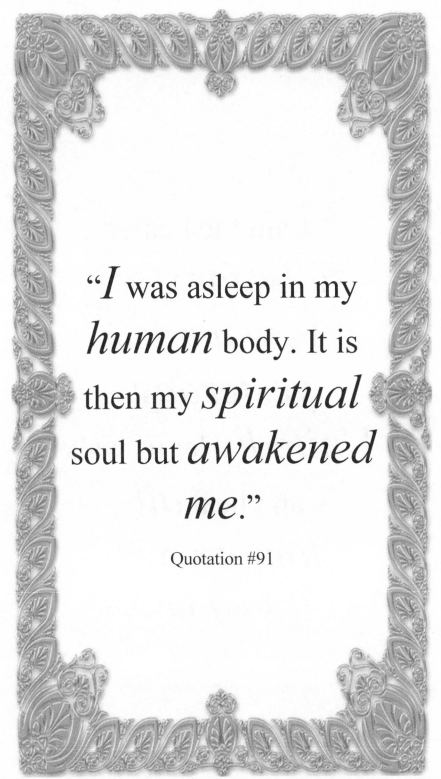

"*I* was asleep in my *human* body. It is then my *spiritual* soul but *awakened me*."

Quotation #91

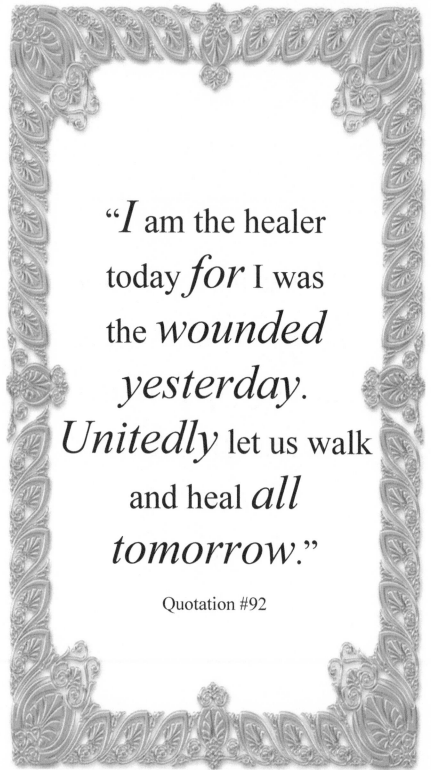

"*I* am the healer today *for* I was the *wounded yesterday*. *Unitedly* let us walk and heal *all tomorrow*."

Quotation #92

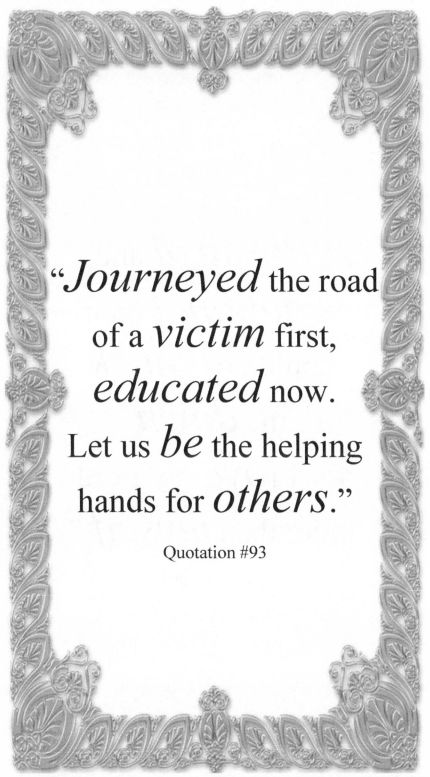

"*Journeyed* the road of a *victim* first, *educated* now. Let us *be* the helping hands for *others*."

Quotation #93

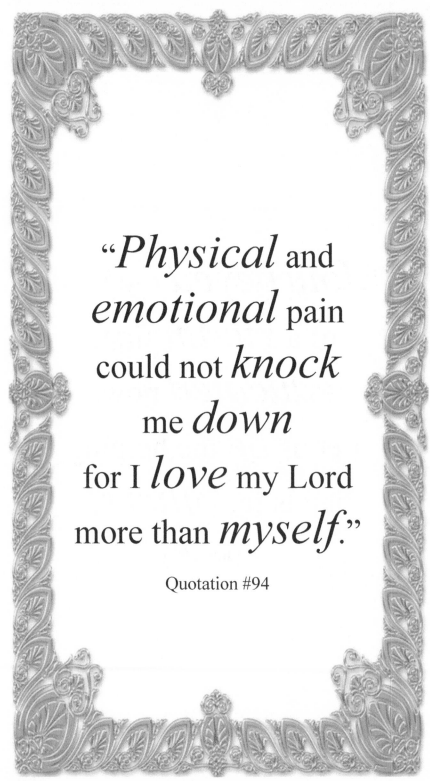

"*Physical* and *emotional* pain could not *knock* me *down* for I *love* my Lord more than *myself*."

Quotation #94

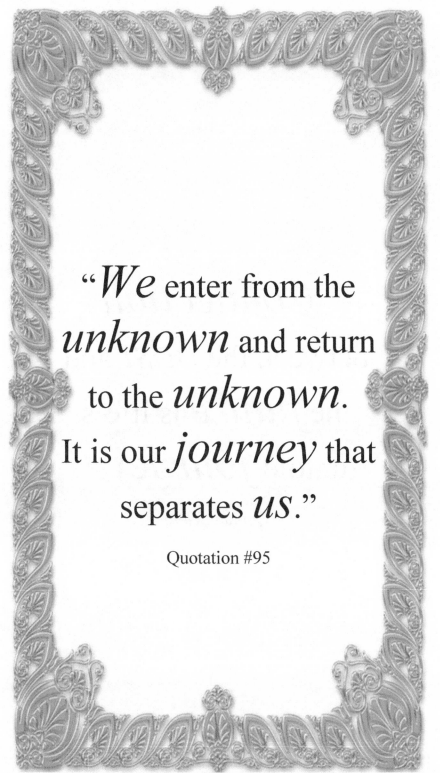

"*We* enter from the *unknown* and return to the *unknown*. It is our *journey* that separates *us*."

Quotation #95

"*Connection* between the *past* and the *future* is life's untold *journey*."

Quotation #96

"*A* walking stranger today, is *your friend* forever *tomorrow.*"

Quotation #97

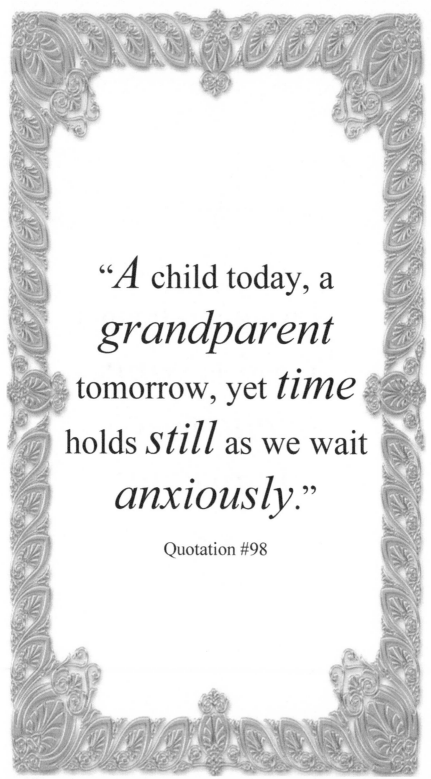

"*A* child today, a *grandparent* tomorrow, yet *time* holds *still* as we wait *anxiously*."

Quotation #98

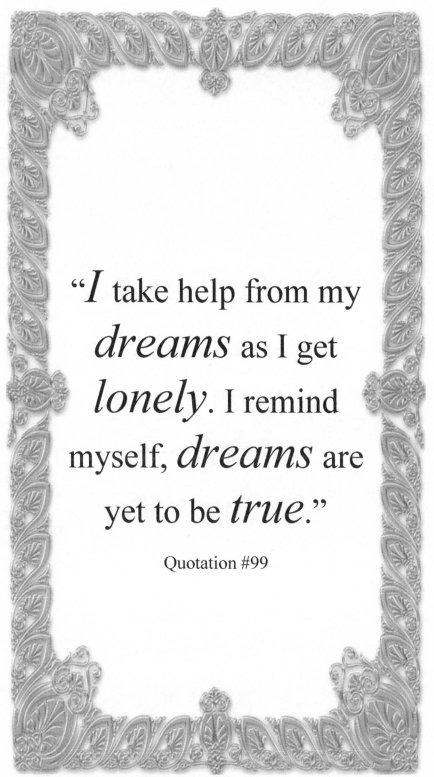

"*I* take help from my *dreams* as I get *lonely*. I remind myself, *dreams* are yet to be *true*."

Quotation #99

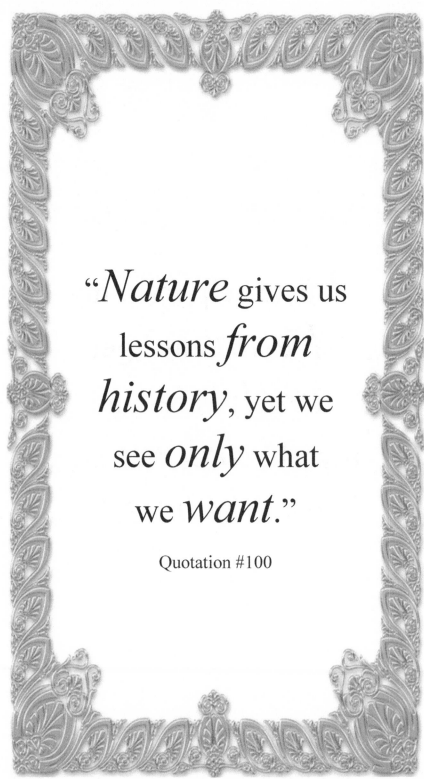

"*Nature* gives us lessons *from history*, yet we see *only* what we *want*."

Quotation #100

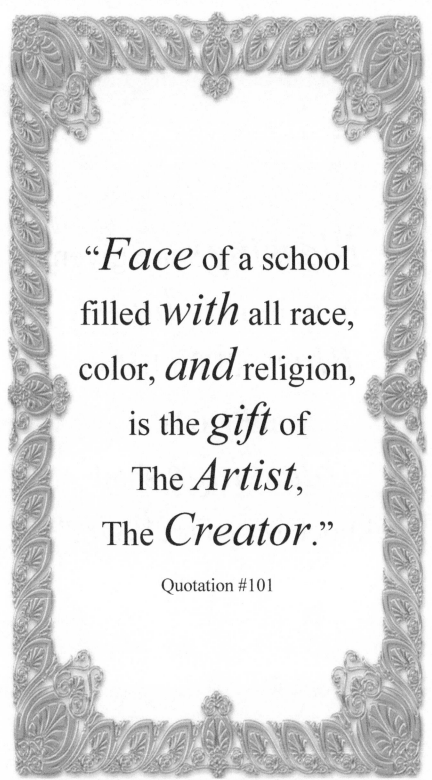

"*Face* of a school filled *with* all race, color, *and* religion, is the *gift* of The *Artist*, The *Creator*."

Quotation #101

"*Blessings* are given from heart to *heart*. *Bless* all for before you *know* it, *blessings* shall knock on your *door*."

Quotation #102

"*Peace* is just one beat away. *Touch* your heart and *find* it. Then, *be* the one to spread *it*."

Quotation #103

"*May* all the children of this world *find* peace *and* spread *peace*."

Quotation #104

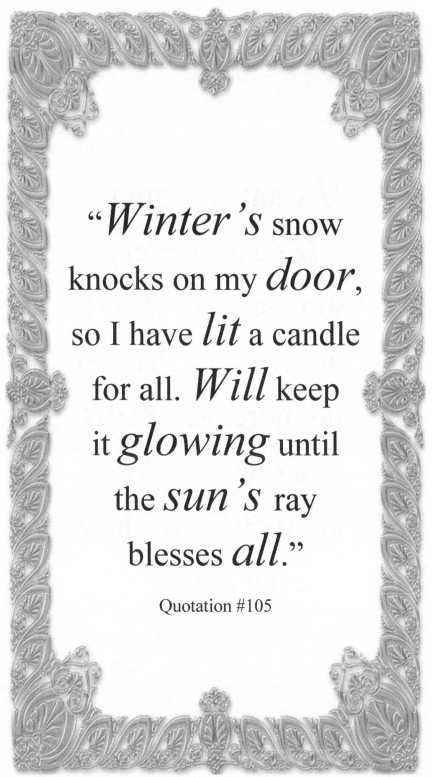

"*Winter's* snow knocks on my *door*, so I have *lit* a candle for all. *Will* keep it *glowing* until the *sun's* ray blesses *all*."

Quotation #105

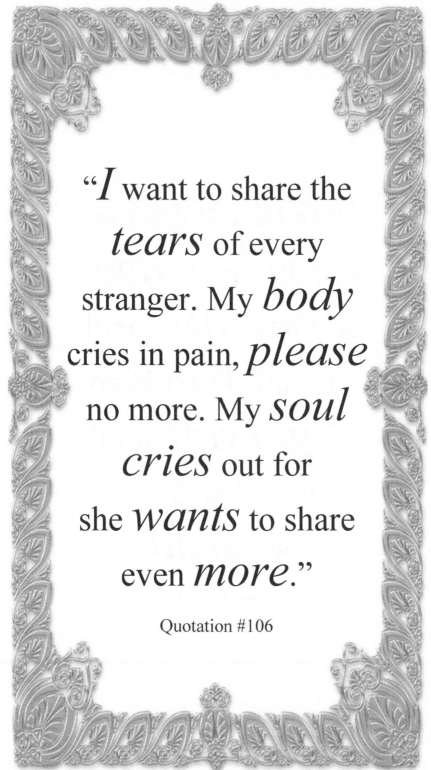

"*I* want to share the *tears* of every stranger. My *body* cries in pain, *please* no more. My *soul cries* out for she *wants* to share even *more*."

Quotation #106

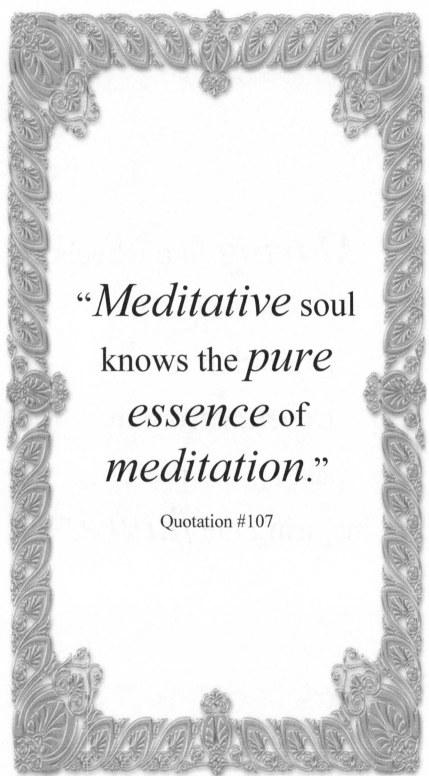

"*Meditative* soul knows the *pure essence* of *meditation*."

Quotation #107

"*Moving* like wheels of a *wagon*, inspiration for *life* *comes* from the past *to* the present, inspiring the *future*."

Quotation #108

"*Let* history be there as a *guide*, but always create your *own* stories as we move *on* and become the *past*."

Quotation #109

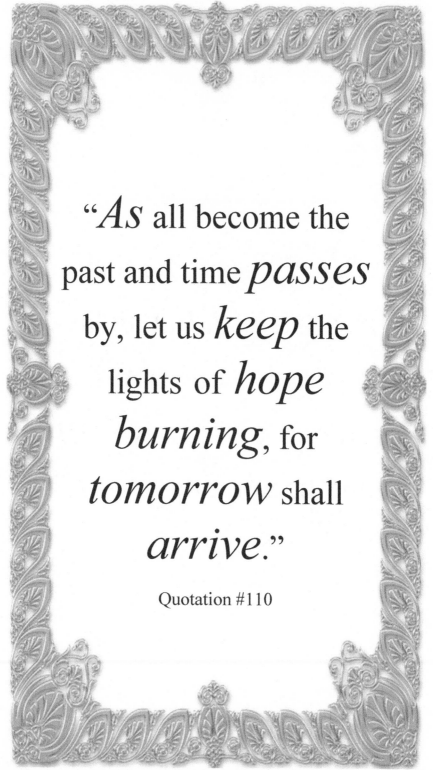

"*As* all become the past and time *passes* by, let us *keep* the lights of *hope burning*, for *tomorrow* shall *arrive*."

Quotation #110

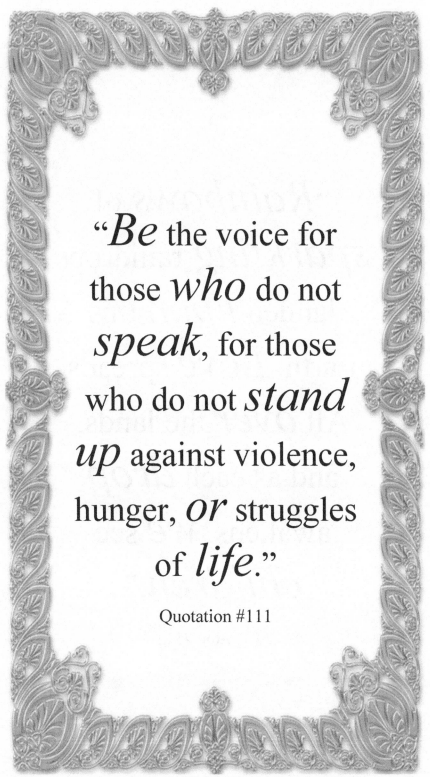

"*Be* the voice for those *who* do not *speak*, for those who do not *stand up* against violence, hunger, *or* struggles of *life*."

Quotation #111

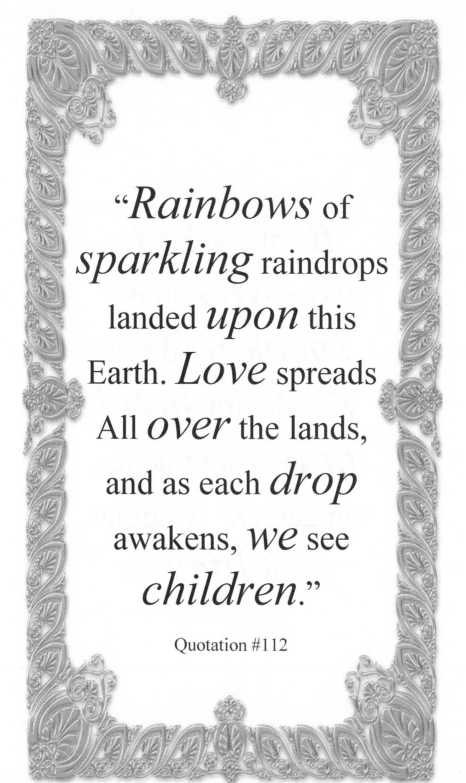

"*Rainbows* of *sparkling* raindrops landed *upon* this Earth. *Love* spreads All *over* the lands, and as each *drop* awakens, *we* see *children*."

Quotation #112

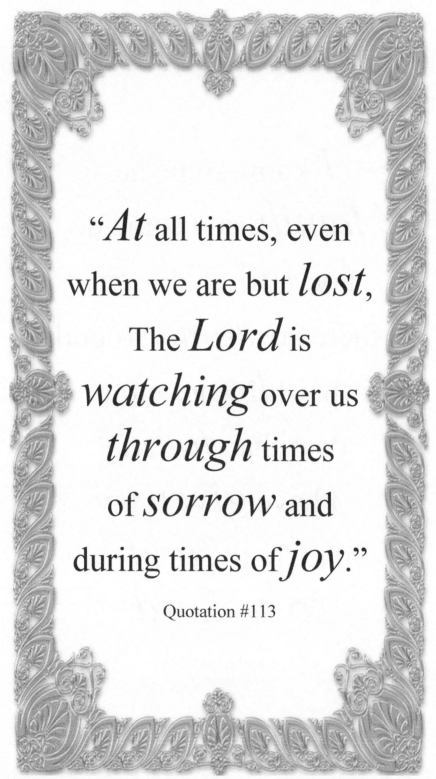

"*At* all times, even when we are but *lost*, The *Lord* is *watching* over us *through* times of *sorrow* and during times of *joy*."

Quotation #113

"*I* know some have *family* and some do not, *but* at all times there are *some* around us *who* are more dear than *family*. I have *given* my mind, body, *and* soul *to* my *Lord*."

Quotation #114

"*Let* us not judge any one for we too *shall* be the *judged*. May we not be the *person* who we *love* to hate, but *let* us be the *one* we all *respect*, honor, and *love*."

Quotation #115

"*What* we do not have in the *pages* of *history* are the people who walk *around* each corner *and* have been *changing* the lives of so *many* throughout *time*."

"*May* we the
present spread this
to the future and
as they the future
awaken and see
the past, they shall
know we have left
onto them, the gift
of love. May the
future be blessed and
may we the past be
the reason for this
blessed *future*."

Quotation #117

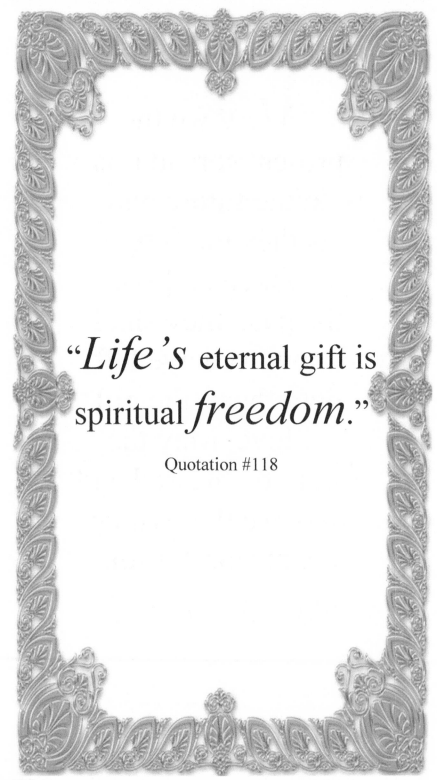

"*Life's* eternal gift is spiritual *freedom.*"

Quotation #118

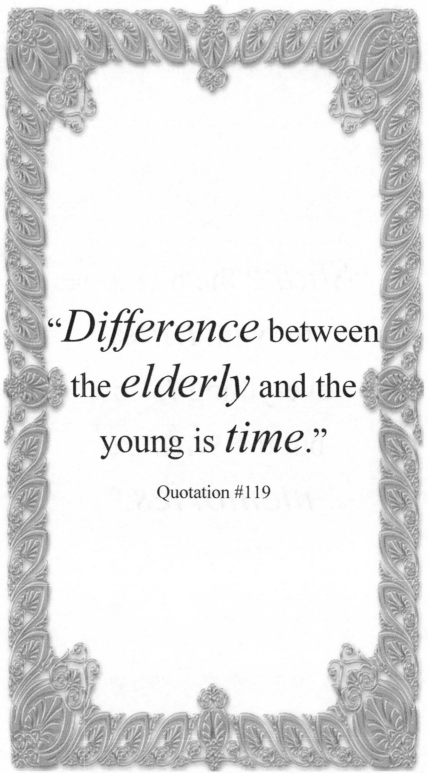

"*Difference* between the *elderly* and the young is *time*."

Quotation #119

"*Share* the memories for with *time*, everything *is* lost but the *shared memories*."

Quotation #120

"*Moon* watches over all the *sweet dreams*, for even when *time* passes by, She keeps an *eye*."

Quotation #121

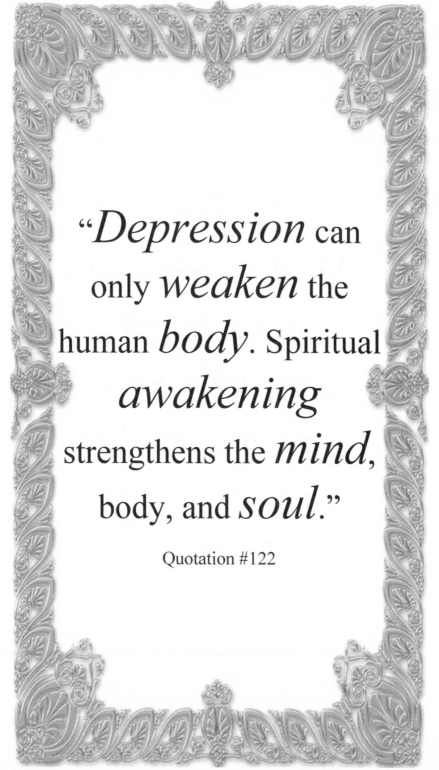

"*Depression* can only *weaken* the human *body*. Spiritual *awakening* strengthens the *mind*, body, and *soul*."

Quotation #122

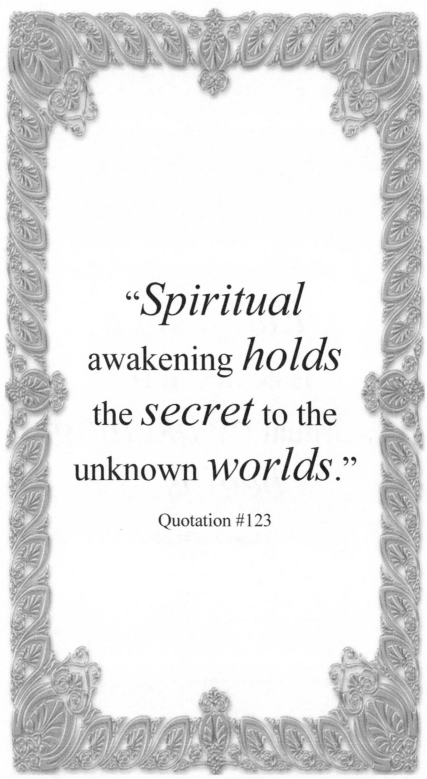

"*Spiritual* awakening *holds* the *secret* to the unknown *worlds*."

Quotation #123

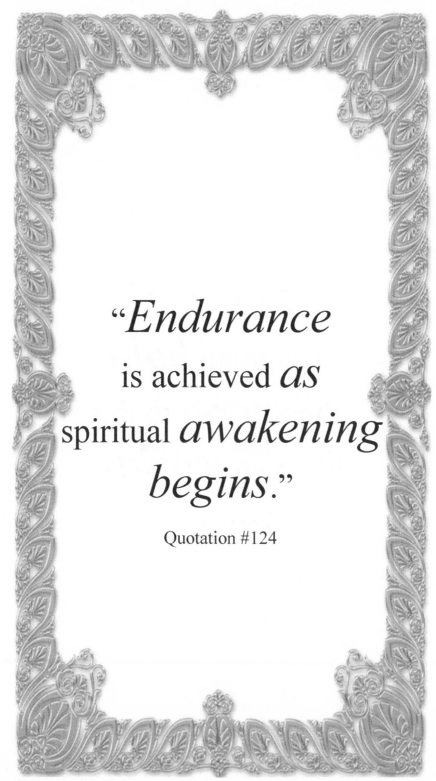

"*Endurance*
is achieved *as*
spiritual *awakening*
begins."

Quotation #124

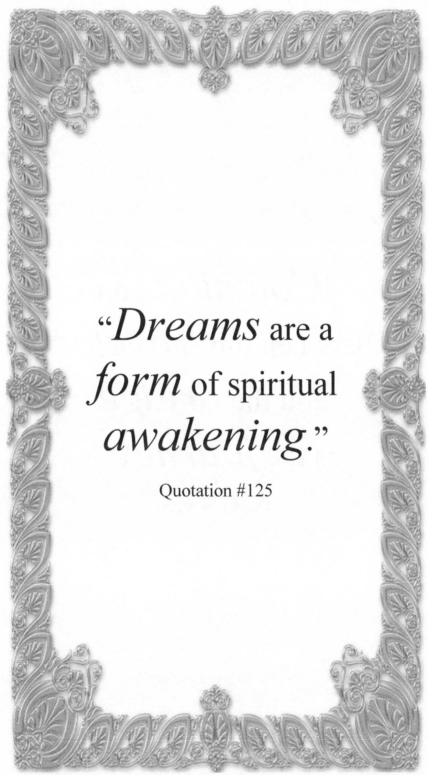

"*Dreams* are a *form* of spiritual *awakening*."

Quotation #125

"*Common* core
between the *traveler*
and the *bridge*
is the *journey*."

Quotation #126

"*Only* thing that remains still as time and tide move on is the memories framed in the hearts of the beholders. People change as does nature. Leaves fall off after giving us a glorious Fall of colors. New leaves bloom as Spring comes around again with new life blooming throughout this *universe*."

Quotation #127

"*The* world
had taught me
everything as I walked
deep into my soul. I had
the realization of how
beautiful this world is.
It is like a Bridge of
Rainbow created by
different race, color,
and religion. Equally
beautiful and with
grace, each creation
is a unique sculpture,
a painting created by
The *Creator*."

Quotation #128

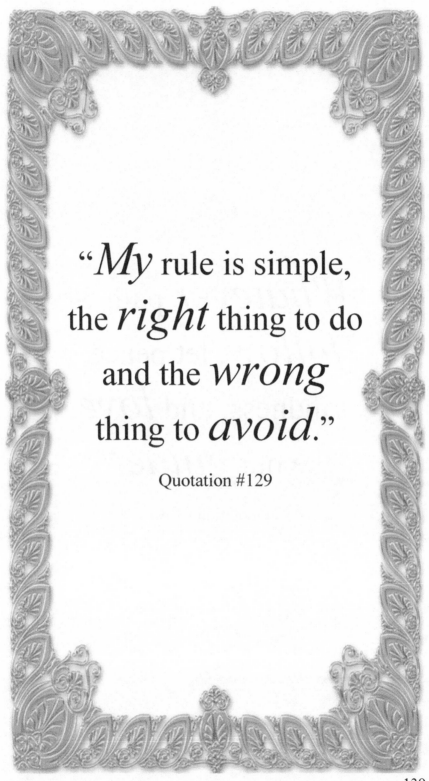

"*My* rule is simple, the *right* thing to do and the *wrong* thing to *avoid*."

Quotation #129

"*Whatever* path we *follow*, let peace, kindness, and *love* be our *guide*."

Quotation #130

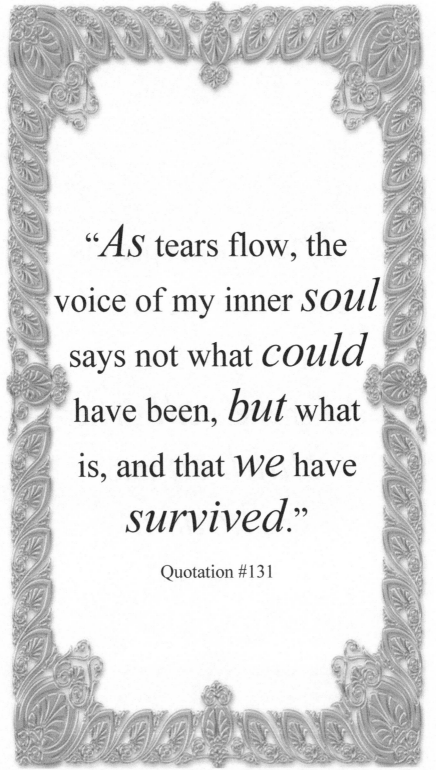

"*As* tears flow, the voice of my inner *soul* says not what *could* have been, *but* what is, and that *we* have *survived*."

Quotation #131

"*The* world spreads herself like the *roots* of a banyan *tree* as she shelters *all* of her *children* into one *house*."

Quotation #132

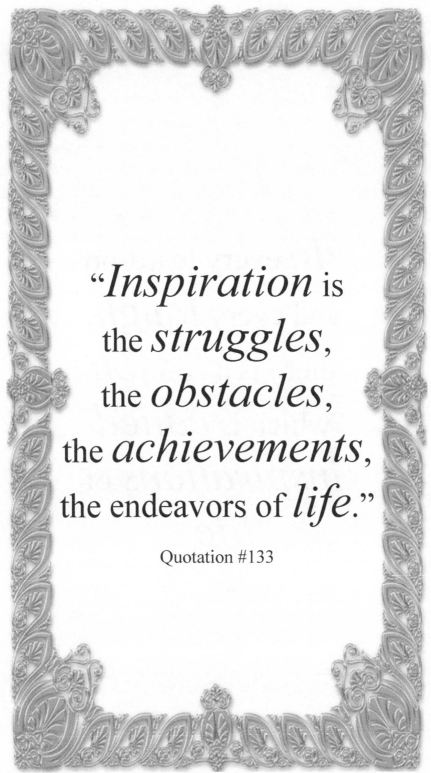

"*Inspiration* is
the *struggles*,
the *obstacles*,
the *achievements*,
the endeavors of *life*."

Quotation #133

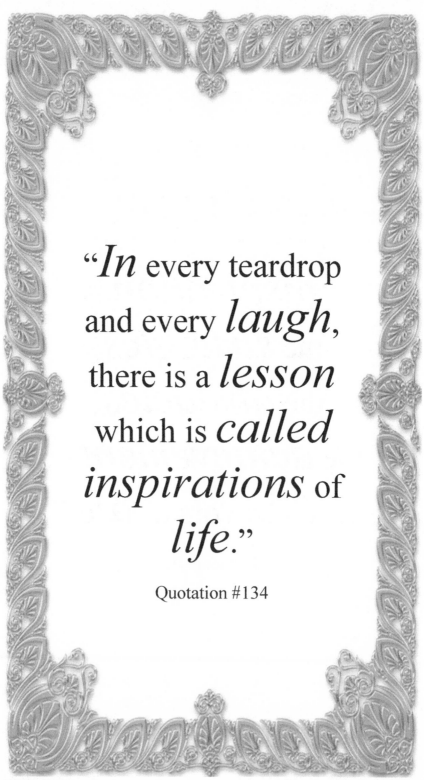

"*In* every teardrop and every *laugh*, there is a *lesson* which is *called* *inspirations* of *life*."

Quotation #134

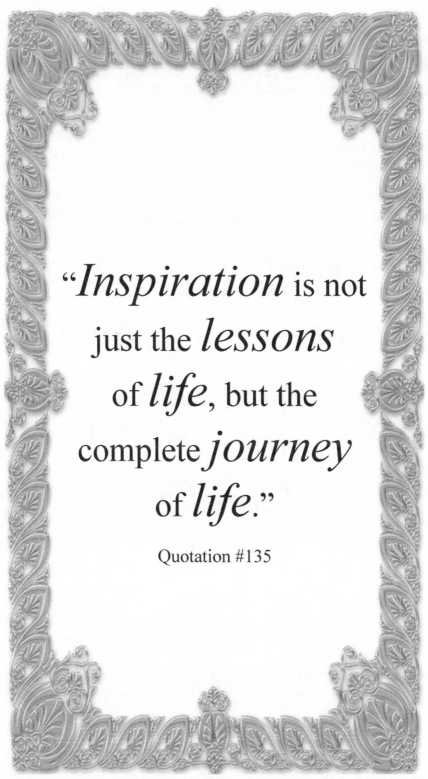

"*Inspiration* is not just the *lessons* of *life*, but the complete *journey* of *life*."

Quotation #135

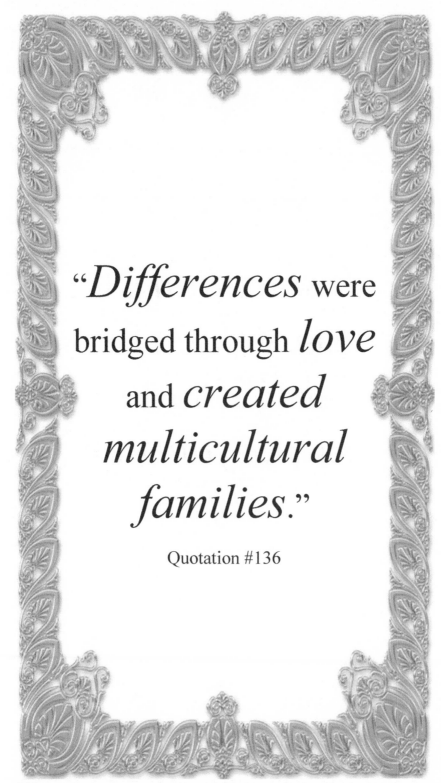

"*Differences* were bridged through *love* and *created multicultural families.*"

Quotation #136

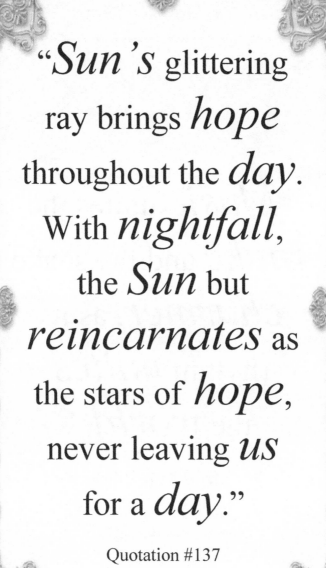

"*Sun's* glittering ray brings *hope* throughout the *day*. With *nightfall*, the *Sun* but *reincarnates* as the stars of *hope*, never leaving *us* for a *day*."

Quotation #137

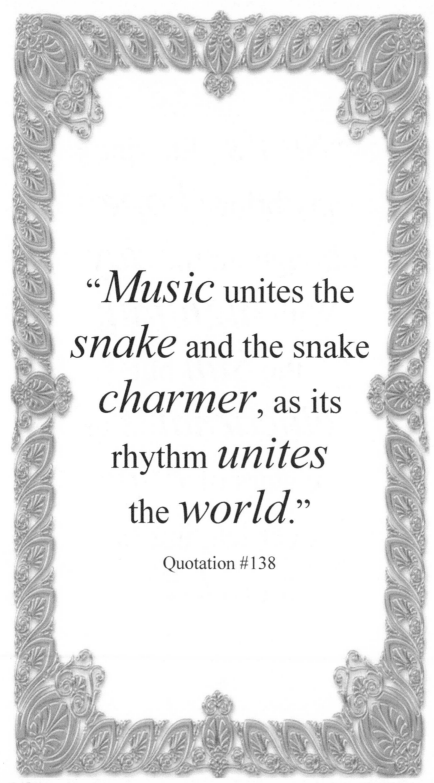

"*Music* unites the *snake* and the snake *charmer*, as its rhythm *unites* the *world*."

Quotation #138

"*As* I was told growing up, all life eventually become stars in the dark skies to guide humans throughout the dark nights. So, my unknown friend shall become a guiding star for all humans. Tomorrow, another unknown friend shall be *born*."

Quotation #139

"*Powerful* words again take me through this dark night. I know daylight comes soon as The Lord's blessings keep me steadfast on my feet. May all be protected throughout the dark nights. My faith is strong and I know at all times, it is

The Lord's *will*."

Quotation #140

"*Love*
all *without*
discrimination, *for* The
Lord created all and
loves all. Let us not
judge the creation
for we are *the* creation
who shall be *judged*
by The *Lord*.
Let there be *peace*."

Quotation #141

"*What* is unknown is a *mystery*, and some question, how *do* you love what is *not* known, or seen, *or heard* by the human ears? I *tell* them because I *love* you and all of *yours*."

Quotation #142

"*All* of these gifts on *Earth* were given to *us*, so you, I, and all *creation* live in *harmony*. These gifts were *created* and *given* by someone *who* loves, *gives*, and wants nothing in *return*."

Quotation #143

"*All* creation *are* scrambling around to find the *truth*, looking at all *doors* as they open *and* close. *For* all who seek, I tell *them* find yourself for *all* of the *knowledge* is in your *heart*."

Quotation #144

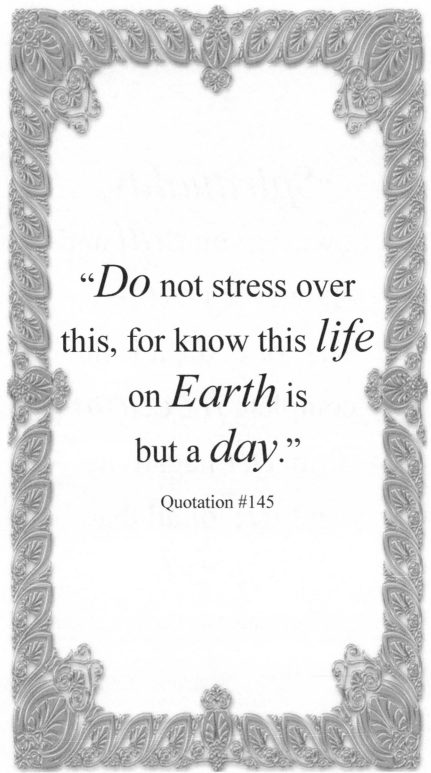

"*Do* not stress over this, for know this *life* on *Earth* is but a *day*."

Quotation #145

"*Spirituality,*
however you *call* and
however *you* see,
hear, or *ask*, it is the
complete *freedom*
from *all* negativity
and *joy* of all that
is *good*."

Quotation #146

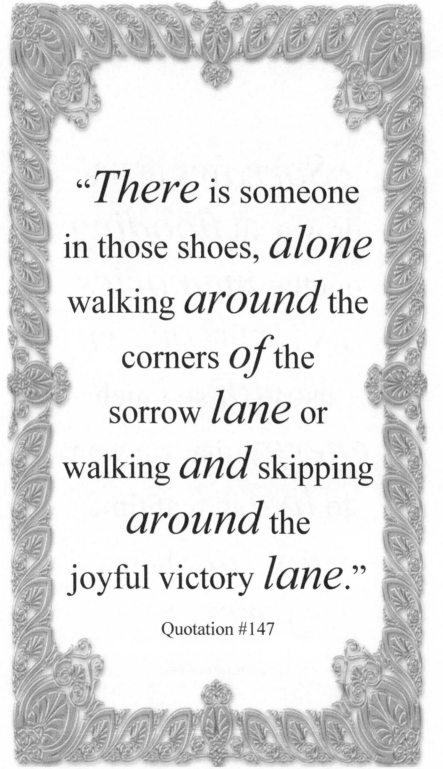

"*There* is someone in those shoes, *alone* walking *around* the corners *of* the sorrow *lane* or walking *and* skipping *around* the joyful victory *lane*."

Quotation #147

"*Sorrows* of life drown all *flooding* out the *memories*. Joys of life *drown* us *with* so much *energy* that we want to *live* in that time, day, *and* hour *forever*."

Quotation #148

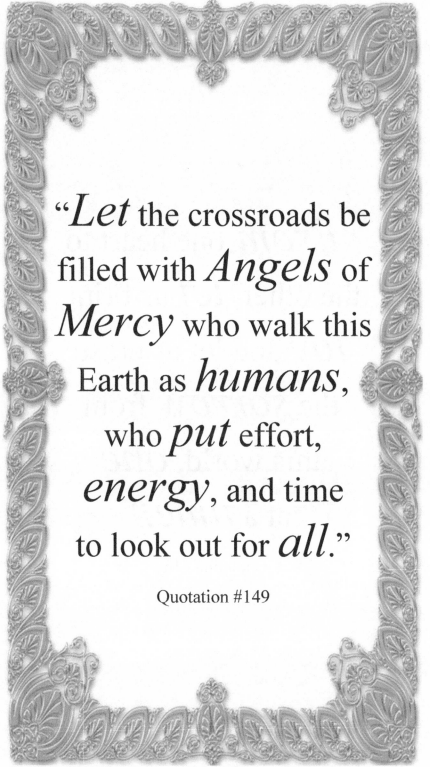

"*Let* the crossroads be filled with *Angels* of *Mercy* who walk this Earth as *humans*, who *put* effort, *energy*, and time to look out for *all*."

Quotation #149

"*From* one heart to the other, *let* us bring *joy* and let us erase the *sorrow* from this world, *one* at a *time*."

Quotation #150

"*I* give you love
from the *inner* of
my *heart* which is the
only *gift* I can give,
and as we *share,*
it *grows*."

Quotation #151

"*Let* us send positive
energy *back* to
this *world* through
a *smile*, a kind word,
a good *deed*,
or like me *plant*
a *tree* with all of your
positive *energy*."

Quotation #152

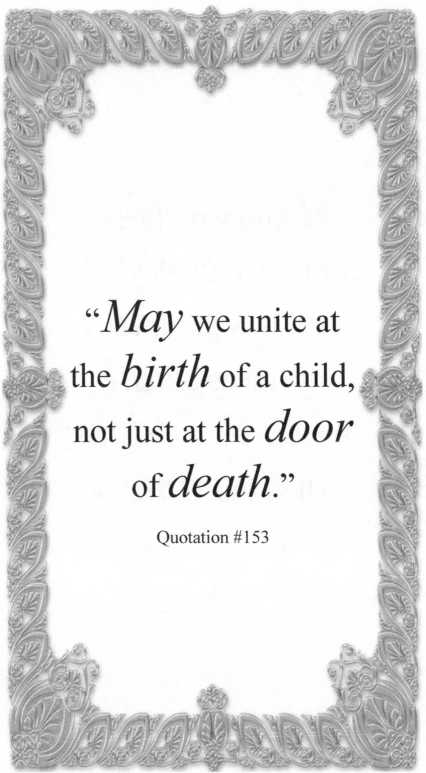

"*May* we unite at the *birth* of a child, not just at the *door* of *death*."

Quotation #153

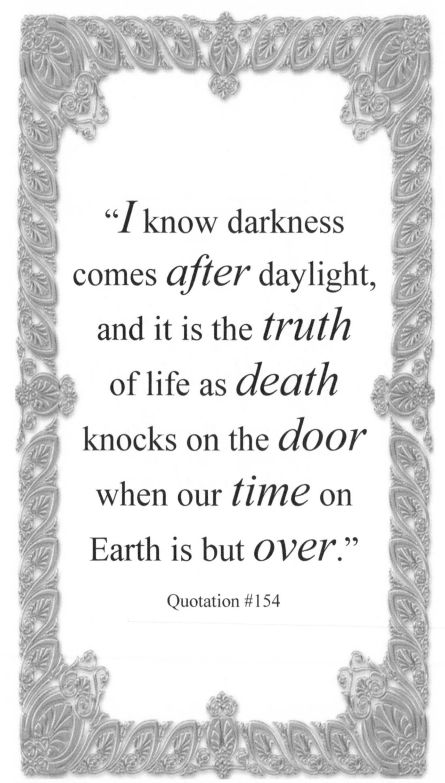

"*I* know darkness comes *after* daylight, and it is the *truth* of life as *death* knocks on the *door* when our *time* on Earth is but *over*."

Quotation #154

"*We* shall triumph over evil *and victory* shall be for all *humans*, as we unite *against* all evil. *Let* religion not be the *focus*, but *union*, peace, and *blessings* flow from one *heart* to the *other*."

Quotation #155

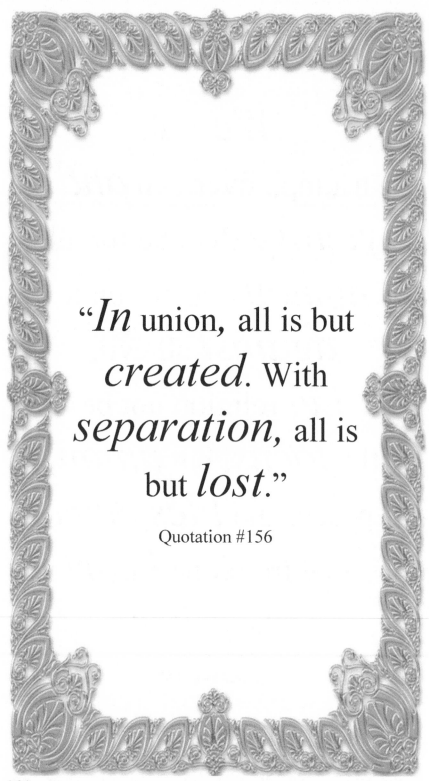

"*In* union, all is but *created*. With *separation*, all is but *lost*."

Quotation #156

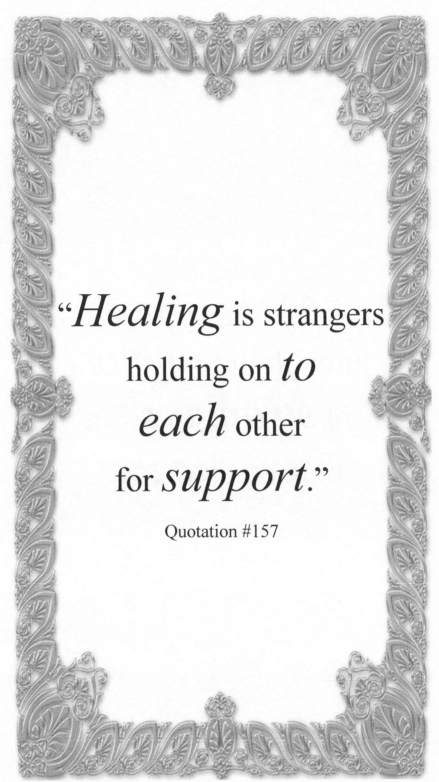

"*Healing* is strangers
holding on *to*
each other
for *support.*"

Quotation #157

"*A* bridge created through the *support* of *strangers* is a blessed *dream*."

Quotation #158

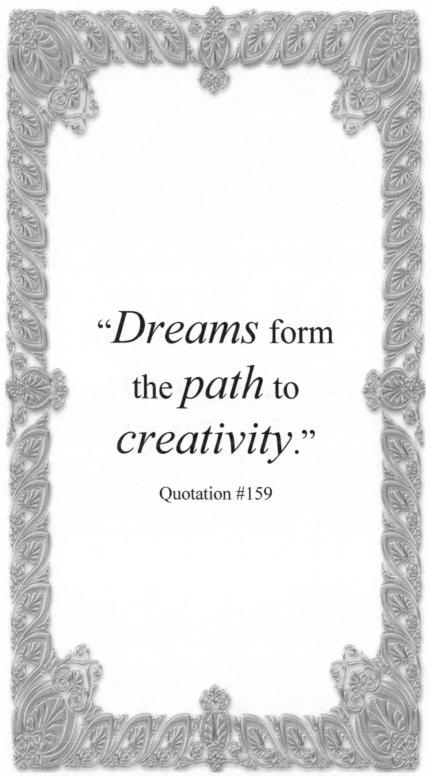

"*Dreams* form
the *path* to
creativity."

Quotation #159

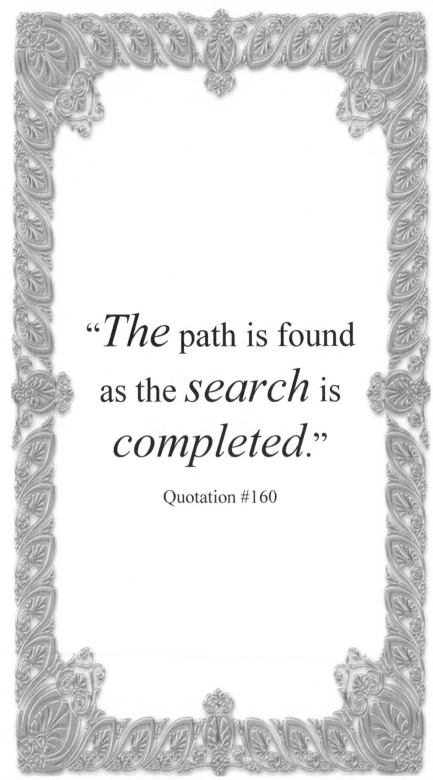

"*The* path is found as the *search* is *completed.*"

Quotation #160

"*The* complete *truth* is a blessed *guide*."

Quotation #161

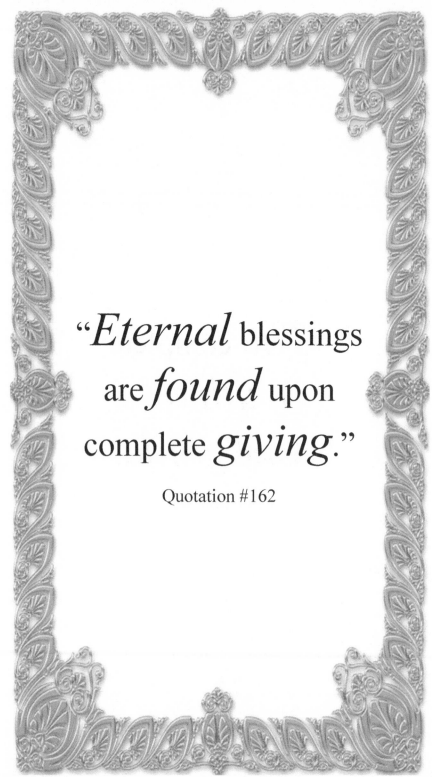

"*Eternal* blessings are *found* upon complete *giving*."

Quotation #162

"Giving is life's *complete journey."*

Quotation #163

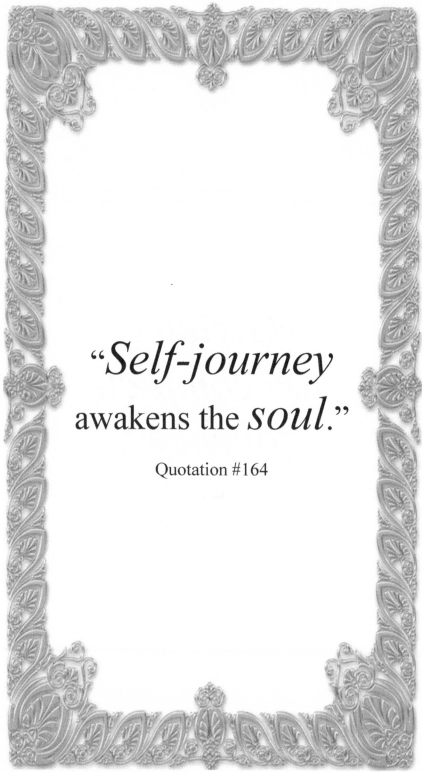

"*Self-journey*
awakens the *soul*."

Quotation #164

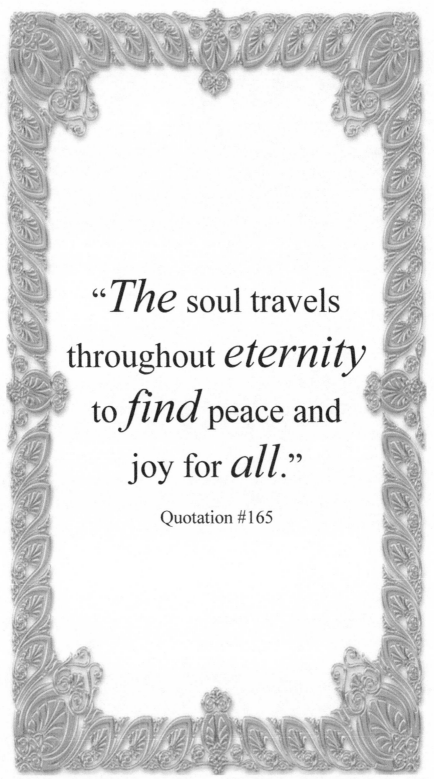

"*The* soul travels throughout *eternity* to *find* peace and joy for *all*."

Quotation #165

BOOK TWO

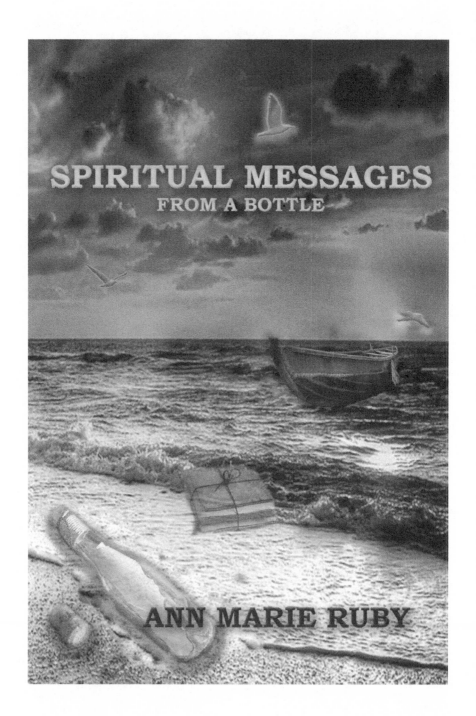

SPIRITUAL MESSAGES
FROM A BOTTLE

ANN MARIE RUBY

DEDICATION

I dedicate this book to all the souls looking for a spiritual message from a friend. Life lands us upon a journey through time. We land upon the doors of strangers, friends, and family. The tunnel continues as life is a lesson to be learned. As we cross the doors and land upon the door of a stranger, please know this stranger gives you a helping hand through my words of inspirational quotations.

I dedicate this book to all of whom need a helping hand. May there always be a helping hand for all of My Lord's creation who have ever fallen down and needed a simple lift from a stranger, your guiding Angel in disguise.

May there be an Angel in disguise at every corner of our lives. I dedicate this book to all of whom needed that inspiration, that helping hand.

Spread peace, be in peace.

BLESSED BE HEAVEN

My Lord, my Creator,

I search for You within the skies.

I see Your eyes watching over,

Keeping me safe from all evil eyes.

I search for You on Earth beneath,

I see my Lord holding on to me,

For it is then, I am but able to walk.

I search for You throughout the blazing desert sun,

Not fearing the burning heat.

I know the winds of my Lord cools my soul,

As the wind blows through the air,

Whispering prayers to keep me going.

I search for You in the deep blue ocean,

As I fear not the waves.

I find my Lord washing my sins away,

As I repent, repent, repent.

At the end of my day, waiting to return Home,

I realize above, around, and beyond me,

All that I see, hear, and feel,

Standing always around me,

My Lord, my Creator.

For I know I have never left Home,

For all of this is,

BLESSED BE HEAVEN.

*From my prayer book, *Spiritual Songs: Letters From My Chest*

"*Journey* of life, I call it *time* of *reflection*, time to repent, *redeem*, *and* spiritually awaken. Leave *all the* negativities behind *and* walk *forward* with peace as our *guide*."

Quotation #166

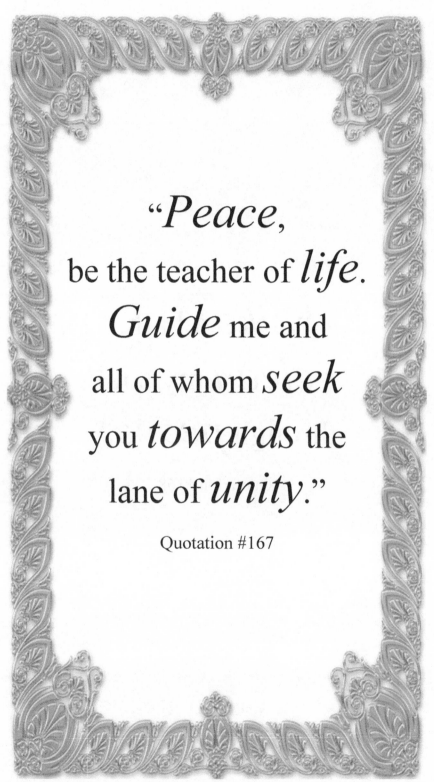

"*Peace,*
be the teacher of *life.*
Guide me and
all of whom *seek*
you *towards* the
lane of *unity.*"

Quotation #167

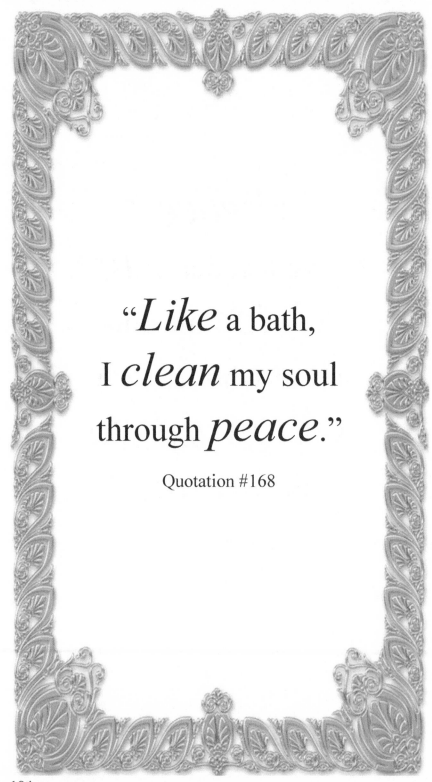

"*Like* a bath,
I *clean* my soul
through *peace.*"

Quotation #168

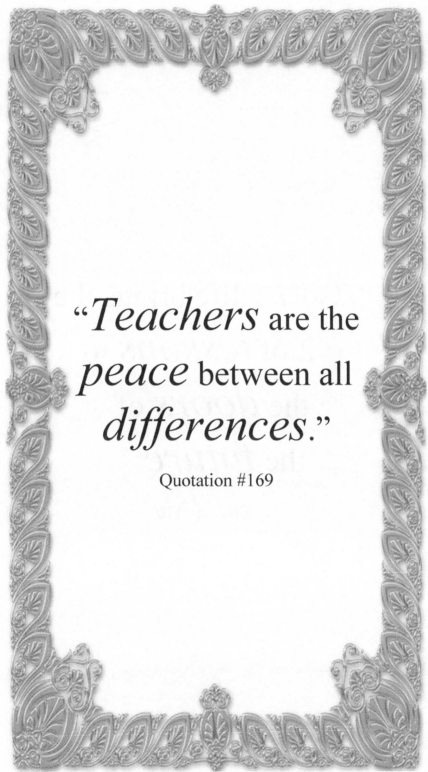

"*Teachers* are the
peace between all
differences."

Quotation #169

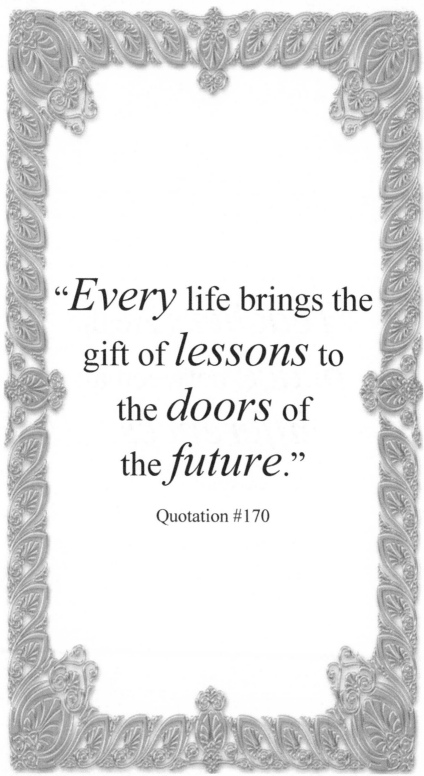

"*Every* life brings the gift of *lessons* to the *doors* of the *future*."

Quotation #170

"*Past*, present, and future become *one* *through* the pages of *history*."

Quotation #171

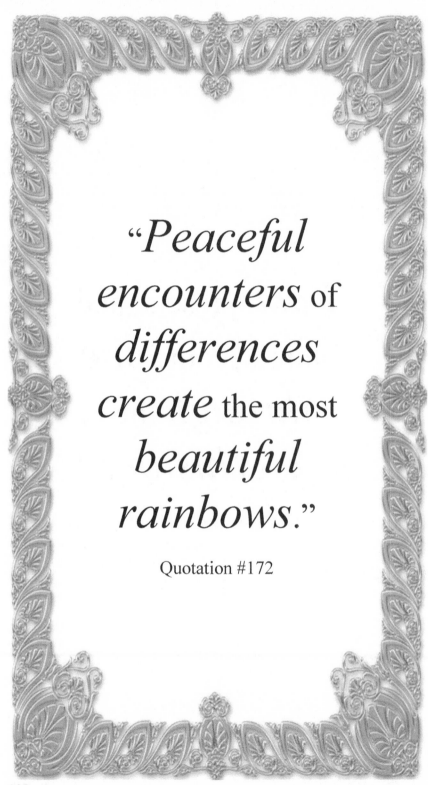

"*Peaceful encounters* of *differences create* the most *beautiful rainbows.*"

Quotation #172

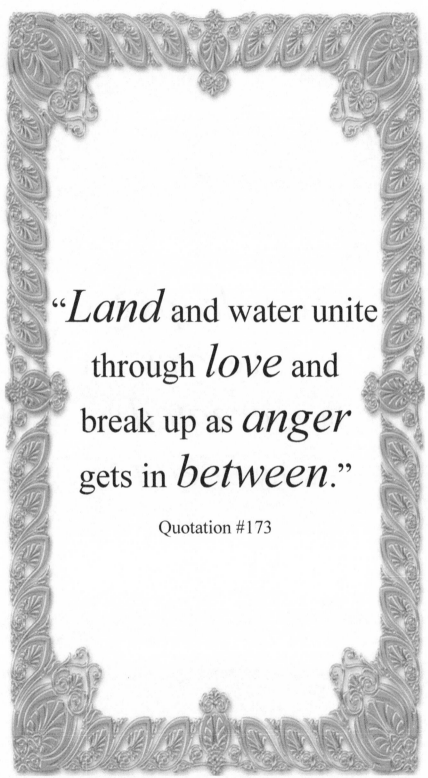

"*Land* and water unite through *love* and break up as *anger* gets in *between*."

Quotation #173

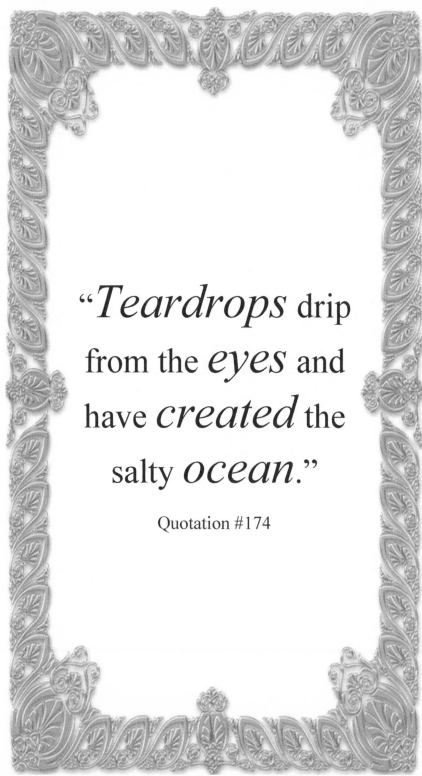

"*Teardrops* drip from the *eyes* and have *created* the salty *ocean*."

Quotation #174

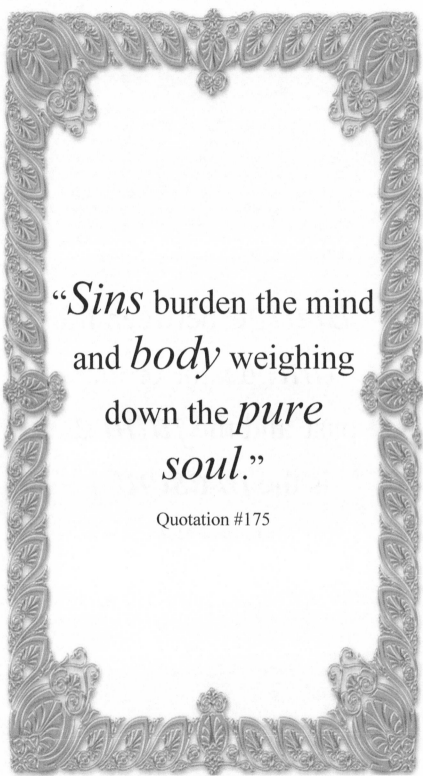

"*Sins* burden the mind and *body* weighing down the *pure soul.*"

Quotation #175

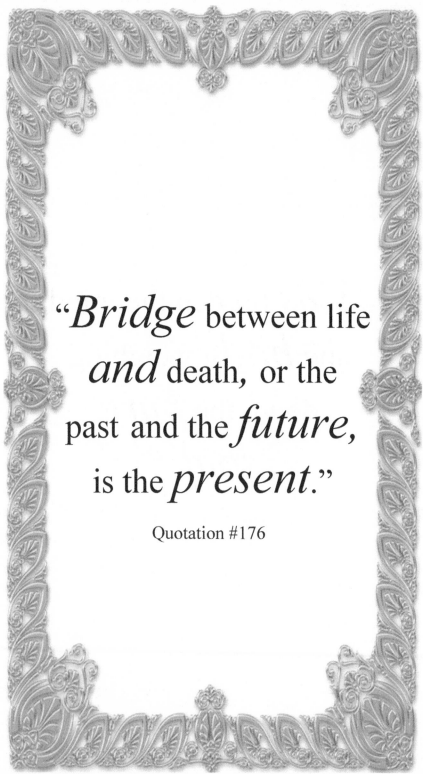

"*Bridge* between life *and* death, or the past and the *future,* is the *present.*"

Quotation #176

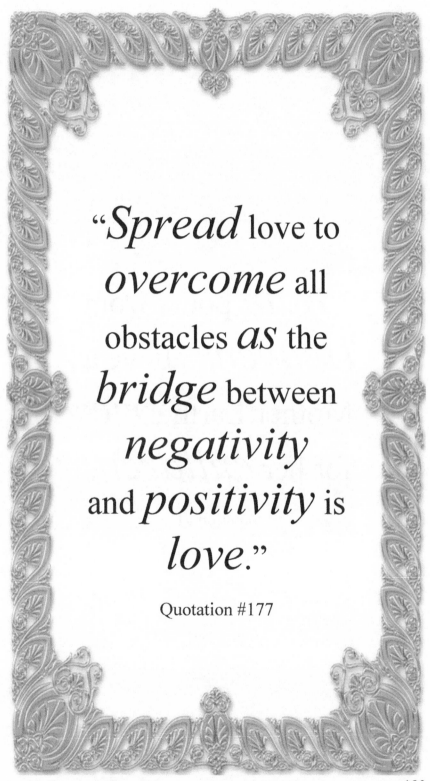

"*Spread* love to *overcome* all obstacles *as* the *bridge* between *negativity* and *positivity* is *love.*"

Quotation #177

"*Rain* pours from *Heavens* above as Mother Earth *cries* for her *children*."

Quotation #178

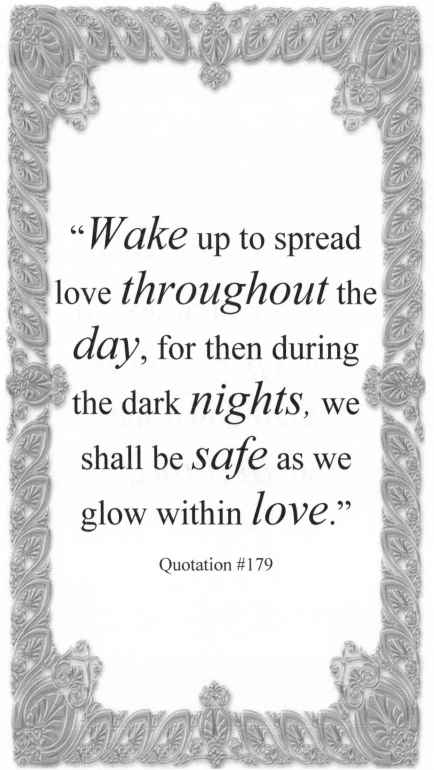

"*Wake* up to spread love *throughout* the *day*, for then during the dark *nights*, we shall be *safe* as we glow within *love*."

Quotation #179

"*Do* not remorse in guilt *for* it brings *you* down and all *around*."

Quotation #180

"*Be* the helping hand
your *soul* seeks, for it
is then *we* shall
find helping *hands*
all *around*."

Quotation #181

"*There* is no orphan on this *Earth* as long *as* there is a *mother* or a father *alive*."

Quotation #182

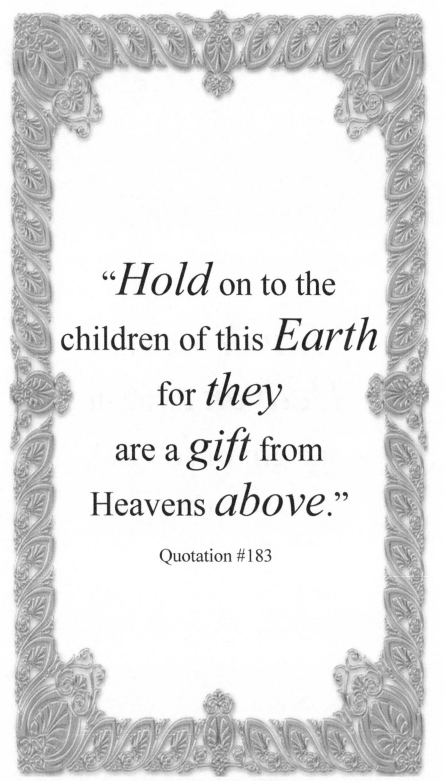

"*Hold* on to the children of this *Earth* for *they* are a *gift* from Heavens *above*."

Quotation #183

"*Earth* becomes *Heaven* through the gift of *love*."

Quotation #184

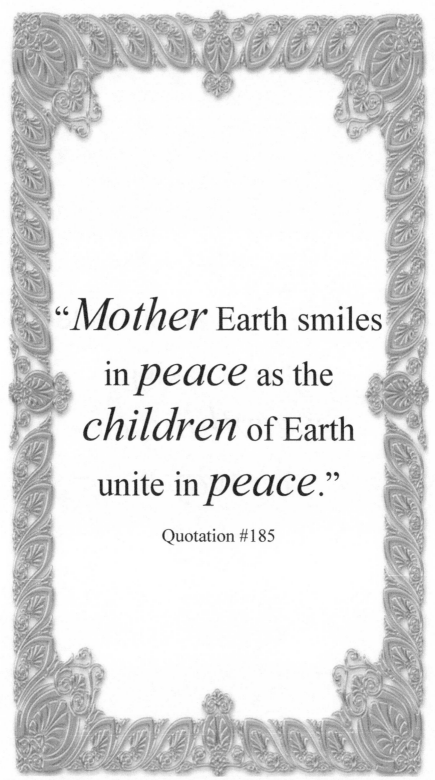

"*Mother* Earth smiles in *peace* as the *children* of Earth unite in *peace*."

Quotation #185

"*Anger* is an obstacle of *life* taking *everything* on her *way*."

Quotation #186

"*Family* is the circle made *through* the past, *the* present, and the *future*."

Quotation #187

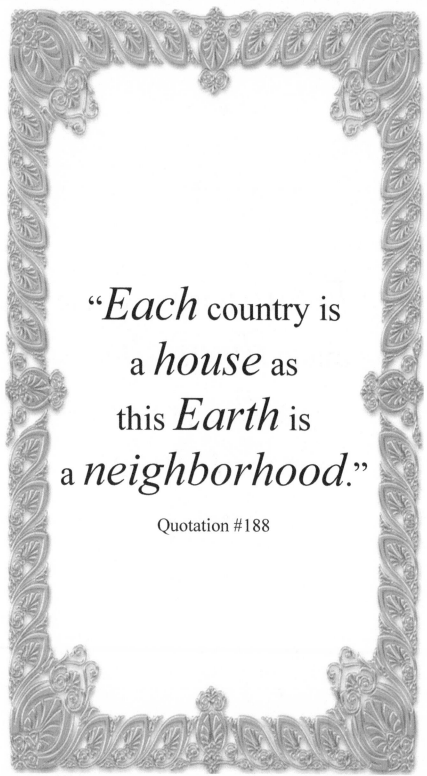

"*Each* country is
a *house* as
this *Earth* is
a *neighborhood.*"

Quotation #188

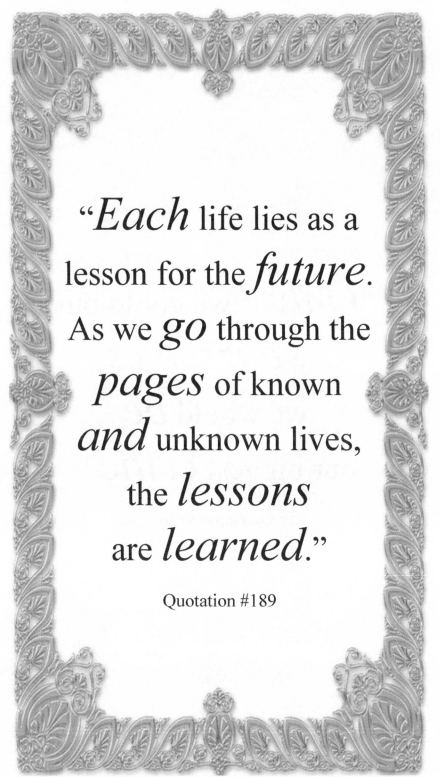

"*Each* life lies as a lesson for the *future*. As we *go* through the *pages* of known *and* unknown lives, the *lessons* are *learned*."

Quotation #189

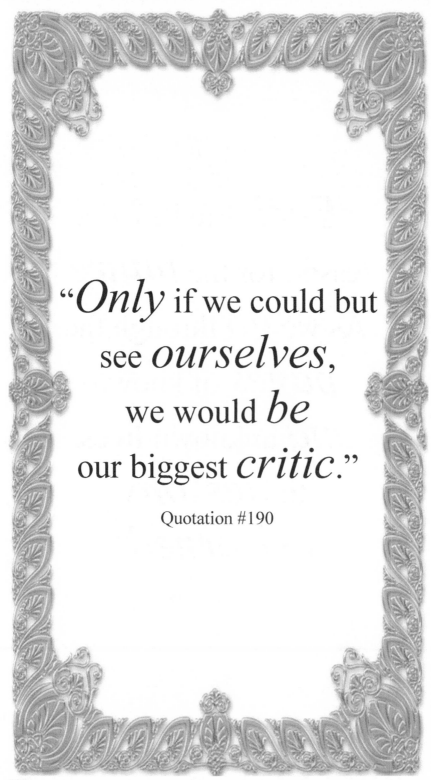

"*Only* if we could but see *ourselves*, we would *be* our biggest *critic.*"

Quotation #190

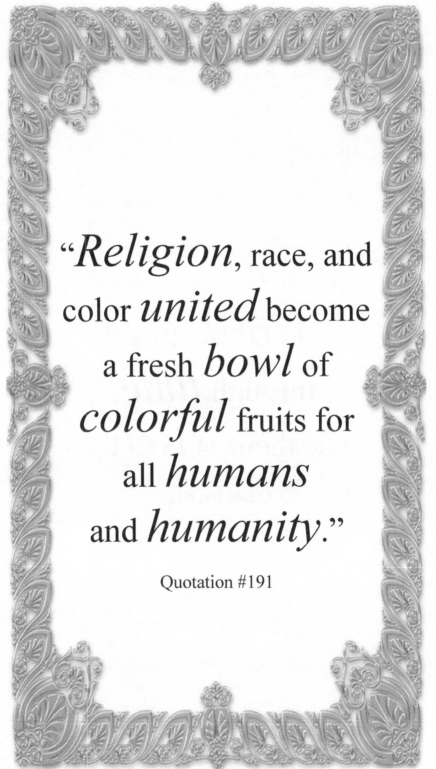

"*Religion*, race, and color *united* become a fresh *bowl* of *colorful* fruits for all *humans* and *humanity*."

Quotation #191

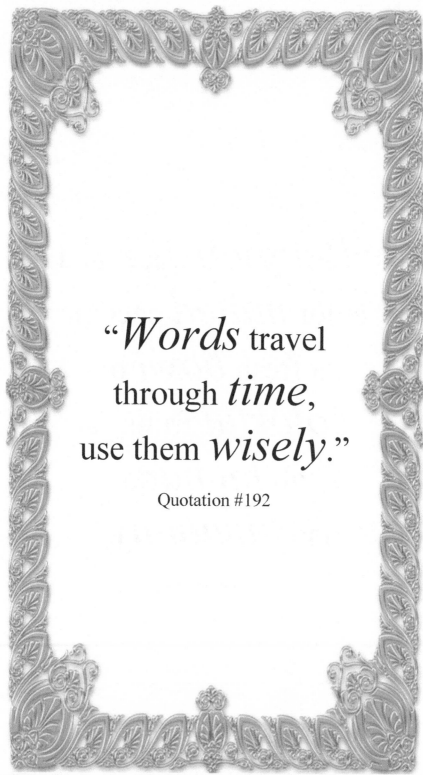

"*Words* travel
through *time*,
use them *wisely*."

Quotation #192

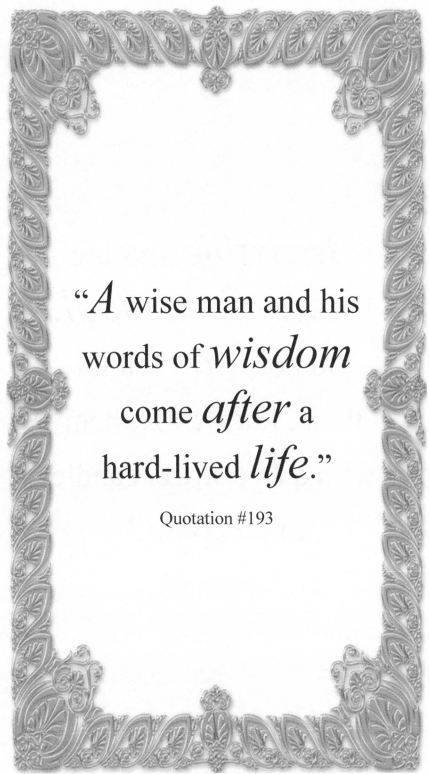

"*A* wise man and his words of *wisdom* come *after* a hard-lived *life*."

Quotation #193

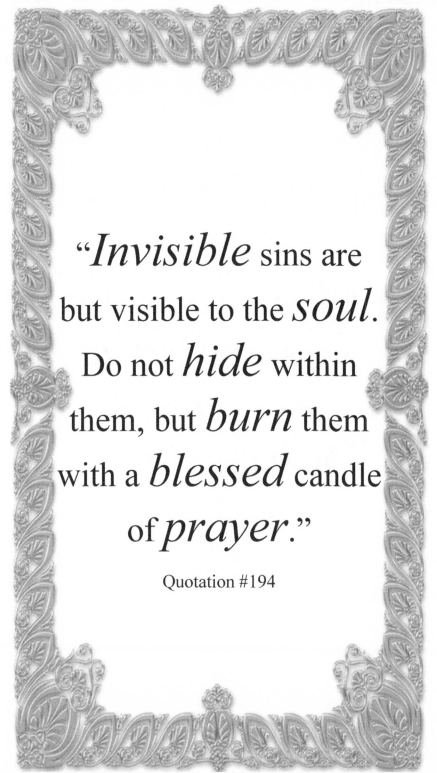

"*Invisible* sins are but visible to the *soul*. Do not *hide* within them, but *burn* them with a *blessed* candle of *prayer*."

Quotation #194

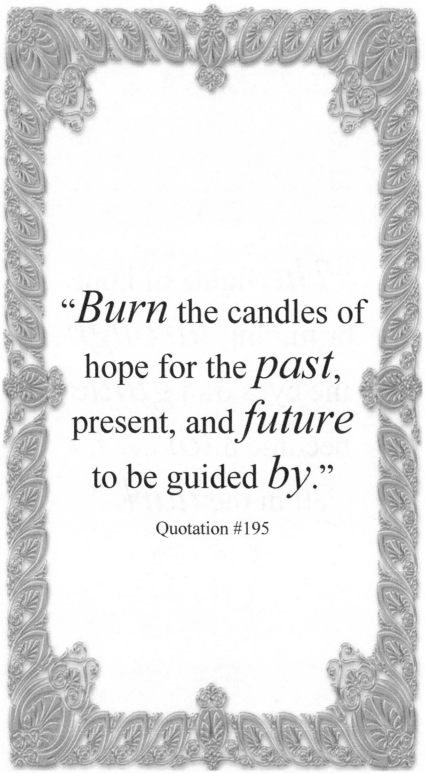

"*Burn* the candles of hope for the *past*, present, and *future* to be guided *by*."

Quotation #195

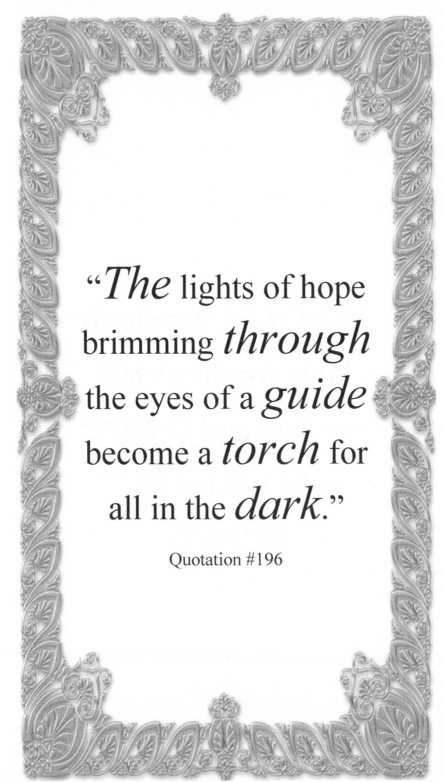

"*The* lights of hope brimming *through* the eyes of a *guide* become a *torch* for all in the *dark*."

Quotation #196

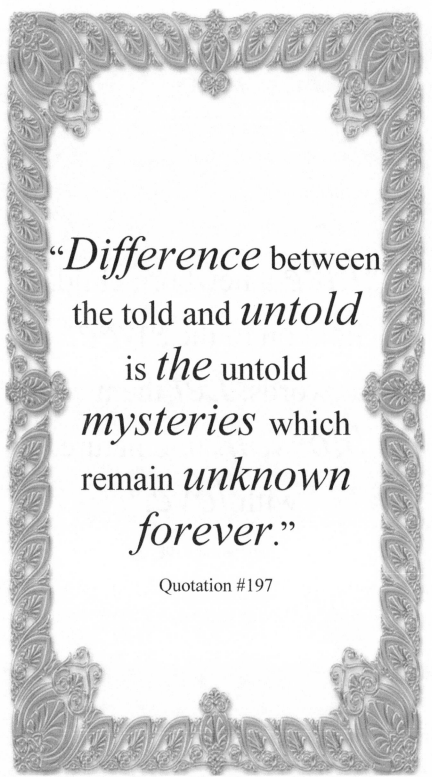

"*Difference* between the told and *untold* is *the* untold *mysteries* which remain *unknown forever.*"

Quotation #197

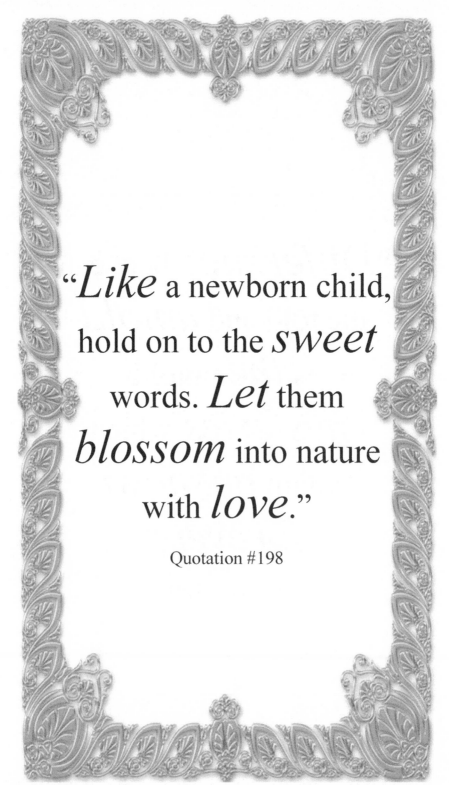

"*Like* a newborn child, hold on to the *sweet* words. *Let* them *blossom* into nature with *love*."

Quotation #198

"*Wind* spreads harmony *from* soul to *soul*. Be the harmony. *Spread harmony*."

Quotation #199

"*Life* is but a day, so on this *day*, be an example. *For* tomorrow, *the* future shall *look* back upon the *past* and *find* you as an *example*."

Quotation #200

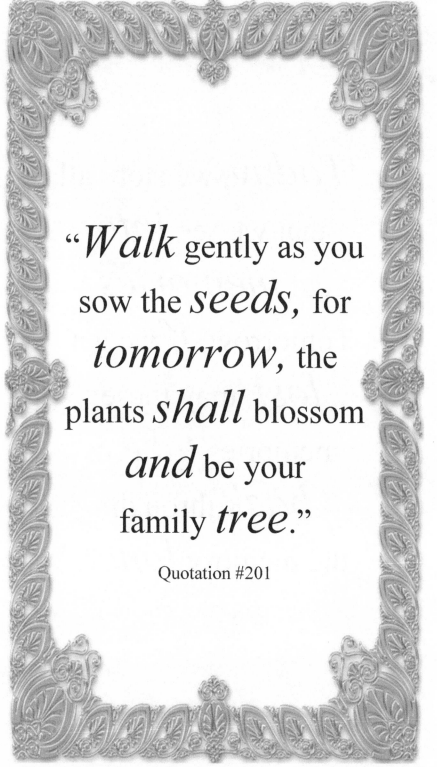

"*Walk* gently as you sow the *seeds,* for *tomorrow,* the plants *shall* blossom *and* be your family *tree*."

Quotation #201

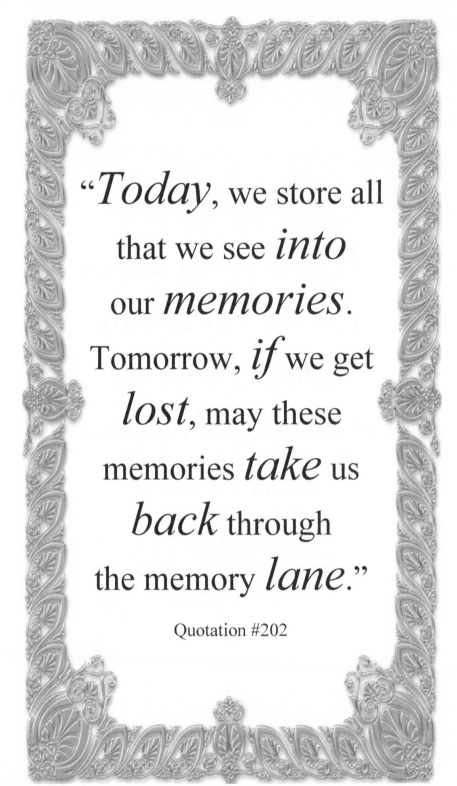

"*Today*, we store all that we see *into* our *memories*. Tomorrow, *if* we get *lost*, may these memories *take* us *back* through the memory *lane*."

Quotation #202

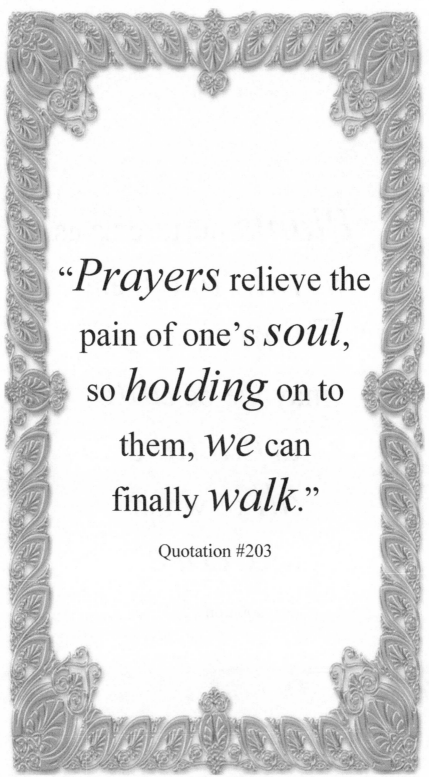

"*Prayers* relieve the pain of one's *soul*, so *holding* on to them, *we* can finally *walk*."

Quotation #203

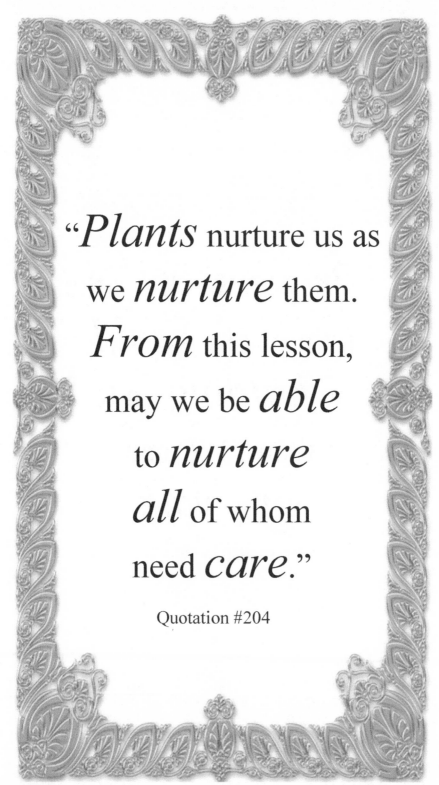

"*Plants* nurture us as we *nurture* them. *From* this lesson, may we be *able* to *nurture* *all* of whom need *care*."

Quotation #204

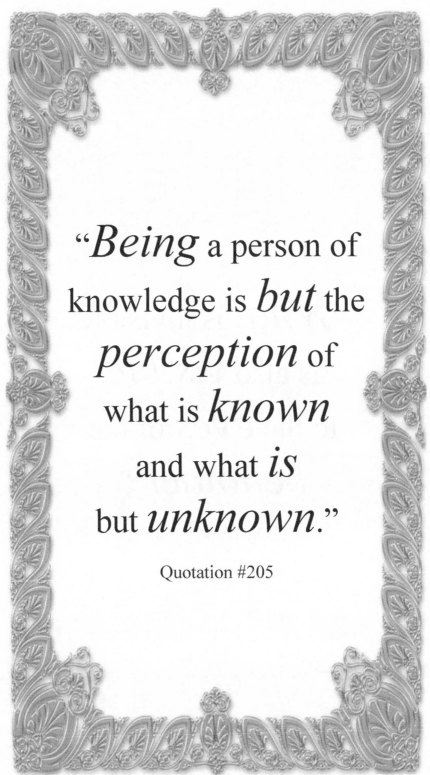

"*Being* a person of knowledge is *but* the *perception* of what is *known* and what *is* but *unknown*."

Quotation #205

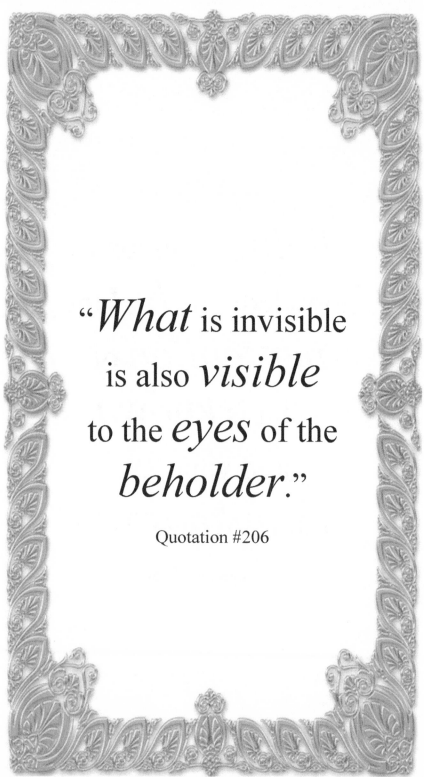

"*What* is invisible
is also *visible*
to the *eyes* of the
beholder."

Quotation #206

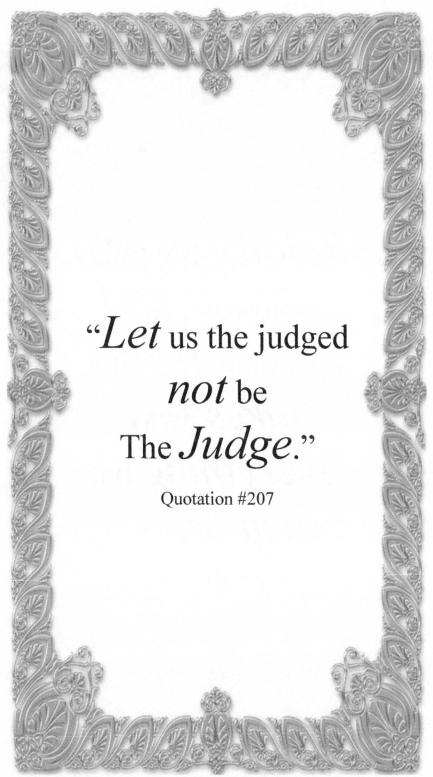

"*Let* us the judged
not be
The *Judge*."

Quotation #207

"*Rejoice* life today, tomorrow, *and* yesterday, *for* time *takes* away *everything* but *memories*."

Quotation #208

"*Waves* come and *break* everything, leaving behind *only* the *memories* as she rebuilds *again*."

Quotation #209

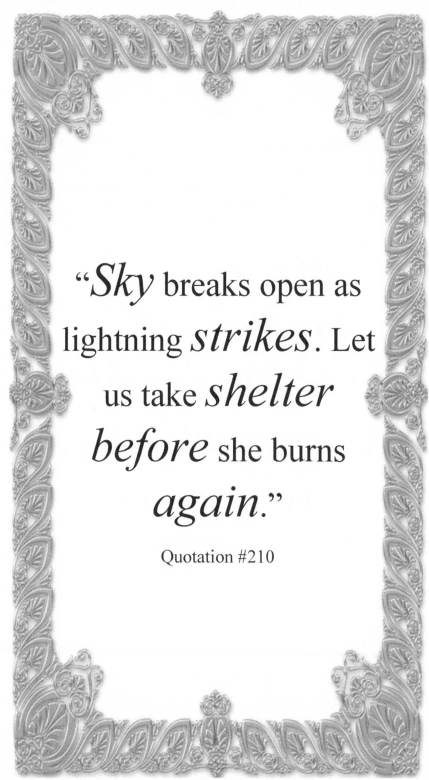

"*Sky* breaks open as lightning *strikes*. Let us take *shelter before* she burns *again*."

Quotation #210

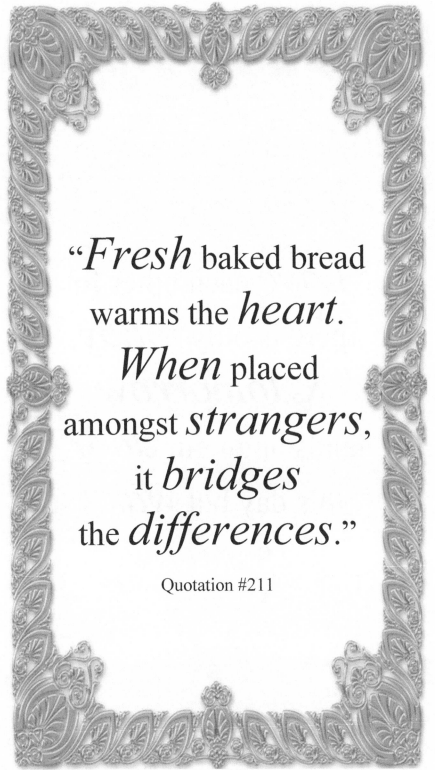

"*Fresh* baked bread warms the *heart*. *When* placed amongst *strangers*, it *bridges* the *differences*."

Quotation #211

"*Love* each other for
there is only *today*.
As *tomorrow*
lands upon our *door*,
this day but *was*."

Quotation #212

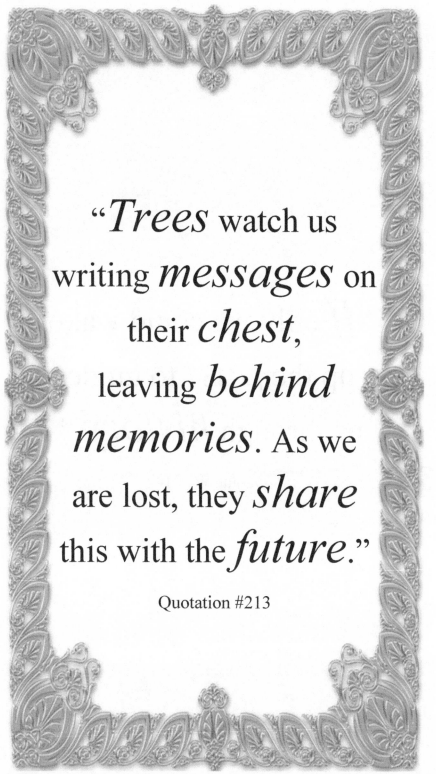

"*Trees* watch us writing *messages* on their *chest*, leaving *behind* *memories*. As we are lost, they *share* this with the *future*."

Quotation #213

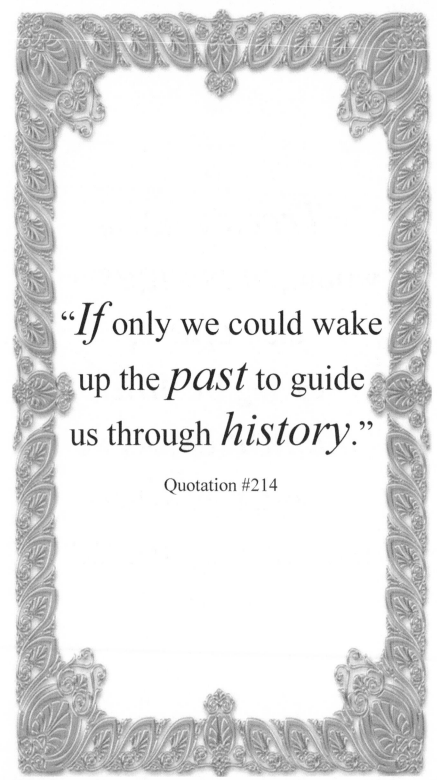

"*If* only we could wake up the *past* to guide us through *history.*"

Quotation #214

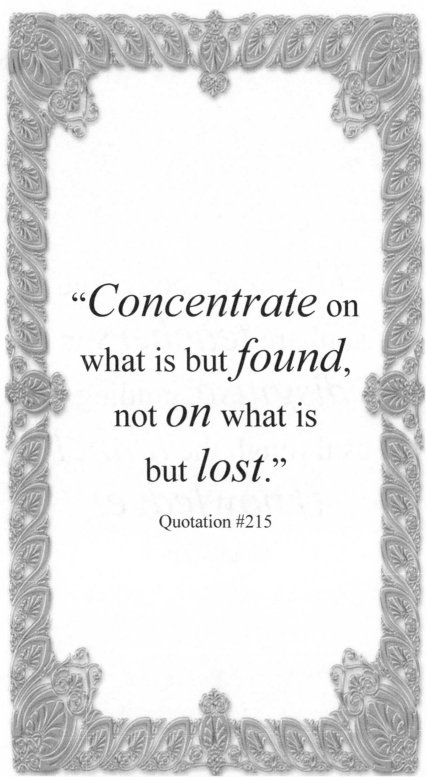

"*Concentrate* on what is but *found*, not *on* what is but *lost*."

Quotation #215

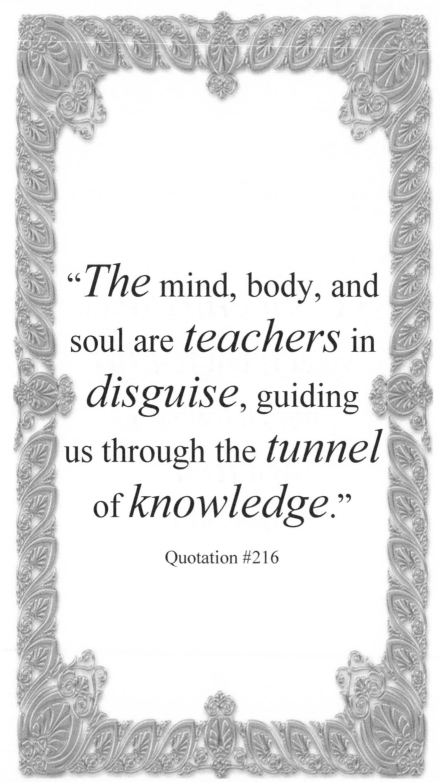

"*The* mind, body, and soul are *teachers* in *disguise*, guiding us through the *tunnel* of *knowledge*."

Quotation #216

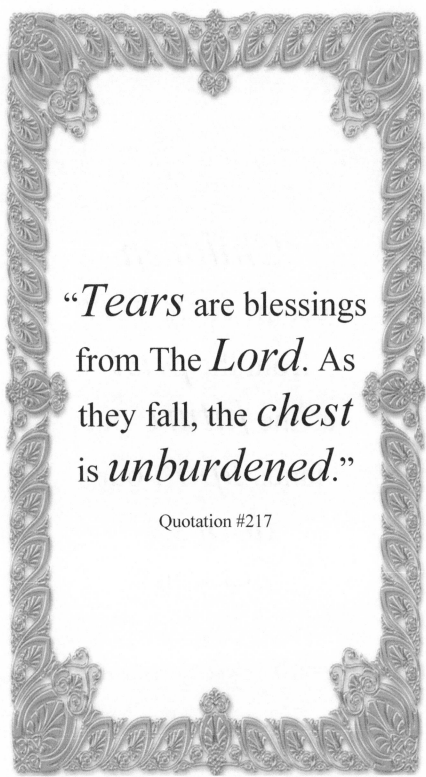

"*Tears* are blessings from The *Lord*. As they fall, the *chest* is *unburdened*."

Quotation #217

"*Children*
become *teachers*
from the *past*
as the *future* but
lands *upon* our
doors."

Quotation #218

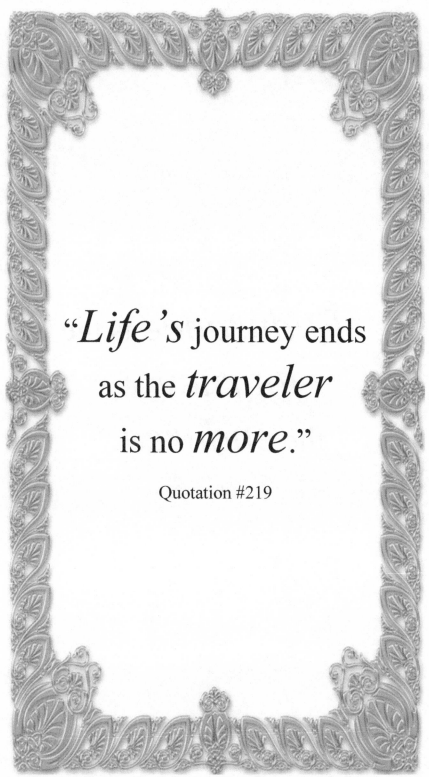

"*Life's* journey ends as the *traveler* is no *more*."

Quotation #219

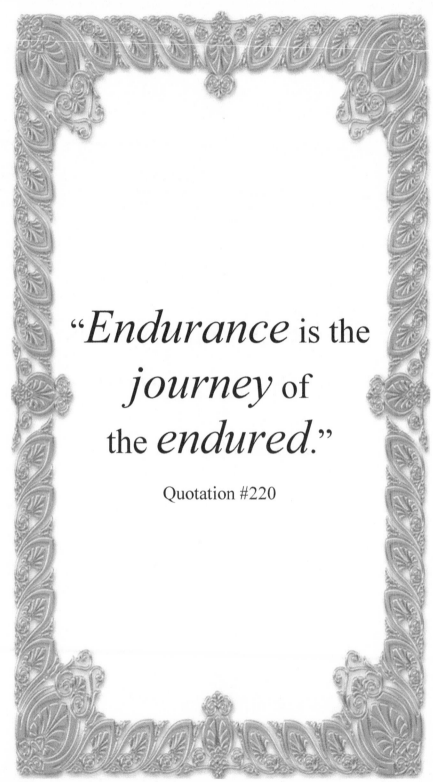

"*Endurance* is the *journey* of the *endured*."

Quotation #220

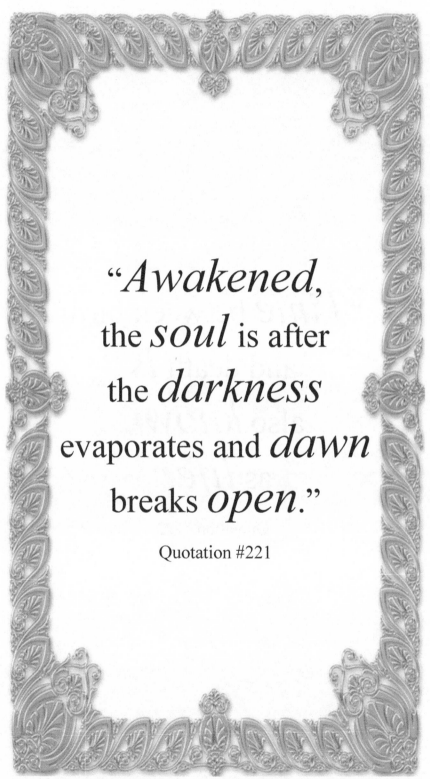

"*Awakened*,
the *soul* is after
the *darkness*
evaporates and *dawn*
breaks *open*."

Quotation #221

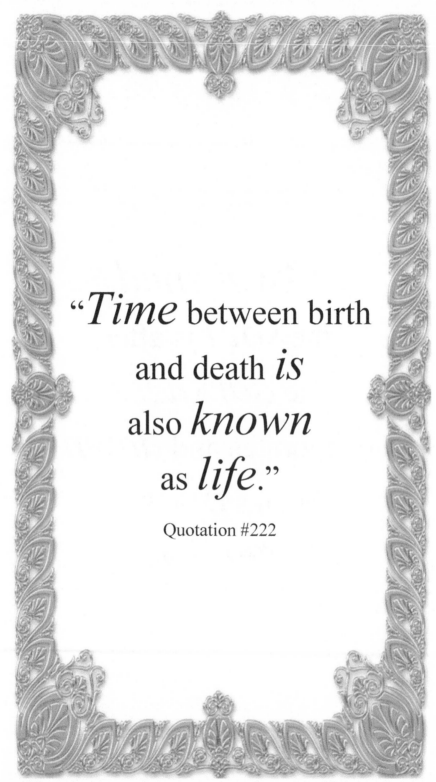

"*Time* between birth
and death *is*
also *known*
as *life.*"

Quotation #222

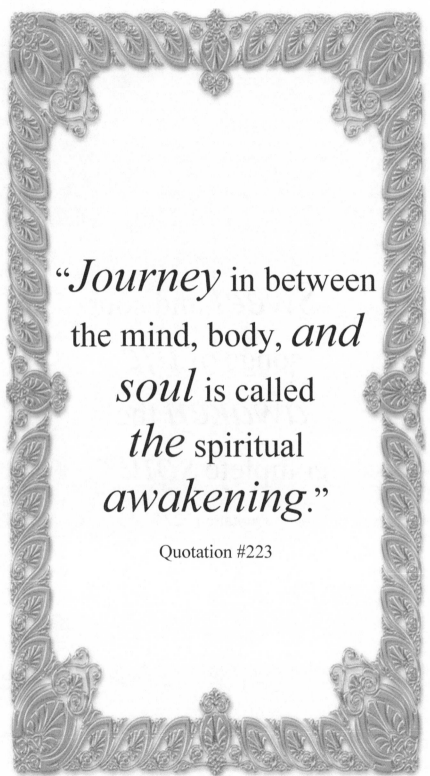

"*Journey* in between the mind, body, *and soul* is called *the* spiritual *awakening*."

Quotation #223

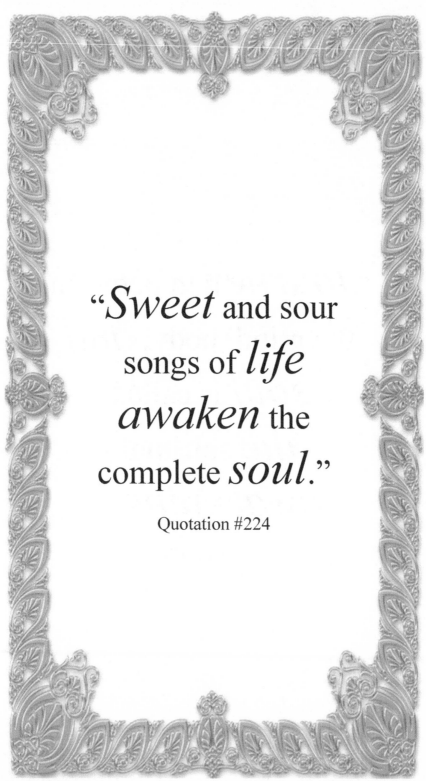

"*Sweet* and sour songs of *life* *awaken* the complete *soul*."

Quotation #224

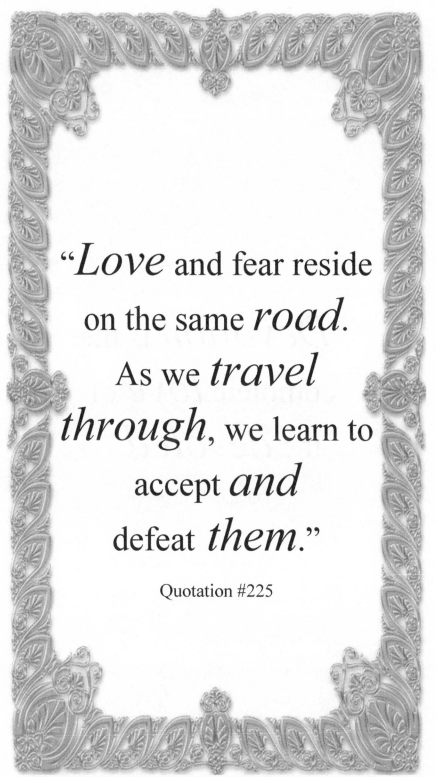

"*Love* and fear reside on the same *road*. As we *travel through*, we learn to accept *and* defeat *them*."

Quotation #225

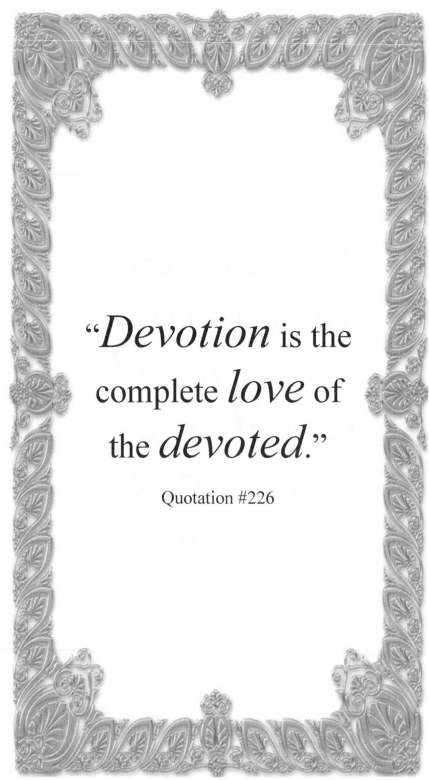

"*Devotion* is the complete *love* of the *devoted*."

Quotation #226

"*In* school, we are until
our life *journey*
but is *complete*."

Quotation #227

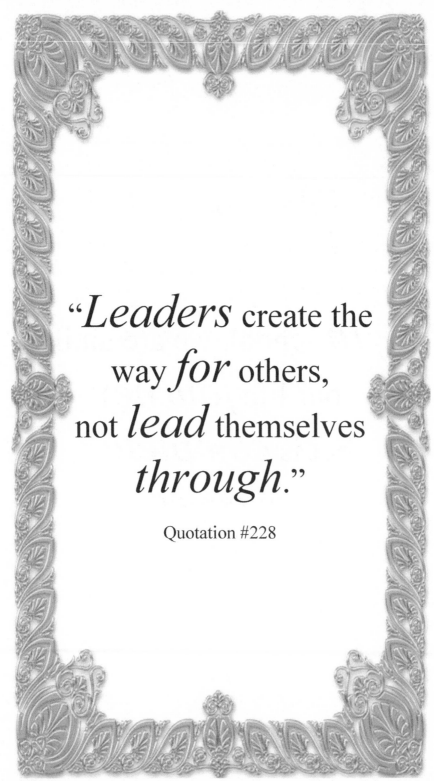

"*Leaders* create the way *for* others, not *lead* themselves *through*."

Quotation #228

"*Giving* up *everything* is not *love*. Trying to *acquire* even something *is*."

Quotation #229

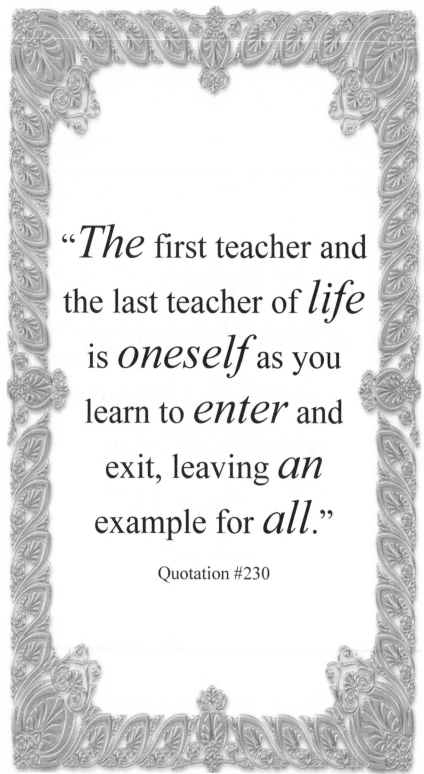

"*The* first teacher and the last teacher of *life* is *oneself* as you learn to *enter* and exit, leaving *an* example for *all*."

Quotation #230

246

"*Kind* words left in the air *spread* far beyond as she *kisses* all throughout *time*."

Quotation #231

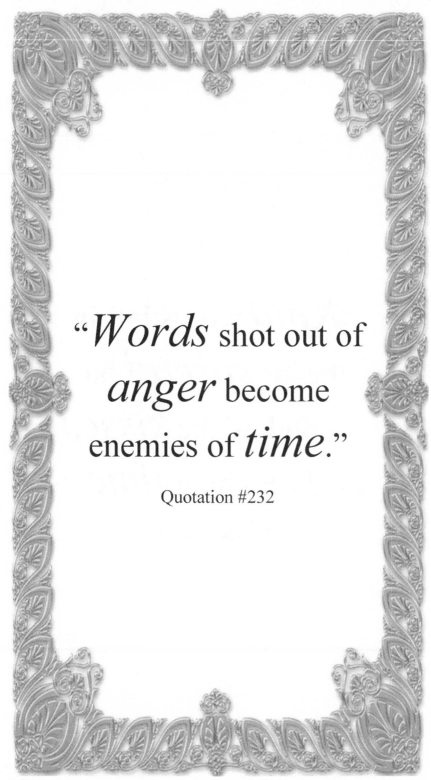

"*Words* shot out of
anger become
enemies of *time*."

Quotation #232

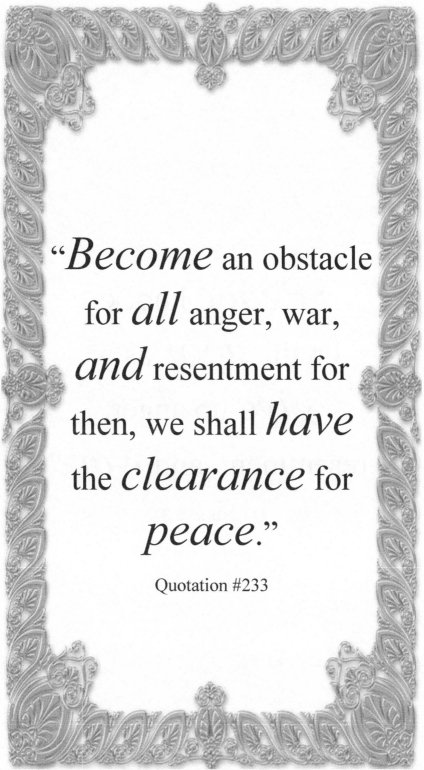

"*Become* an obstacle for *all* anger, war, *and* resentment for then, we shall *have* the *clearance* for *peace.*"

Quotation #233

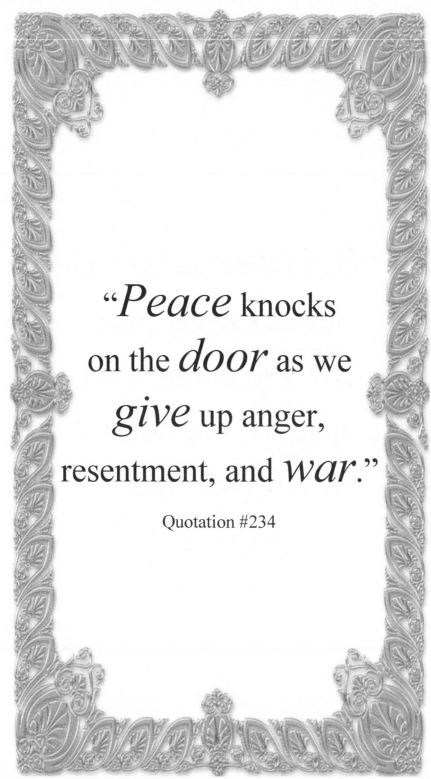

"*Peace* knocks on the *door* as we *give* up anger, resentment, and *war*."

Quotation #234

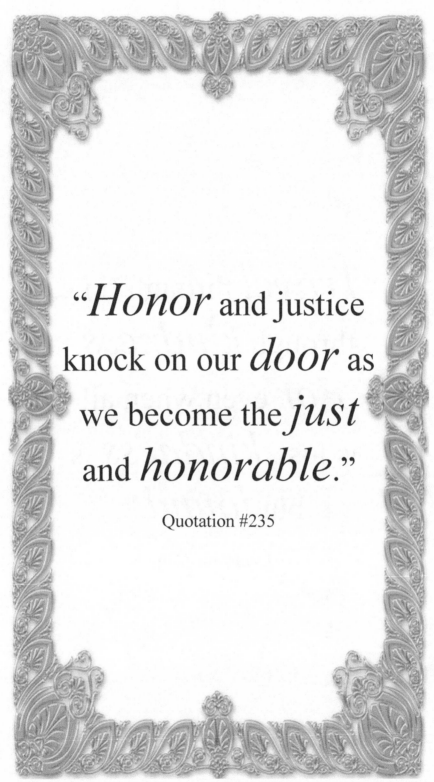

"*Honor* and justice knock on our *door* as we become the *just* and *honorable*."

Quotation #235

"*Travel* through time, through *kindness*. *For* even when all is lost, *kindness* is but *found*."

Quotation #236

"*The* ocean, the land, and the *skies* are all *witnesses* of the past, *present*, and the *future.*"

Quotation #237

"*The* ark carries all
life *throughout* the
storms, if only
we can *make*
it *aboard*."

Quotation #238

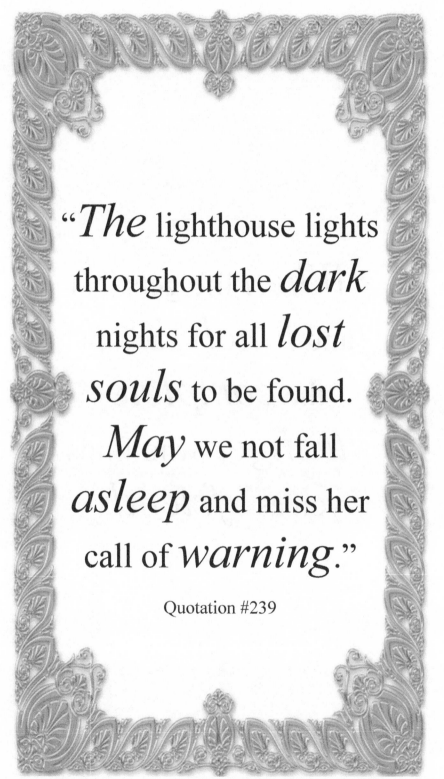

"*The* lighthouse lights throughout the *dark* nights for all *lost souls* to be found. *May* we not fall *asleep* and miss her call of *warning*."

Quotation #239

"*When* life gets lost and *lonely*, accept the *complete stranger* who finds you as a *friend*."

Quotation #240

"*Do* not hide
in a *tunnel* for then
you *shall* be
lost."

Quotation #241

"*Forever*
there is *love* amongst
strangers who
wait for a *friend*."

Quotation #242

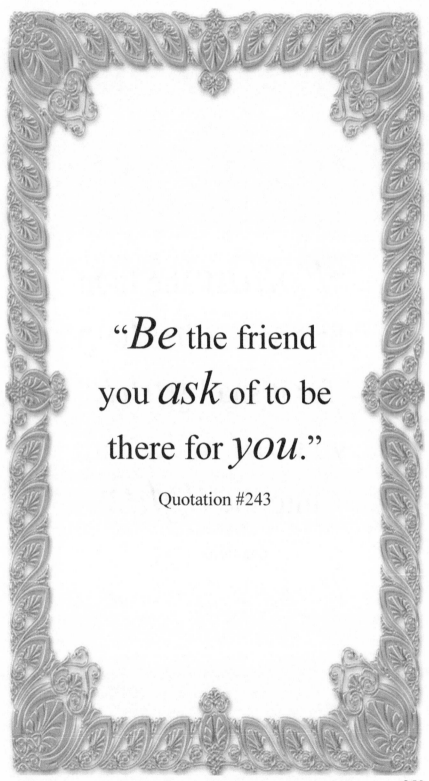

"*Be* the friend
you *ask* of to be
there for *you*."

Quotation #243

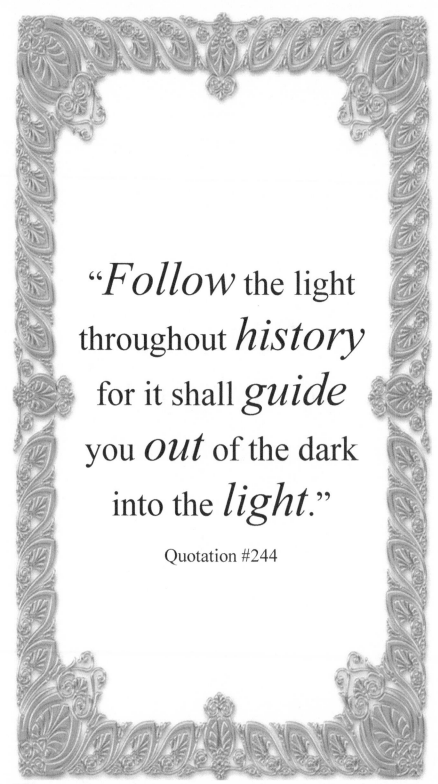

"*Follow* the light throughout *history* for it shall *guide* you *out* of the dark into the *light*."

Quotation #244

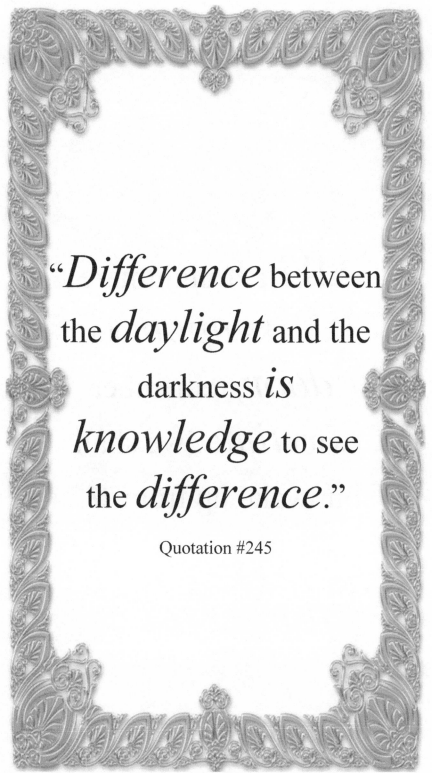

"*Difference* between the *daylight* and the darkness *is* *knowledge* to see the *difference*."

Quotation #245

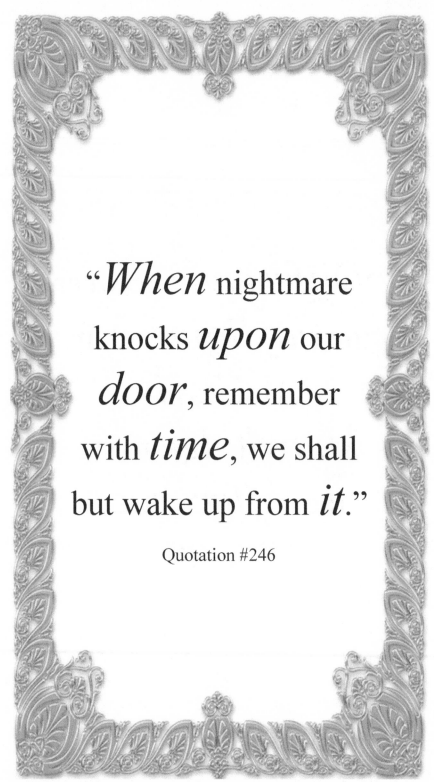

"*When* nightmare knocks *upon* our *door*, remember with *time*, we shall but wake up from *it*."

Quotation #246

"*Dreams* are a form of *blessings* from the *unknown*."

Quotation #247

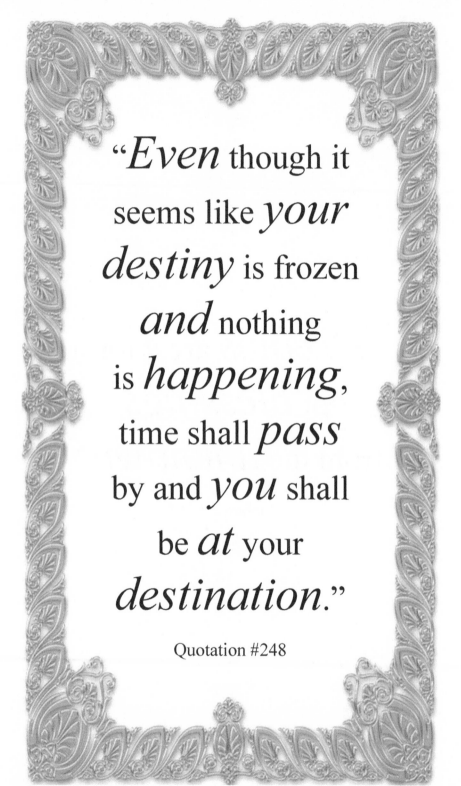

"*Even* though it seems like *your destiny* is frozen *and* nothing is *happening*, time shall *pass* by and *you* shall be *at* your *destination*."

Quotation #248

"*Peace* is achieved *every* day through give and *take*."

Quotation #249

"*Life* stays still as *everything* else *moves* on. What is *found* is not needed *until* it too is but *gone*."

Quotation #250

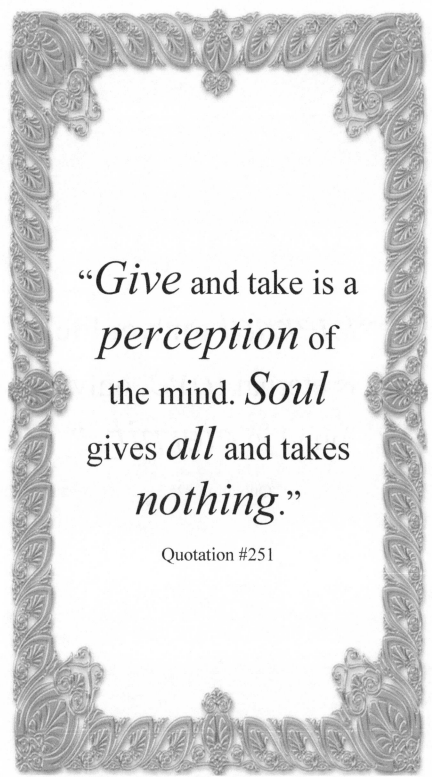

"*Give* and take is a *perception* of the mind. *Soul* gives *all* and takes *nothing*."

Quotation #251

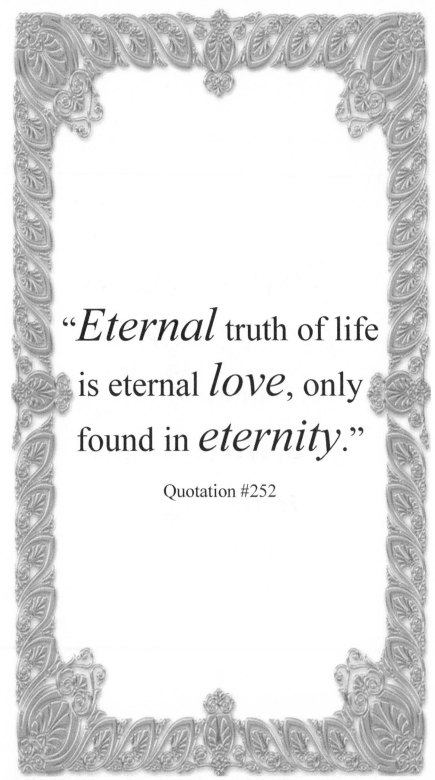

"*Eternal* truth of life is eternal *love*, only found in *eternity*."

Quotation #252

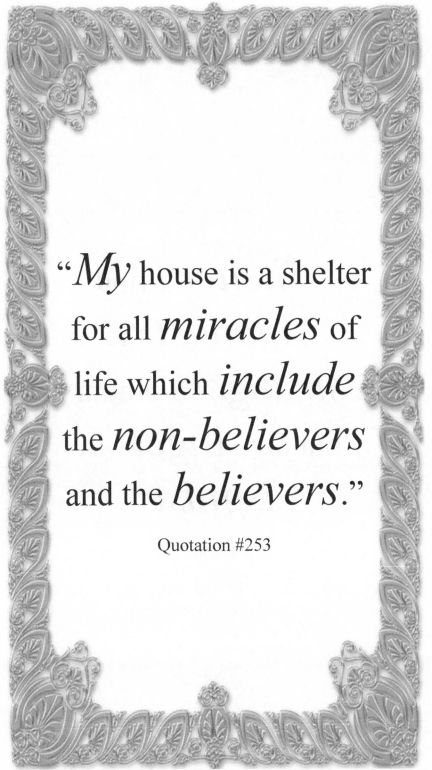

"*My* house is a shelter for all *miracles* of life which *include* the *non-believers* and the *believers*."

Quotation #253

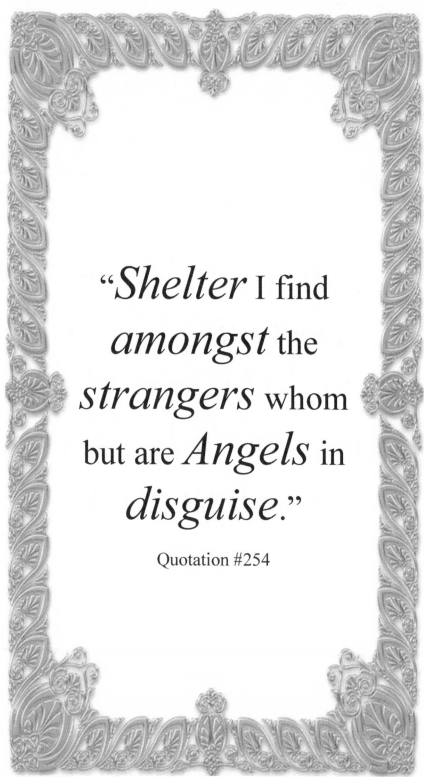

"*Shelter* I find *amongst* the *strangers* whom but are *Angels* in *disguise*."

Quotation #254

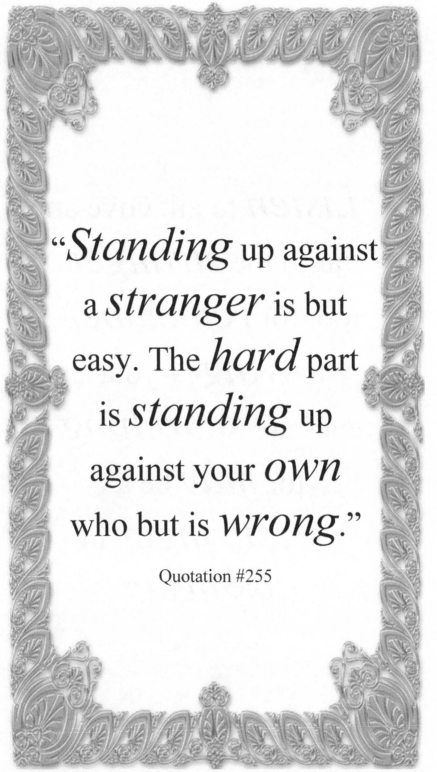

"*Standing* up against a *stranger* is but easy. The *hard* part is *standing* up against your *own* who but is *wrong*."

Quotation #255

"*Listen* to all. Give an ear to the *stranger* too, for *remember* the *Angel* your eyes are *searching* for *may* be a total *stranger* in *disguise*."

Quotation #256

"*The* goal of life is not the *achievements*, but the *journey* through *it*."

Quotation #257

"*Do* not give up on *hope* for remember hope is *but immortal.*"

Quotation #258

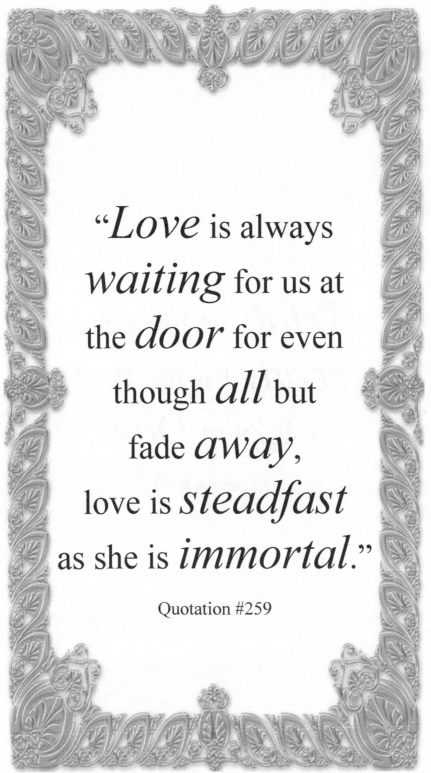

"*Love* is always *waiting* for us at the *door* for even though *all* but fade *away*, love is *steadfast* as she is *immortal*."

Quotation #259

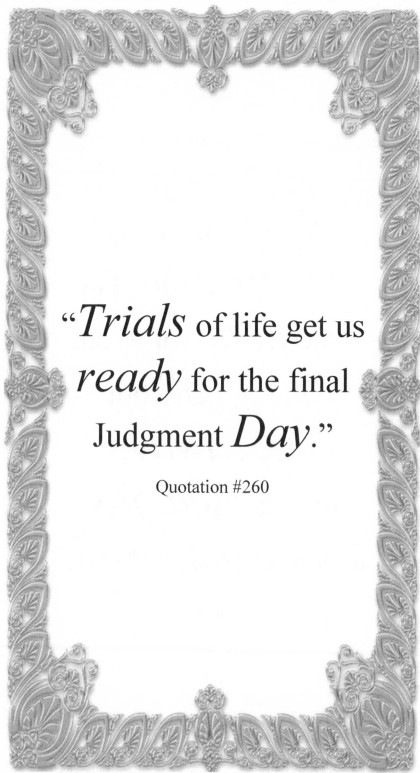

"*Trials* of life get us *ready* for the final Judgment *Day*."

Quotation #260

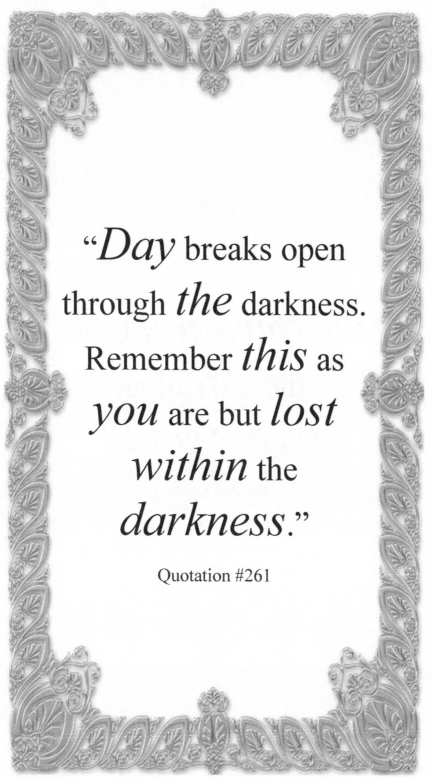

"*Day* breaks open through *the* darkness. Remember *this* as *you* are but *lost within* the *darkness.*"

Quotation #261

"*Inspiration* is but the *gift* of an inspired *soul*."

Quotation #262

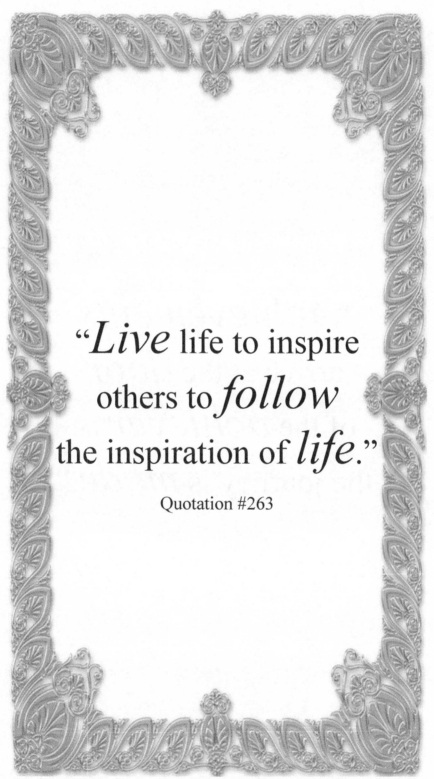

"*Live* life to inspire
others to *follow*
the inspiration of *life.*"

Quotation #263

"*Achievements* arrive at the *door* of the *achiever* as the journey is *made*."

Quotation #264

"*Mercy* is but found
at the *door* of the
merciful."

Quotation #265

"*Time* passes by us. *Words* stay forever as a *guide* and *become* a guide for the *future*."

Quotation #266

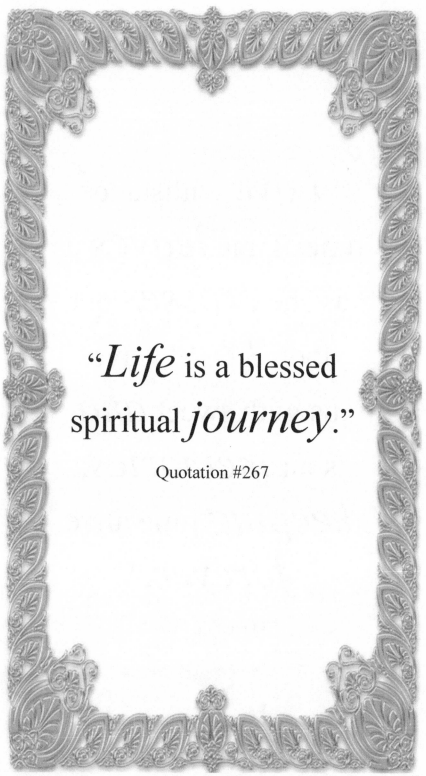

"*Life* is a blessed
spiritual *journey*."

Quotation #267

"*Love* withstands time. Time *leaves* us as she *crosses* our door. *Love* leaves us with sweet *and* sour *memories*, *keeping* time alive *forever.*"

Quotation #268

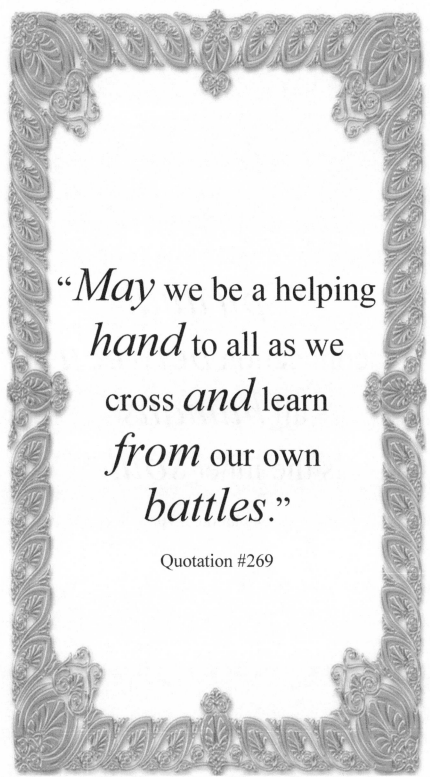

"*May* we be a helping *hand* to all as we cross *and* learn *from* our own *battles.*"

Quotation #269

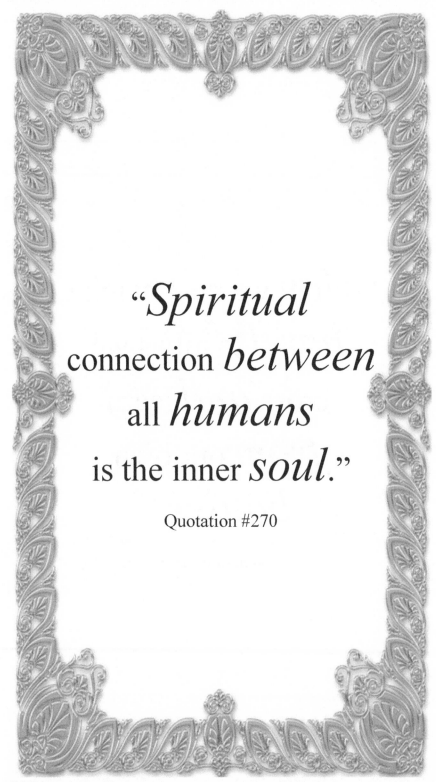

"*Spiritual*
connection *between*
all *humans*
is the inner *soul.*"

Quotation #270

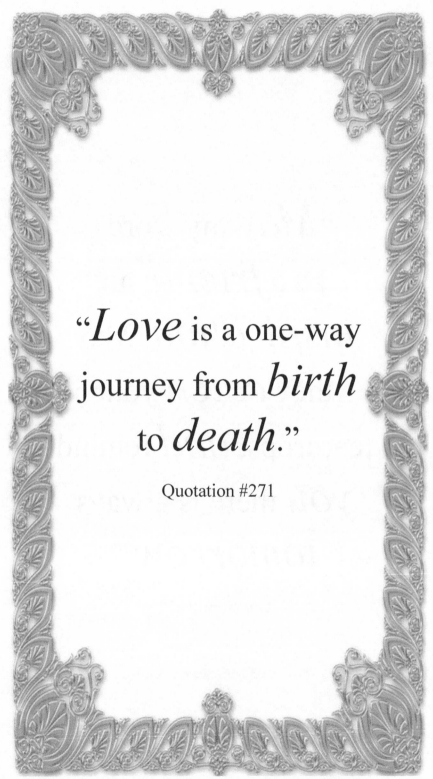

"*Love* is a one-way journey from *birth* to *death*."

Quotation #271

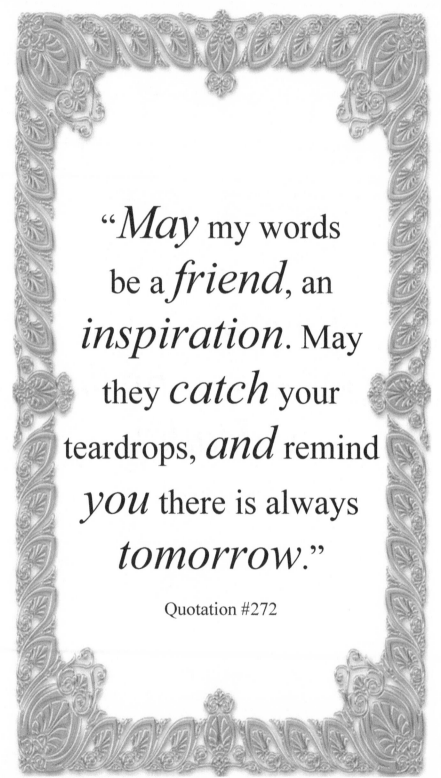

"*May* my words be a *friend*, an *inspiration*. May they *catch* your teardrops, *and* remind *you* there is always *tomorrow*."

Quotation #272

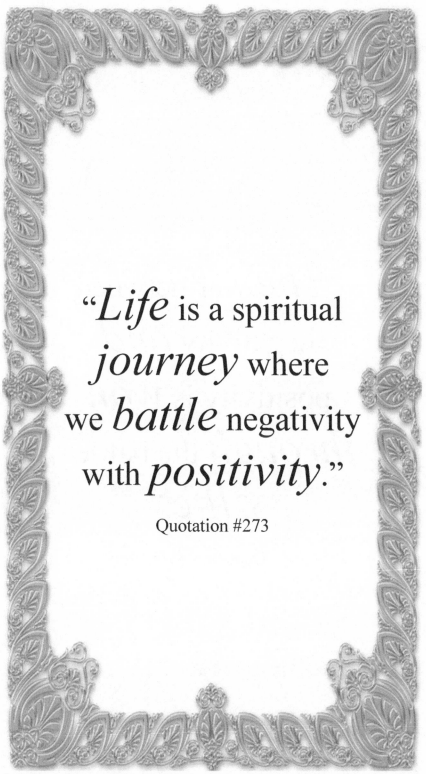

"*Life* is a spiritual *journey* where we *battle* negativity with *positivity*."

Quotation #273

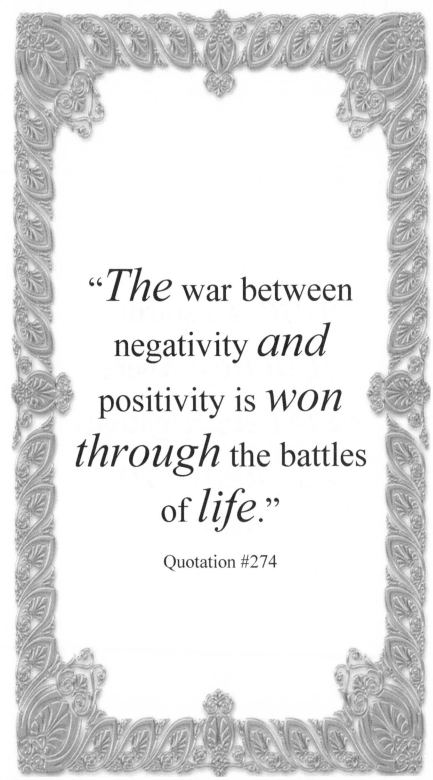

"*The* war between negativity *and* positivity is *won through* the battles of *life*."

Quotation #274

"*Come* and join
me on this journey
of giving and maybe
together, we can be
the hope, the
motivation, the
inspiration for a
stranger waiting for a
knock on the door from
a stranger who I call
my Angel in
disguise."

Quotation #275

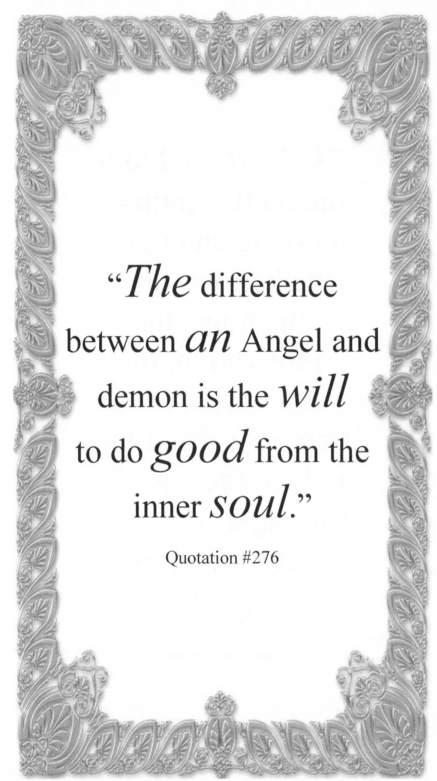

"*The* difference between *an* Angel and demon is the *will* to do *good* from the inner *soul*."

Quotation #276

"*My* life is a journey through *struggles* and *achievements* of *life*. Throughout *all*, it was a test as to see if I *could withstand* the winds *of* obstacles and hold *on*."

Quotation #277

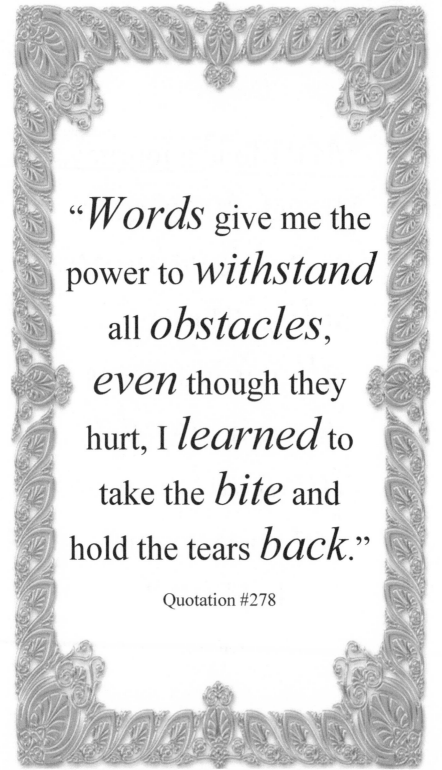

"*Words* give me the power to *withstand* all *obstacles*, *even* though they hurt, I *learned* to take the *bite* and hold the tears *back*."

Quotation #278

294

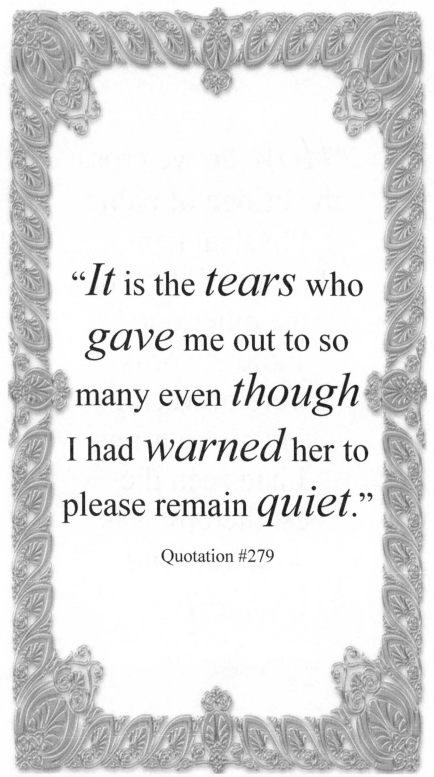

"*It* is the *tears* who *gave* me out to so many even *though* I had *warned* her to please remain *quiet*."

Quotation #279

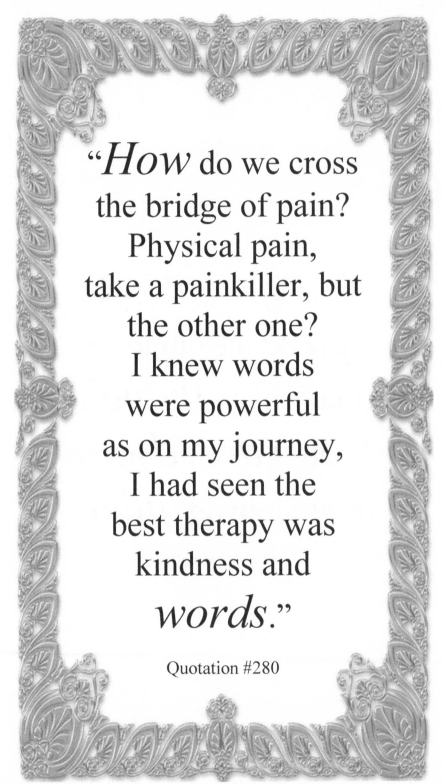

"*How* do we cross
the bridge of pain?
Physical pain,
take a painkiller, but
the other one?
I knew words
were powerful
as on my journey,
I had seen the
best therapy was
kindness and
words."

Quotation #280

296

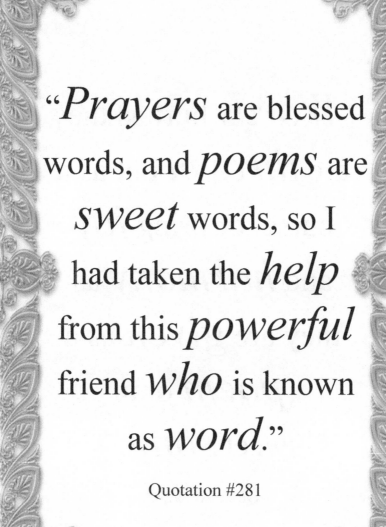

"*Prayers* are blessed words, and *poems* are *sweet* words, so I had taken the *help* from this *powerful* friend *who* is known as *word*."

Quotation #281

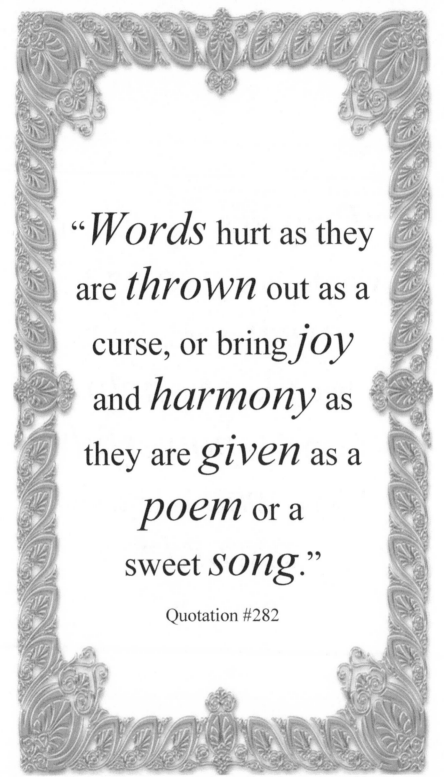

"*Words* hurt as they are *thrown* out as a curse, or bring *joy* and *harmony* as they are *given* as a *poem* or a sweet *song*."

Quotation #282

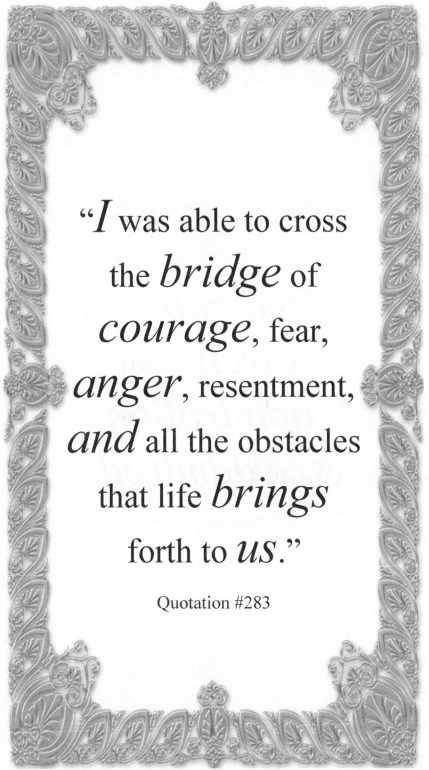

"*I* was able to cross the *bridge* of *courage*, fear, *anger*, resentment, *and* all the obstacles that life *brings* forth to *us*."

Quotation #283

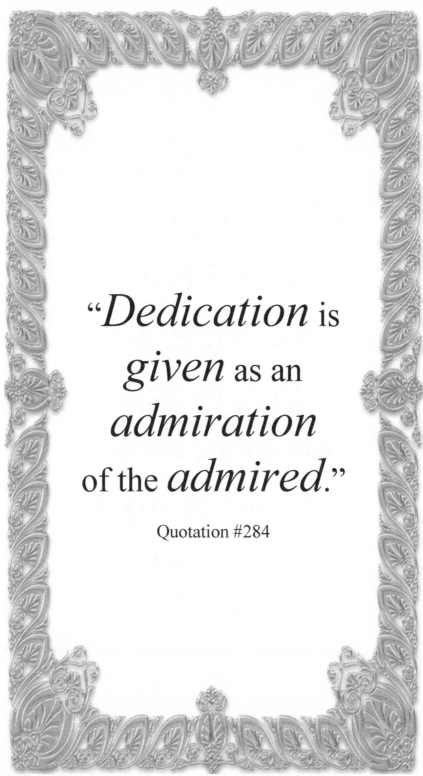

"*Dedication* is *given* as an *admiration* of the *admired*."

Quotation #284

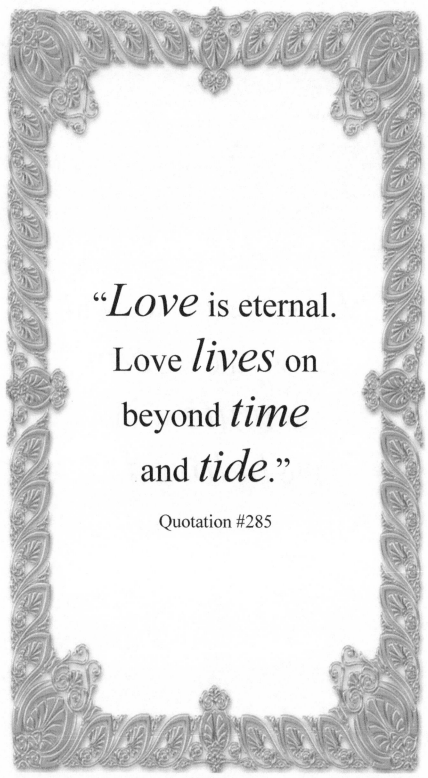

"*Love* is eternal.
Love *lives* on
beyond *time*
and *tide*."

Quotation #285

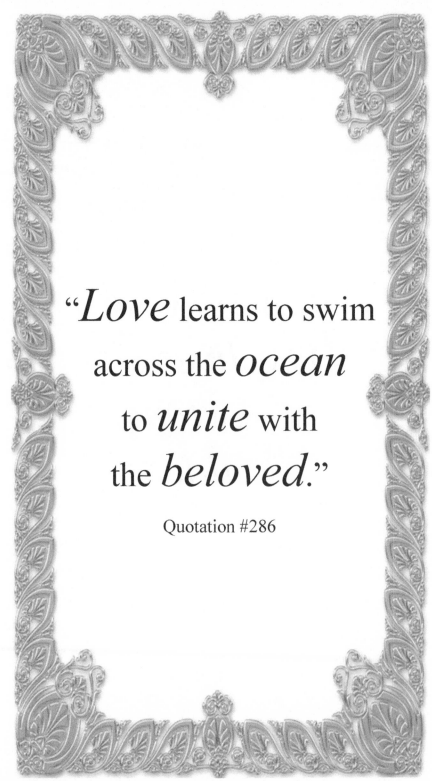

"*Love* learns to swim
across the *ocean*
to *unite* with
the *beloved.*"

Quotation #286

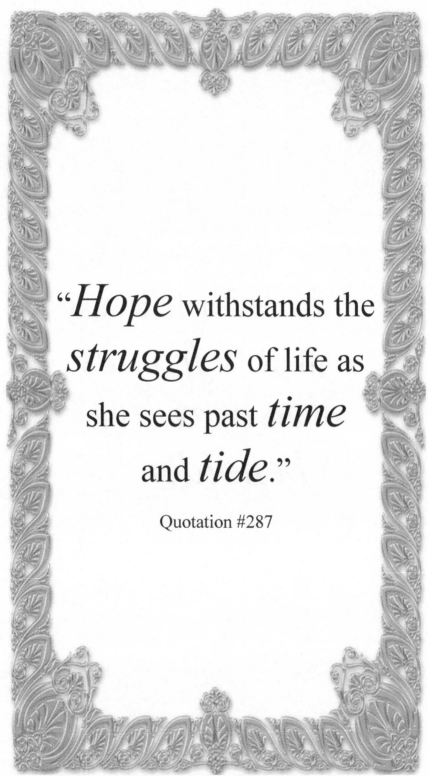

"*Hope* withstands the *struggles* of life as she sees past *time* and *tide*."

Quotation #287

"*Time* is held to stay
still in the *frames*
of the *eyes* of the
beholder."

Quotation #288

"*The* soul remains *forever* within the *heart* of the true *beloved*."

Quotation #289

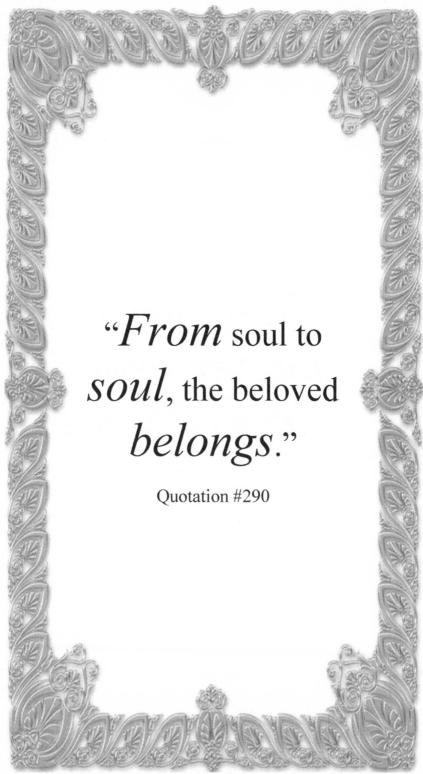

"*From* soul to
soul, the beloved
belongs."

Quotation #290

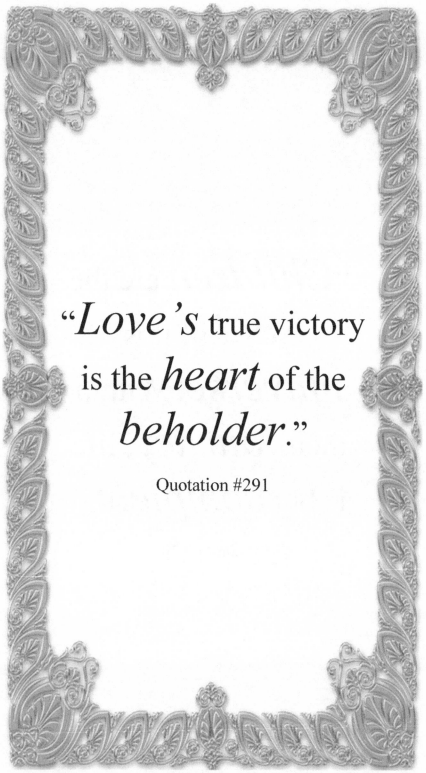

"*Love's* true victory
is the *heart* of the
beholder."

Quotation #291

"*Children* are the *soul* of this *universe*. Within their *journey*, life is but *complete*."

Quotation #292

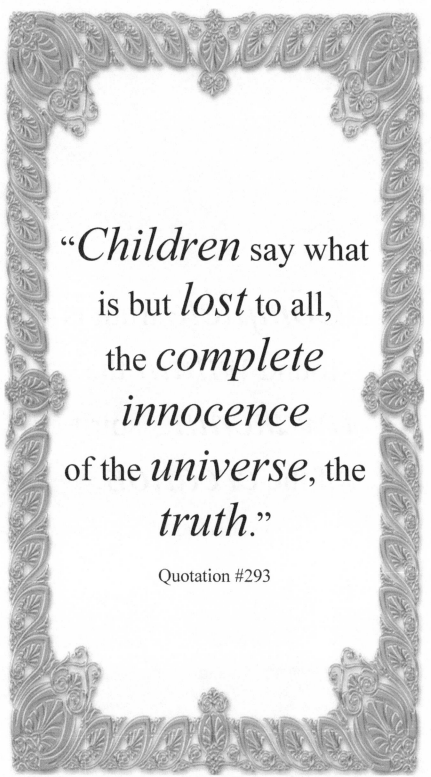

"*Children* say what is but *lost* to all, the *complete innocence* of the *universe*, the *truth*."

Quotation #293

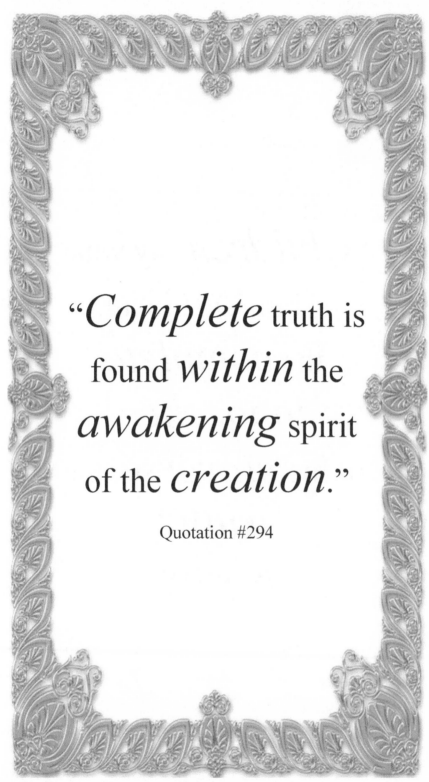

"*Complete* truth is found *within* the *awakening* spirit of the *creation*."

Quotation #294

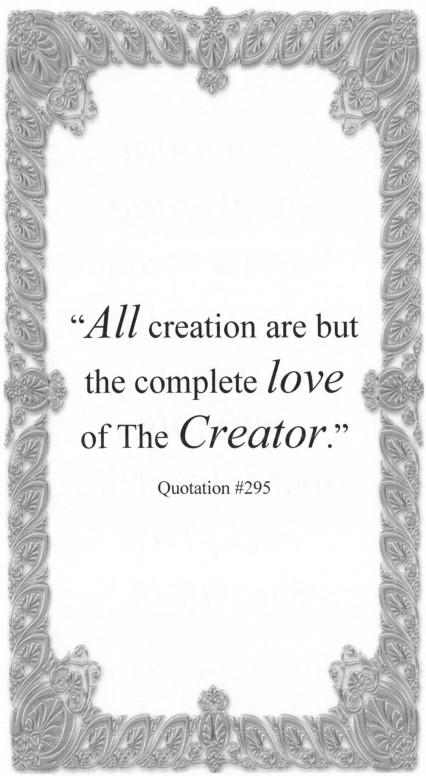

"*All* creation are but the complete *love* of The *Creator*."

Quotation #295

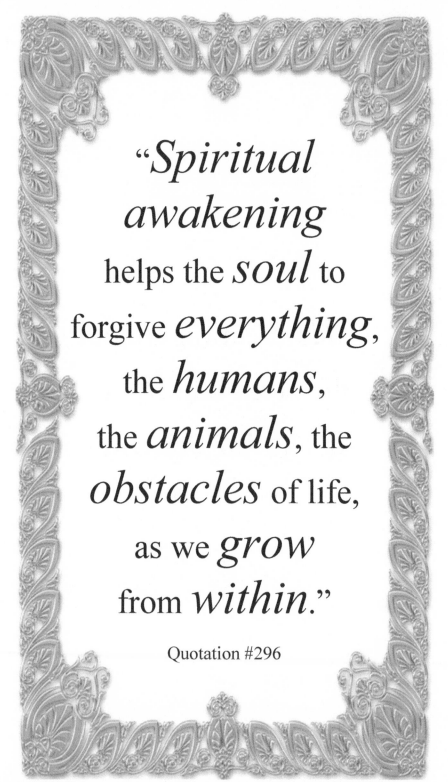

"*Spiritual awakening* helps the *soul* to forgive *everything*, the *humans*, the *animals*, the *obstacles* of life, as we *grow* from *within*."

Quotation #296

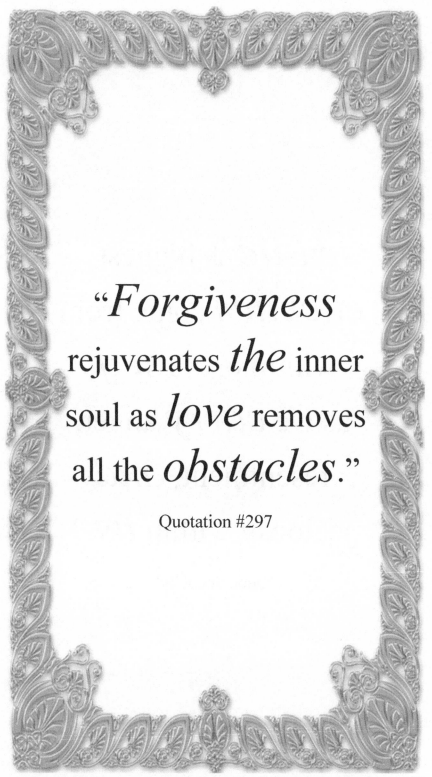

"*Forgiveness*
rejuvenates *the* inner
soul as *love* removes
all the *obstacles*."

Quotation #297

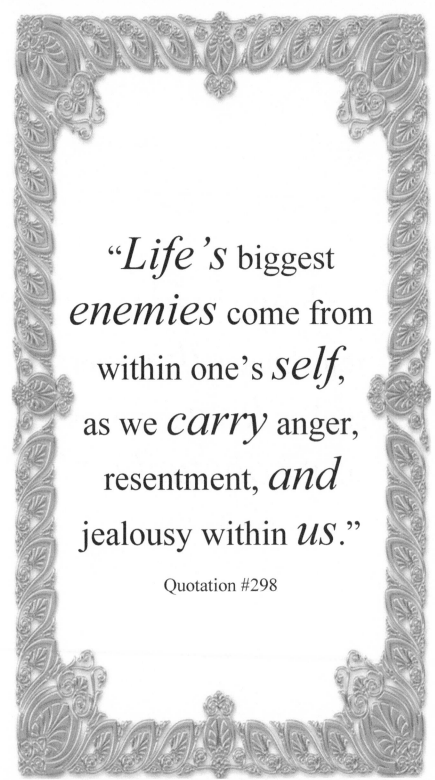

"*Life's* biggest *enemies* come from within one's *self*, as we *carry* anger, resentment, *and* jealousy within *us*."

Quotation #298

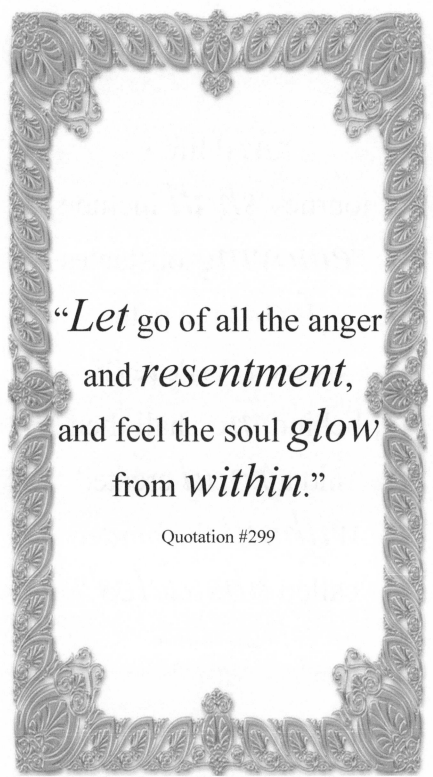

"*Let* go of all the anger and *resentment*, and feel the soul *glow* from *within*."

Quotation #299

"*My* life's journey *shall* include *removing* obstacles *from* the path as the *travelers* behind *me* shall then find a *road* created *without* the burden called *obstacles*."

Quotation #300

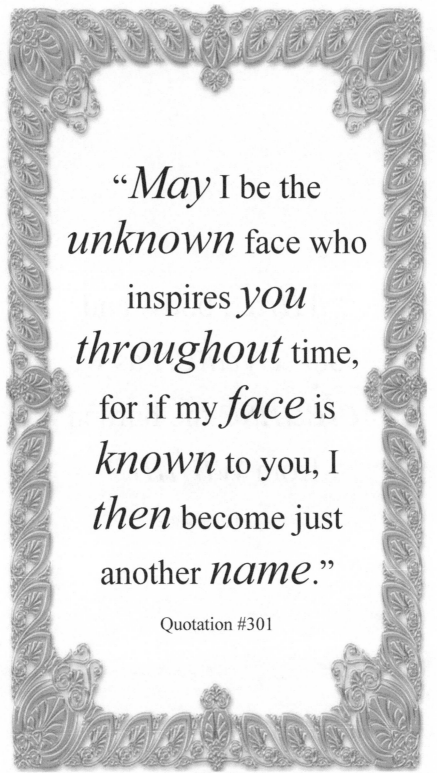

"*May* I be the *unknown* face who inspires *you* *throughout* time, for if my *face* is *known* to you, I *then* become just another *name*."

Quotation #301

317

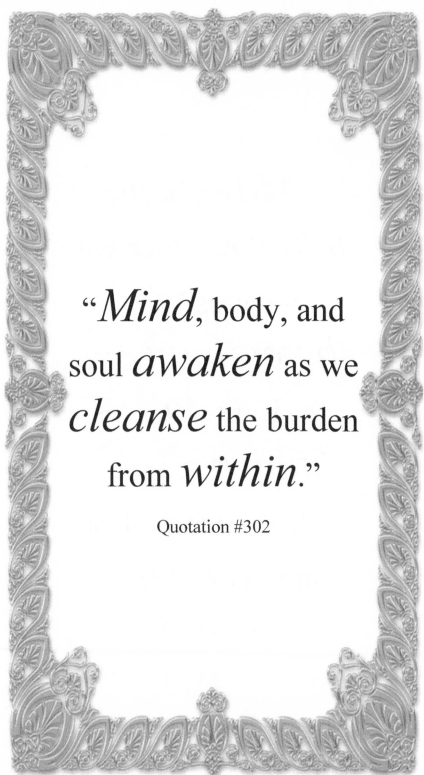

"*Mind*, body, and soul *awaken* as we *cleanse* the burden from *within*."

Quotation #302

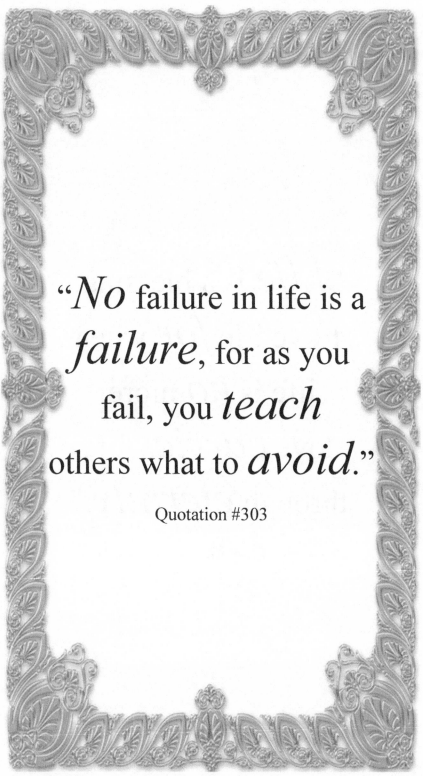

"*No* failure in life is a
failure, for as you
fail, you *teach*
others what to *avoid*."

Quotation #303

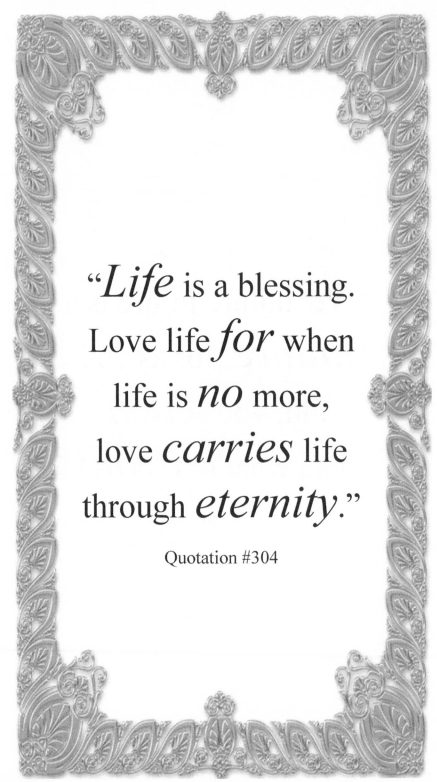

"*Life* is a blessing.
Love life *for* when
life is *no* more,
love *carries* life
through *eternity*."

Quotation #304

"*Love* is all about *giving* and the feeling to give more, *for* with the *gift* of giving, *love* becomes *eternal*."

Quotation #305

"*Mother* Earth *embraces* all of her *children* under one *blanket* as we *sleep* on our Earthly *bed*."

Quotation #306

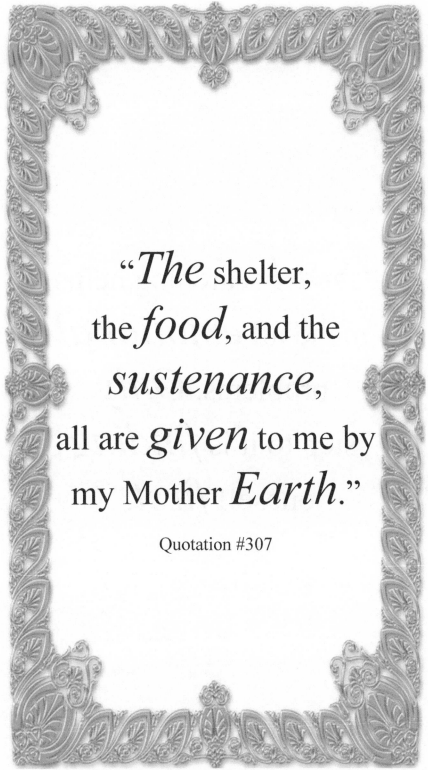

"*The* shelter,
the *food*, and the
sustenance,
all are *given* to me by
my Mother *Earth*."

Quotation #307

"*Soul* searching helps mend all *emotional* problems. *Only* step to it is *finding* oneself *first*."

Quotation #308

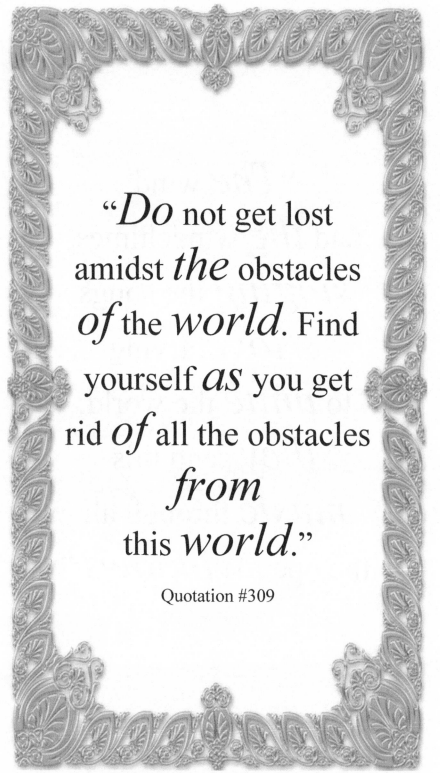

"*Do* not get lost amidst *the* obstacles *of* the *world*. Find yourself *as* you get rid *of* all the obstacles *from* this *world*."

Quotation #309

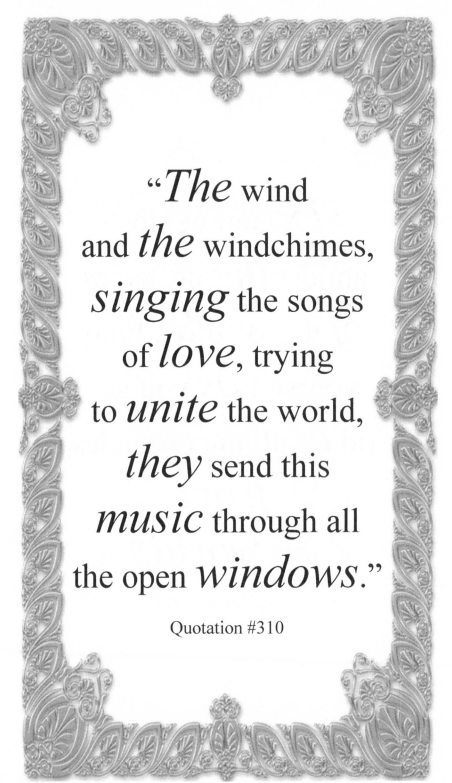

"*The* wind
and *the* windchimes,
singing the songs
of *love*, trying
to *unite* the world,
they send this
music through all
the open *windows*."

Quotation #310

"*Time* is not a friend as he *passes* us by. *Take* this moment, *catch* him through your *memories* forever. So *even* after his *departure*, memories *frame* him *forever*."

Quotation #311

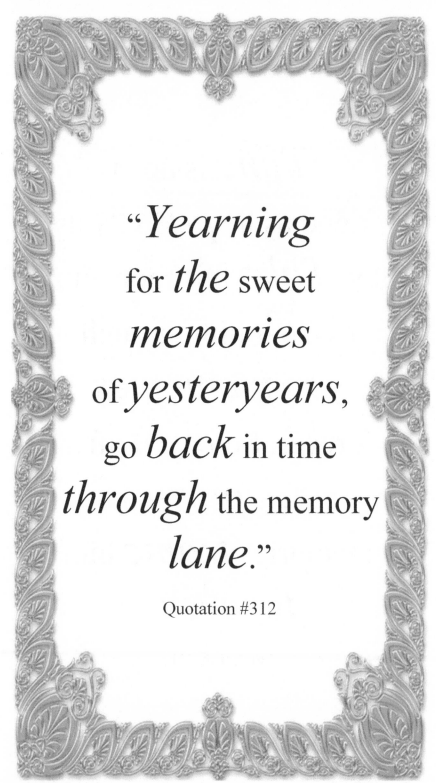

"*Yearning* for *the* sweet *memories* of *yesteryears*, go *back* in time *through* the memory *lane.*"

Quotation #312

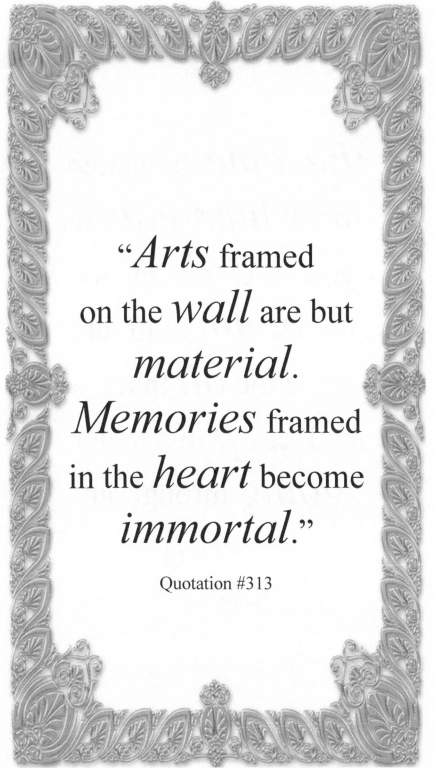

"*Arts* framed on the *wall* are but *material*. *Memories* framed in the *heart* become *immortal*."

Quotation #313

"*Become* the lantern for all *humanity* as your *words* carried by *mouth* to mouth is the *oil* that shall *keep* this lantern *going* throughout *eternity*."

Quotation #314

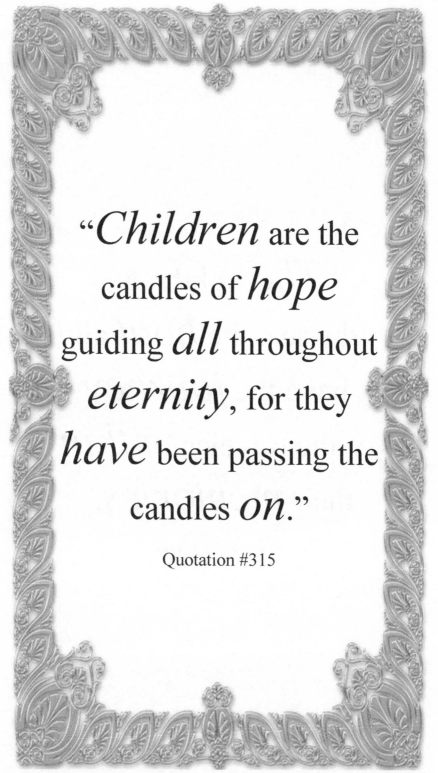

"*Children* are the candles of *hope* guiding *all* throughout *eternity*, for they *have* been passing the candles *on*."

Quotation #315

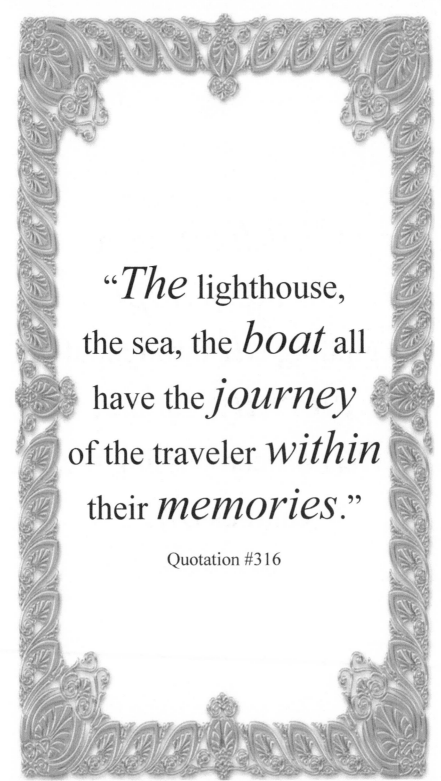

"*The* lighthouse, the sea, the *boat* all have the *journey* of the traveler *within* their *memories*."

Quotation #316

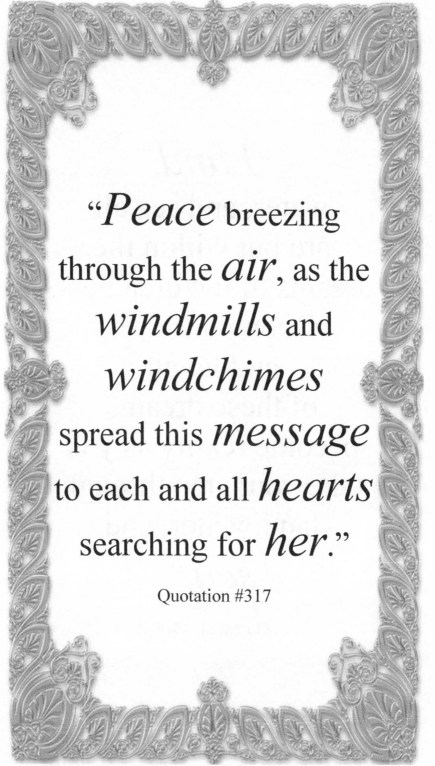

"*Peace* breezing through the *air*, as the *windmills* and *windchimes* spread this *message* to each and all *hearts* searching for *her*."

Quotation #317

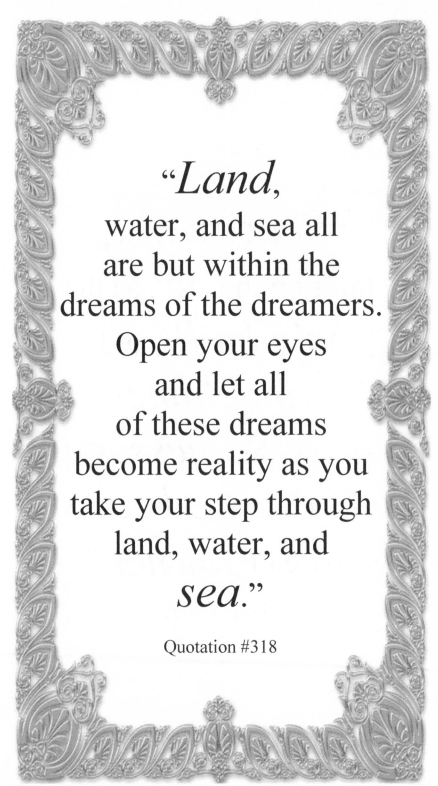

"*Land*,
water, and sea all
are but within the
dreams of the dreamers.
Open your eyes
and let all
of these dreams
become reality as you
take your step through
land, water, and
sea."

Quotation #318

BOOK THREE

Spiritual
Journey
Life's Eternal Blessings

Ann Marie Ruby

DEDICATION

I dedicate this book to all of whom do not have a family and are looking for a family. Please consider me your spiritual family. I believe as long as there is a spiritually awakened soul in this universe, we are a family. I am your family as you are mine. I shall always be there for all spiritually awakened souls. May we spread peace as we find peace. Like I always say, "Spread peace, be in peace."

JOURNEY OF MY LIFE

My Lord,

My Creator,

You have but placed us, the travelers,

Upon this journey,

With struggles, agony, pain, health, wealth, Wisdom,

love, and victory

As our companions of life.

May I, Your devotee, the traveler,

Have as my companion only Your blessings

As I embark upon this blessed

JOURNEY OF MY LIFE.

*From my prayer book, *Spiritual Songs: Letters From My Chest.*

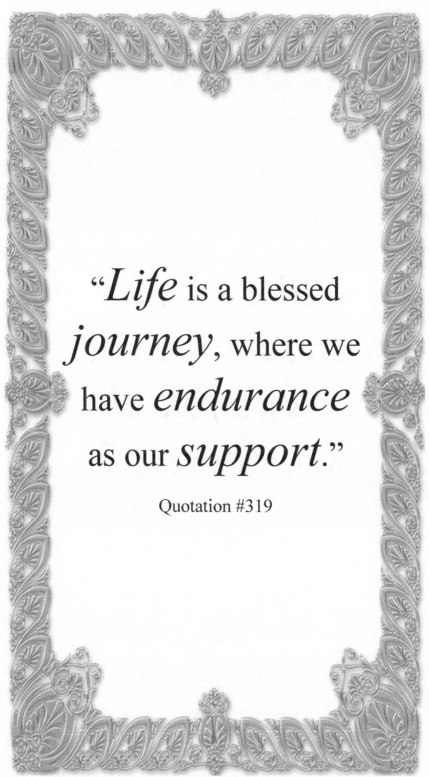

"*Life* is a blessed
journey, where we
have *endurance*
as our *support*."

Quotation #319

"*Focus* on the *complete* truth only, as it is *found* within each *soul*."

Quotation #320

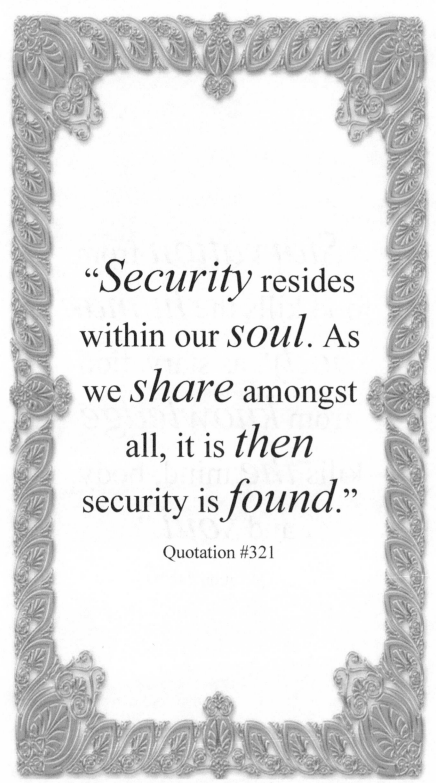

"*Security* resides within our *soul*. As we *share* amongst all, it is *then* security is *found*."

Quotation #321

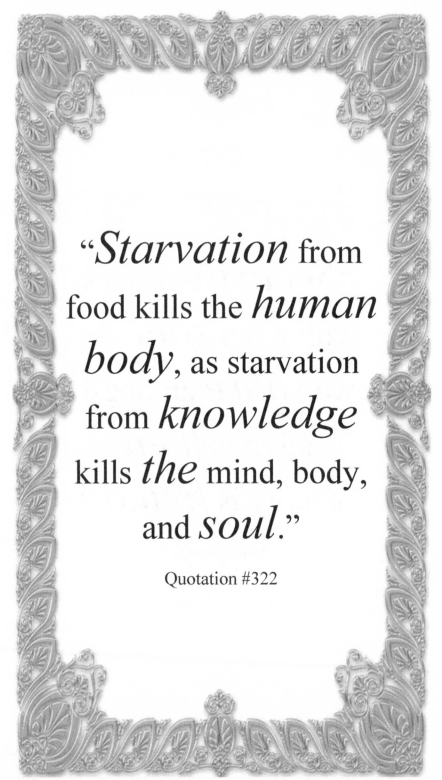

"*Starvation* from food kills the *human body*, as starvation from *knowledge* kills *the* mind, body, and *soul*."

Quotation #322

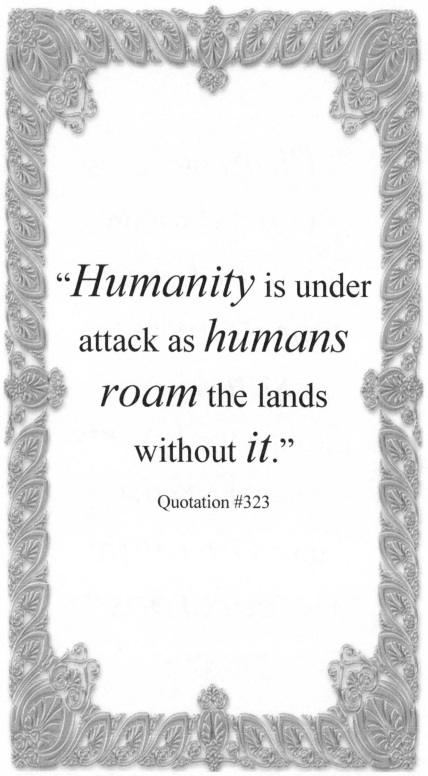

"*Humanity* is under attack as *humans roam* the lands without *it.*"

Quotation #323

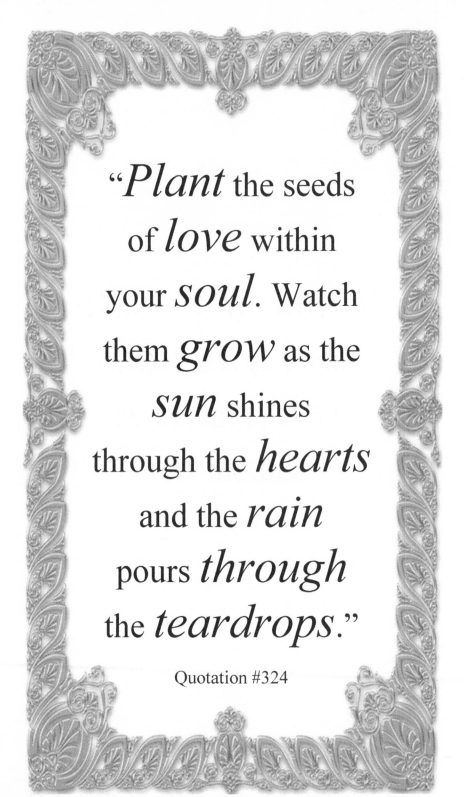

"*Plant* the seeds of *love* within your *soul*. Watch them *grow* as the *sun* shines through the *hearts* and the *rain* pours *through* the *teardrops*."

Quotation #324

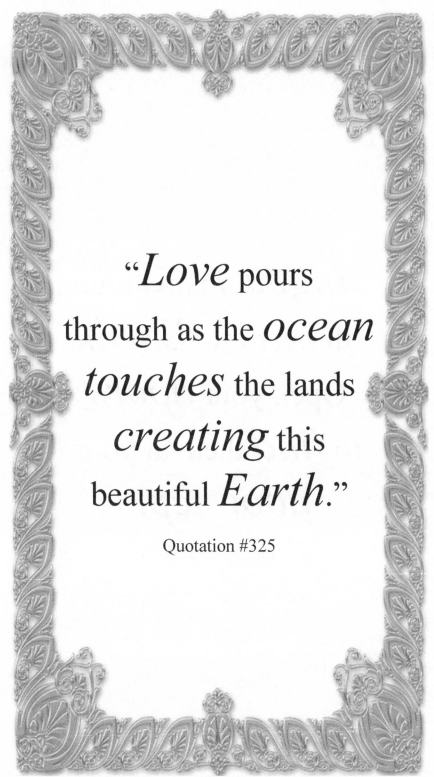

"*Love* pours through as the *ocean touches* the lands *creating* this beautiful *Earth*."

Quotation #325

"*Angels* roam around all over this *Earth*. Open your *doors* to *find* them at your *doorstep*."

Quotation #326

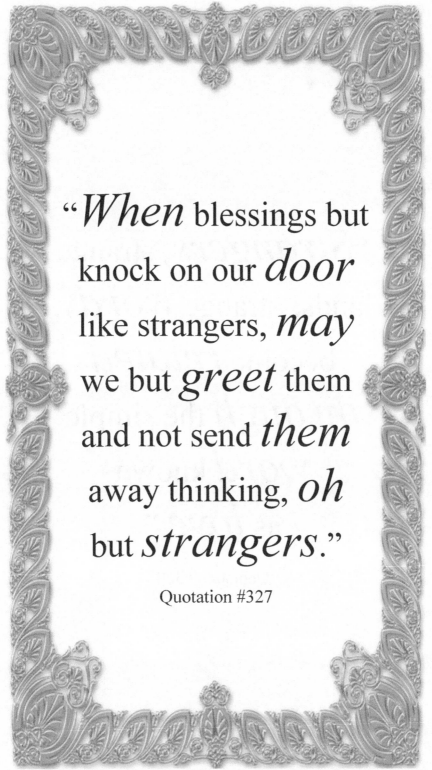

"*When* blessings but knock on our *door* like strangers, *may* we but *greet* them and not send *them* away thinking, *oh* but *strangers*."

Quotation #327

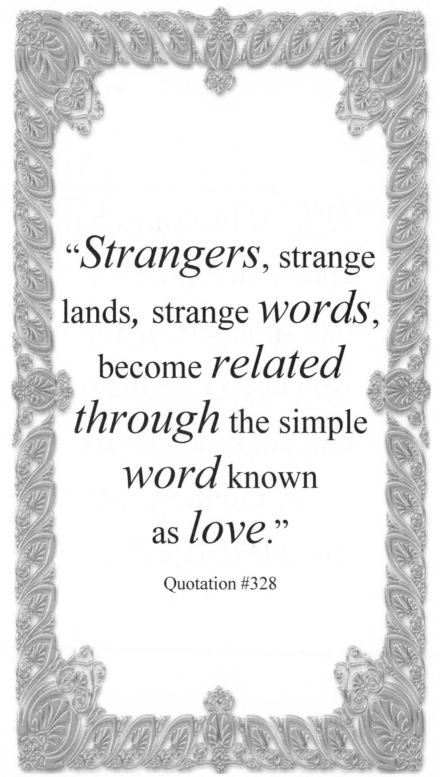

"*Strangers*, strange lands, strange *words*, become *related through* the simple *word* known as *love*."

Quotation #328

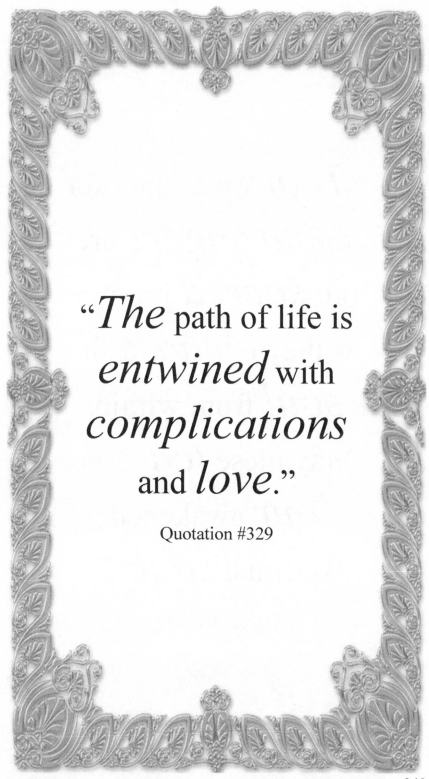

"*The* path of life is *entwined* with *complications* and *love.*"

Quotation #329

"*Tears* we share for the *strangers* are our *sacred* journey as they *cleanse* the *soul* from within. May these *tears* be *our* awakened spiritual *souls*."

Quotation #330

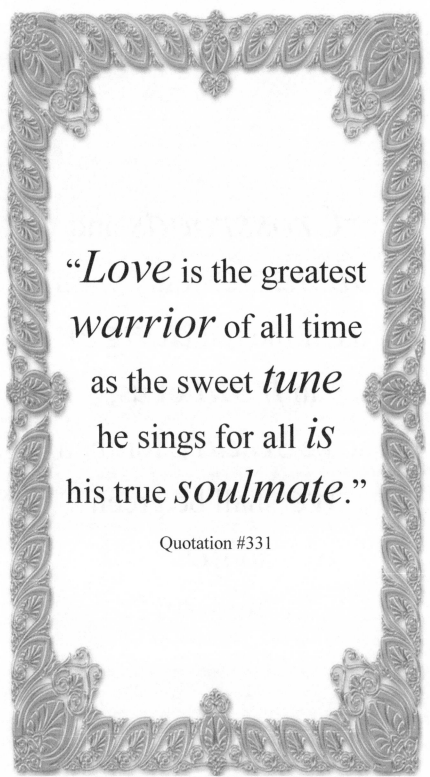

"*Love* is the greatest *warrior* of all time as the sweet *tune* he sings for all *is* his true *soulmate*."

Quotation #331

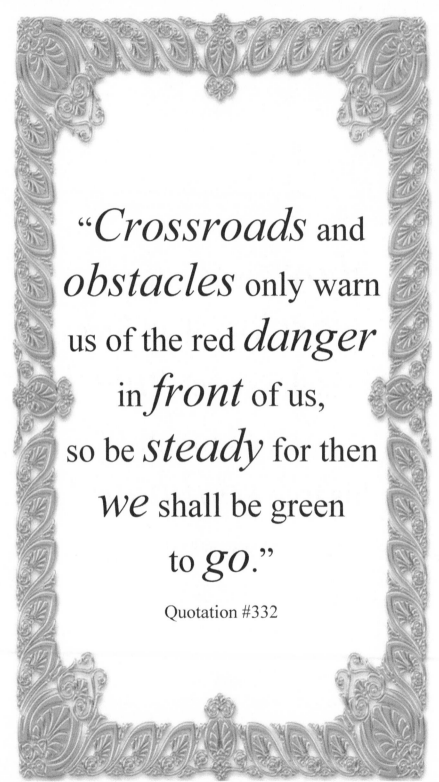

"*Crossroads* and *obstacles* only warn us of the red *danger* in *front* of us, so be *steady* for then *we* shall be green to *go*."

Quotation #332

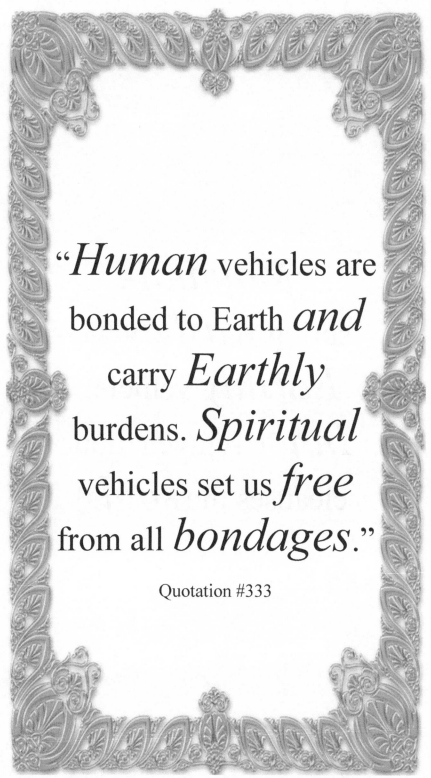

"*Human* vehicles are bonded to Earth *and* carry *Earthly* burdens. *Spiritual* vehicles set us *free* from all *bondages*."

Quotation #333

"*Mountain* spring *washes* the *Earthly* vehicle. *Inner* rejuvenation cleanses the *soul*."

Quotation #334

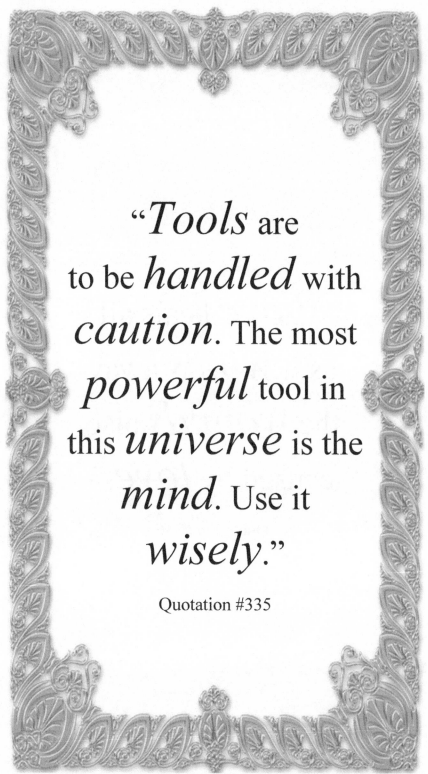

"*Tools* are to be *handled* with *caution*. The most *powerful* tool in this *universe* is the *mind*. Use it *wisely*."

Quotation #335

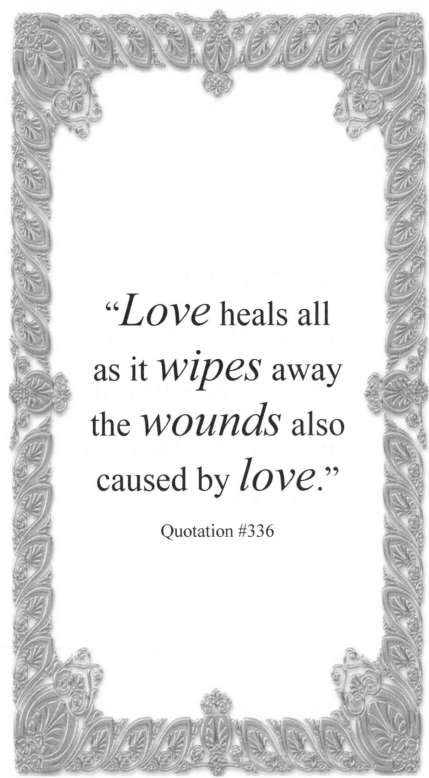

"*Love* heals all
as it *wipes* away
the *wounds* also
caused by *love*."

Quotation #336

"*A* mystery book is only a *mystery* until it is *read.* *Take* the effort and *open* the *pages.*"

Quotation #337

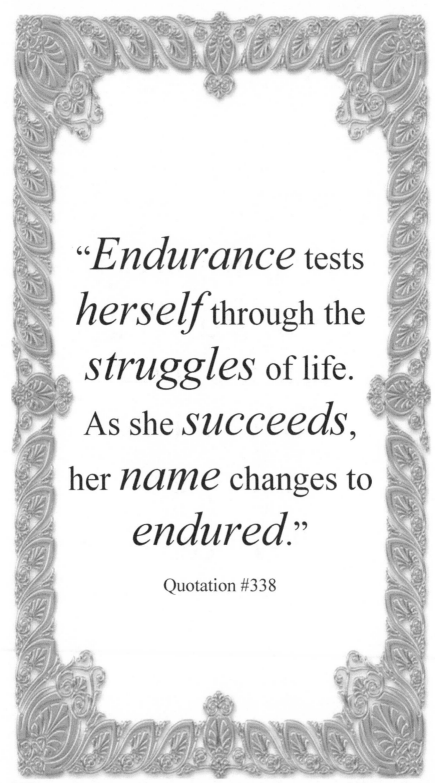

"*Endurance* tests *herself* through the *struggles* of life. As she *succeeds*, her *name* changes to *endured*."

Quotation #338

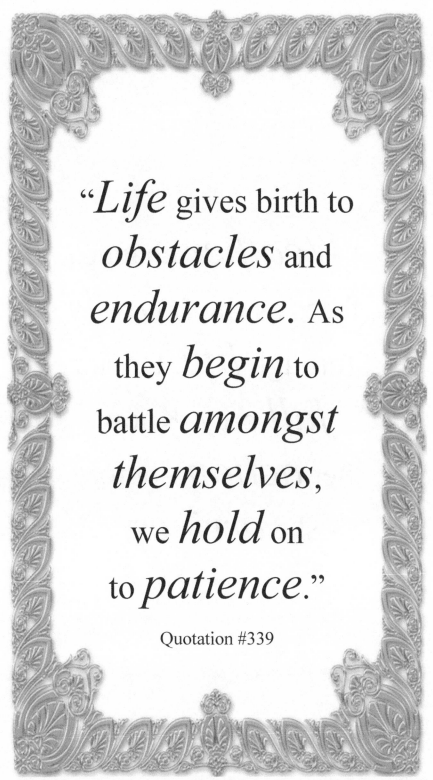

"*Life* gives birth to *obstacles* and *endurance*. As they *begin* to battle *amongst themselves*, we *hold* on to *patience*."

Quotation #339

"*Weather* changes faces as she *travels* through *life*. Do not *fall* prey. Know her *actions* before she *arrives*."

Quotation #340

"'*Weather* can be a *friend* in disguise as long as *you* are *prepared* for her,' say the *wise*."

Quotation #341

"*From* amongst the dark clouds *hiding* behind the *fog,* *pouring* like a *glimpse* of hope, the biggest star the *sun* but *appears*."

Quotation #342

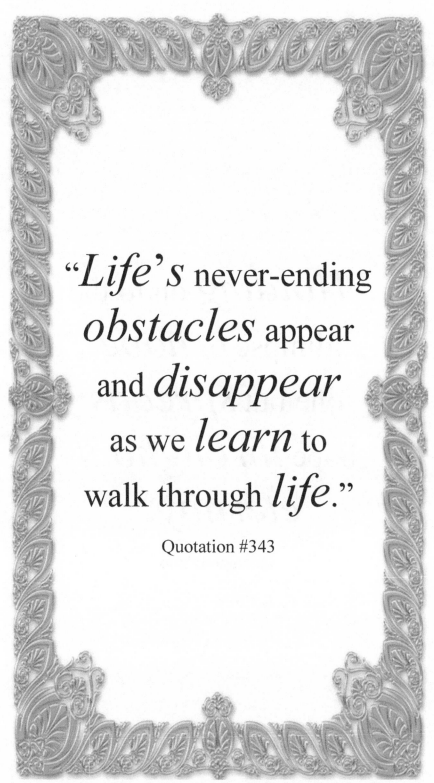

"*Life's* never-ending *obstacles* appear and *disappear* as we *learn* to walk through *life*."

Quotation #343

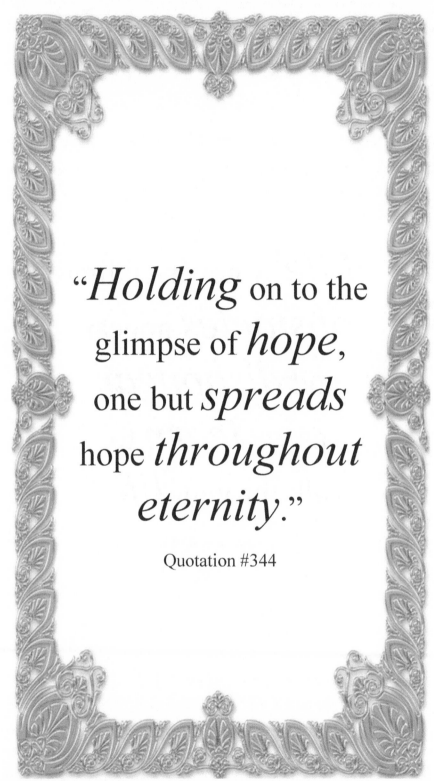

"*Holding* on to the glimpse of *hope*, one but *spreads* hope *throughout eternity*."

Quotation #344

"*Hold* on to the glimpse of *hope* for dawn *breaks* open *through* the dark night's *sky*."

Quotation #345

"*Memories* made,
pull us *backwards*,
when we *must*
walk *forward*
towards *making*
more *memories*."

Quotation #346

"*Waiting* for the *achievements* is the only *way* the *achiever* but *achieves*."

Quotation #347

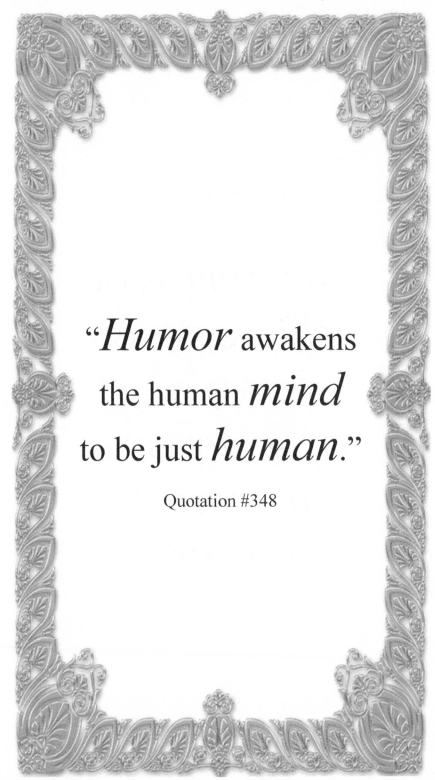

"*Humor* awakens
the human *mind*
to be just *human*."

Quotation #348

"*Life* turns around at all obstacles and wants help from within the soul. The soul then guides all through dreams. Awaken yourself and live life's eternal dreams. As all obstacles are overcome, life completes the blessed *dreams*."

Quotation #349

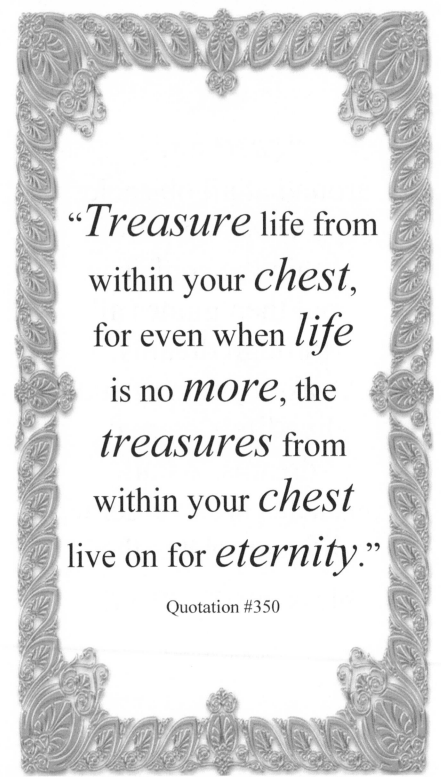

"*Treasure* life from within your *chest*, for even when *life* is no *more*, the *treasures* from within your *chest* live on for *eternity*."

Quotation #350

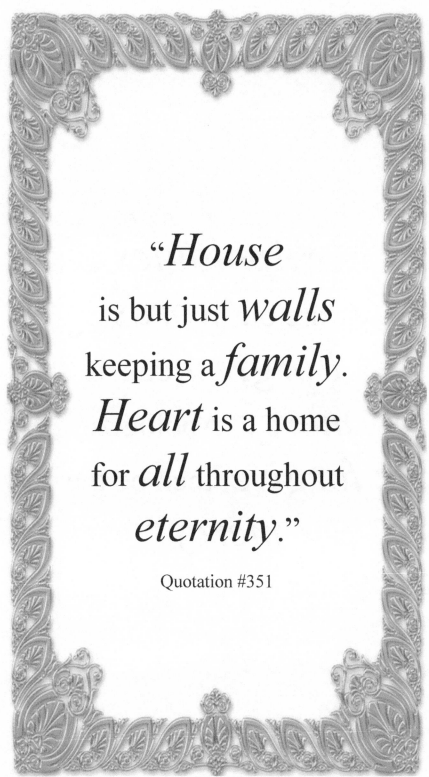

"*House*
is but just *walls*
keeping a *family*.
Heart is a home
for *all* throughout
eternity."

Quotation #351

"*Apologies*
are but *words*.
Forgiveness is
mercy. Apologize,
forgive, then be the
mercy."

Quotation #352

"*The* human mind and *body* fight to *survive* each day as the spiritual *soul* fights *to* be awakened *from* within the *body*. As this journey is *completed*, the mind, body, *and* soul are but *united*."

Quotation #353

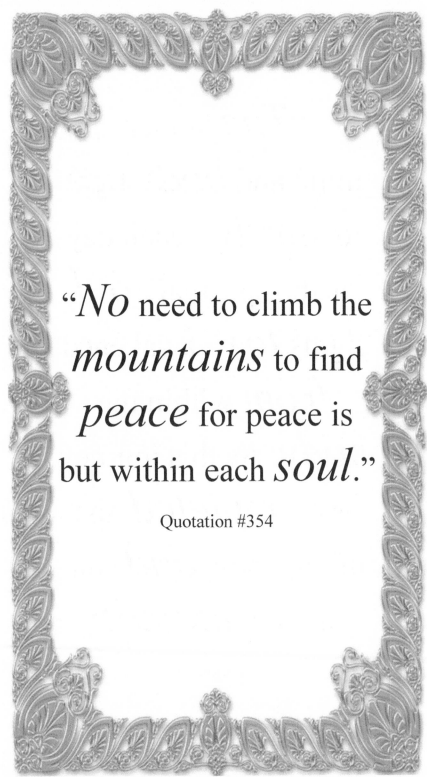

"*No* need to climb the *mountains* to find *peace* for peace is but within each *soul*."

Quotation #354

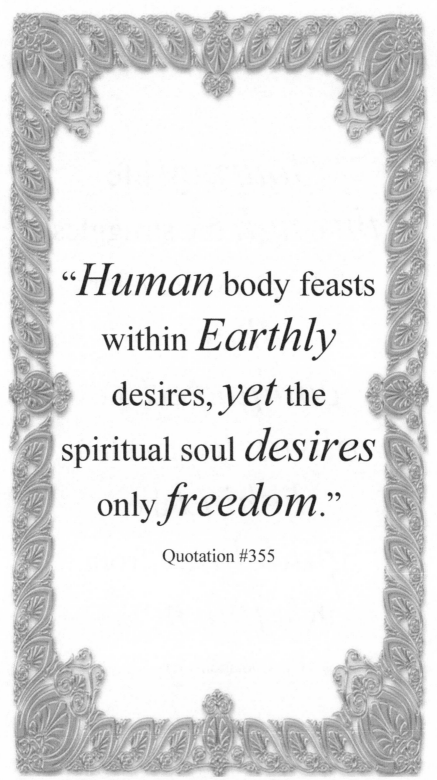

"*Human* body feasts within *Earthly* desires, *yet* the spiritual soul *desires* only *freedom*."

Quotation #355

"*Journey* life *through* the struggles of the *past* travelers, as *they* have *conquered* the *obstacles* and left *behind* the *guidelines* from their *journey*."

Quotation #356

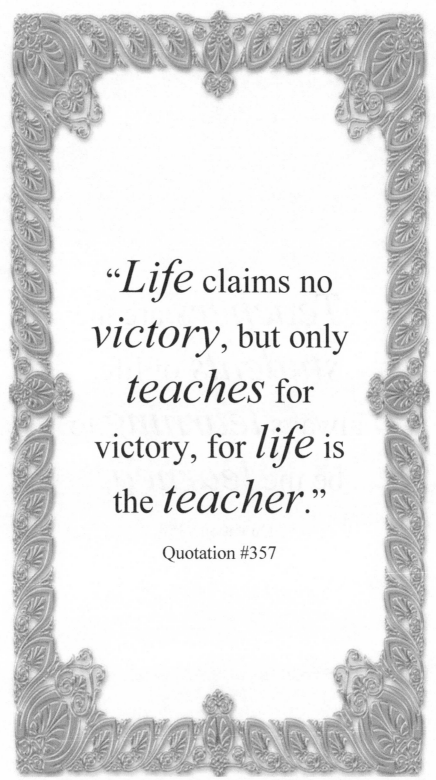

"*Life* claims no *victory*, but only *teaches* for victory, for *life* is the *teacher*."

Quotation #357

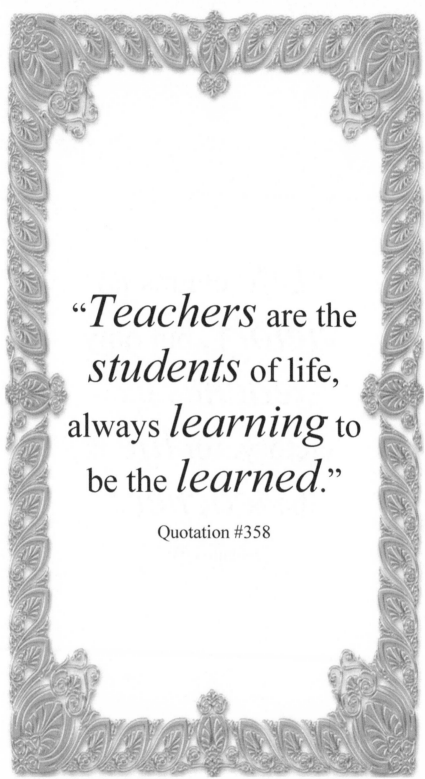

"*Teachers* are the
students of life,
always *learning* to
be the *learned*."

Quotation #358

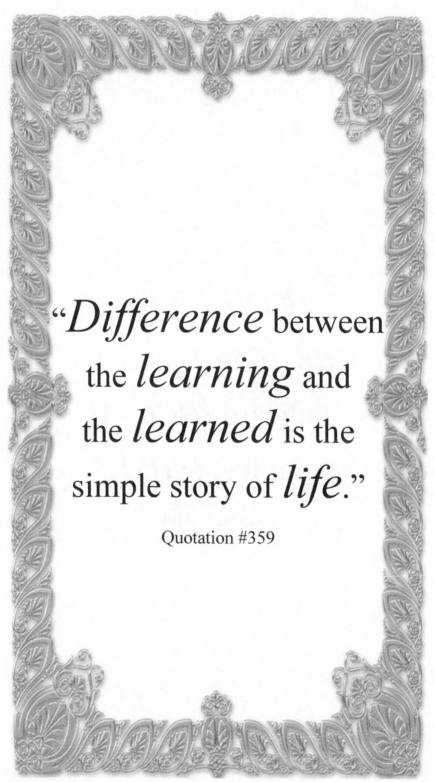

"*Difference* between the *learning* and the *learned* is the simple story of *life*."

Quotation #359

"*Faith* is the *unknown*, unseen, unheard *face* of complete *trust*."

Quotation #360

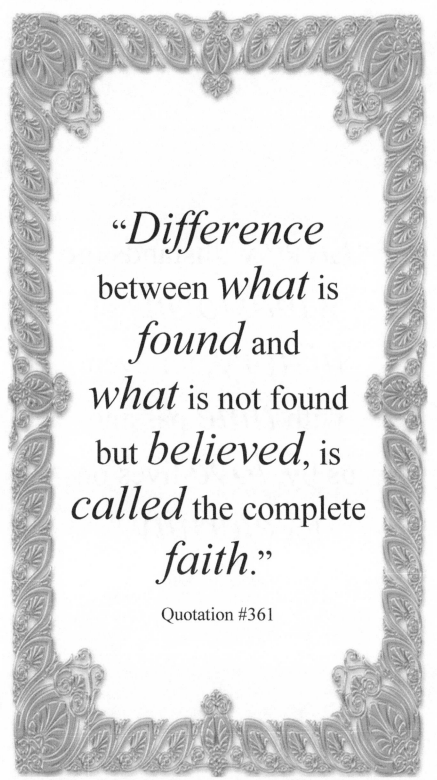

"*Difference* between *what* is *found* and *what* is not found but *believed*, is *called* the complete *faith*."

Quotation #361

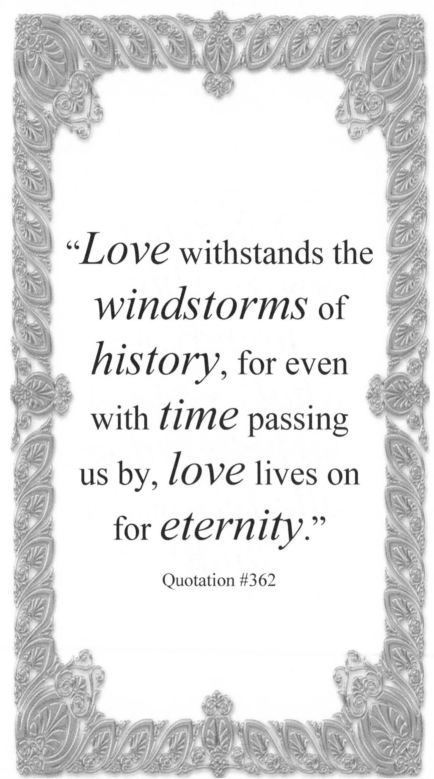

"*Love* withstands the *windstorms* of *history*, for even with *time* passing us by, *love* lives on for *eternity*."

Quotation #362

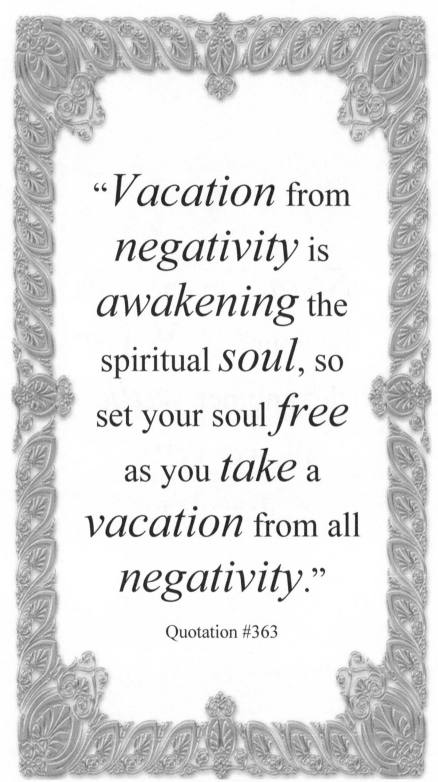

"*Vacation* from *negativity* is *awakening* the spiritual *soul*, so set your soul *free* as you *take* a *vacation* from all *negativity*."

Quotation #363

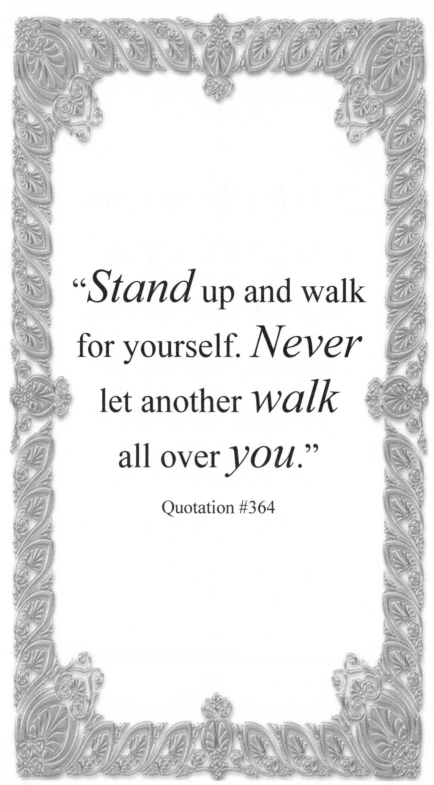

"*Stand* up and walk for yourself. *Never* let another *walk* all over *you*."

Quotation #364

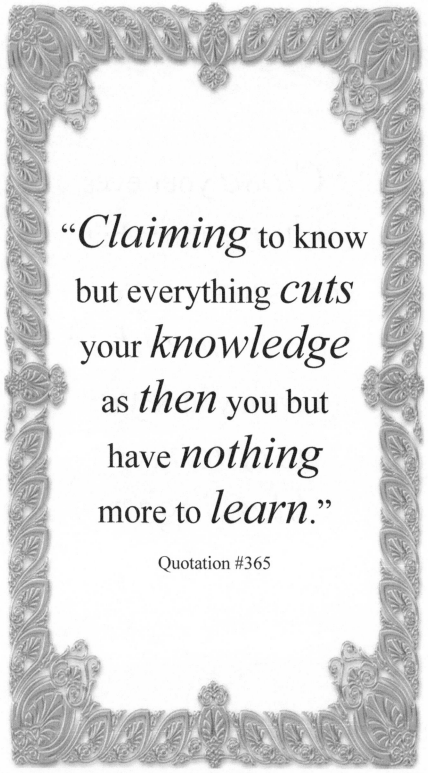

"*Claiming* to know but everything *cuts* your *knowledge* as *then* you but have *nothing* more to *learn*."

Quotation #365

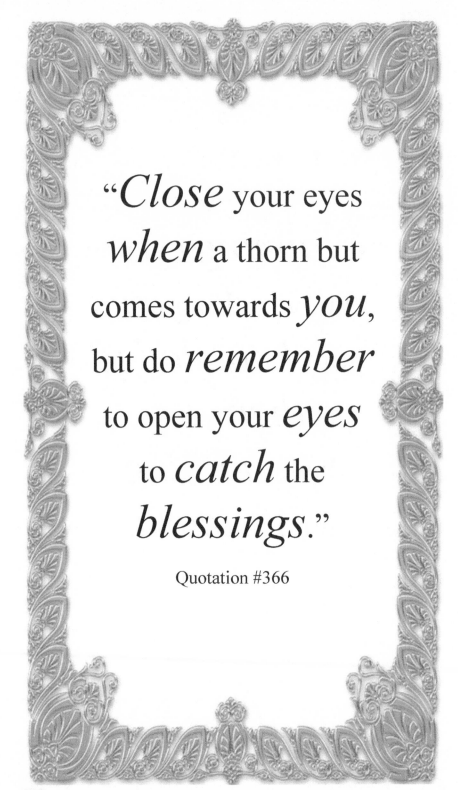

"*Close* your eyes *when* a thorn but comes towards *you*, but do *remember* to open your *eyes* to *catch* the *blessings*."

Quotation #366

"*Keep* the lantern glowing all *night* so the lost *souls* find their way back. *With* each *household glowing* one after another, *there* will be no lost *souls*."

Quotation #367

"*The* ocean, the *mountain*, and the trees *share* the same Mother *Earth*. May we learn from *them* and *share* her in *union* amongst all *humans*."

Quotation #368

"*Memories* cross time to be *made*. May *we* leave them *behind* with *love*."

Quotation #369

"*Criticizing* a grown-up is *easy*, but *let* us get back to the *present* and hold on *to* each *child* so they do not go *astray*. Then, in the *future*, there shall be no *criticism*."

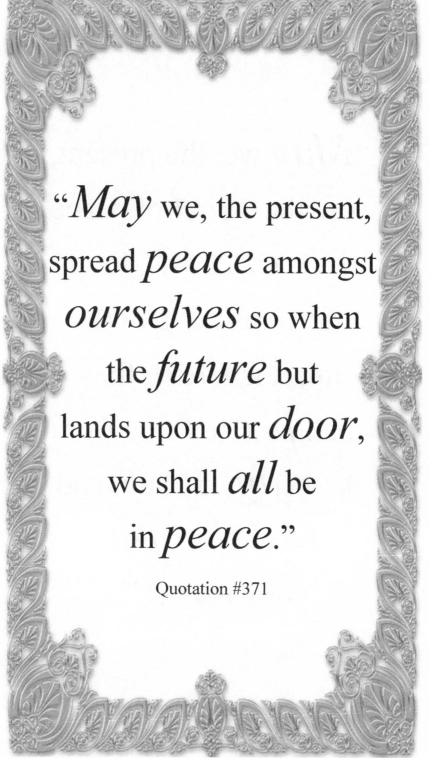

"*May* we, the present, spread *peace* amongst *ourselves* so when the *future* but lands upon our *door*, we shall *all* be in *peace*."

Quotation #371

"*May* we, the present, sow the *seed* of peace all *around* us, for as the trees but *grow* up, it is *then*, they shall *protect* us from the *rain*, the sun, and be the *bearer* of *peace*."

Quotation #372

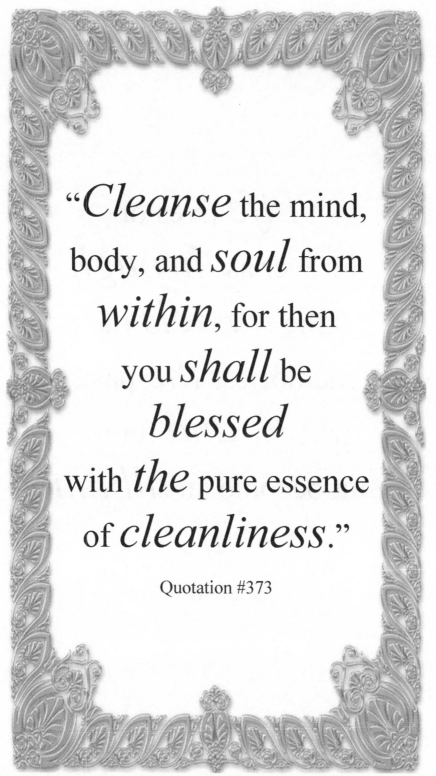

"*Cleanse* the mind, body, and *soul* from *within*, for then you *shall* be *blessed* with *the* pure essence of *cleanliness*."

Quotation #373

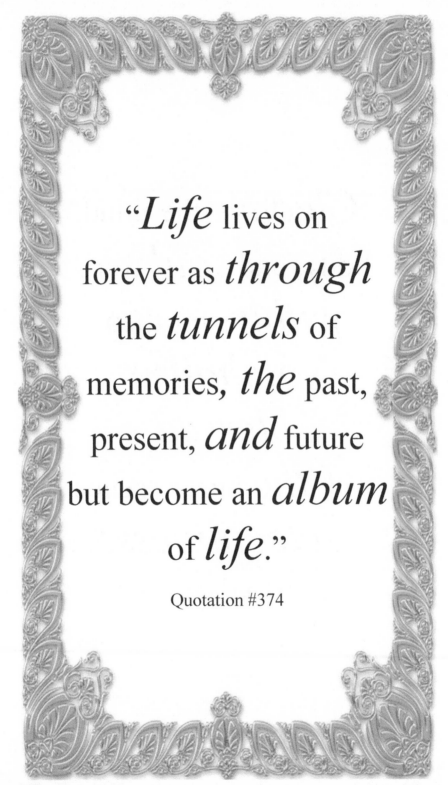

"*Life* lives on forever as *through* the *tunnels* of memories, *the* past, present, *and* future but become an *album* of *life*."

Quotation #374

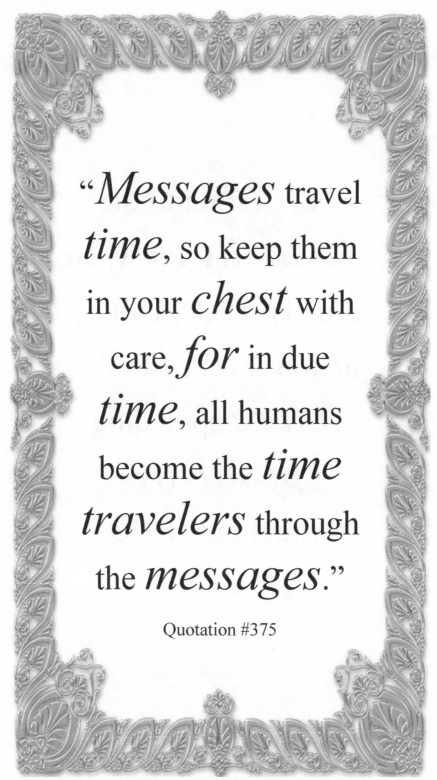

"*Messages* travel *time*, so keep them in your *chest* with care, *for* in due *time*, all humans become the *time travelers* through the *messages*."

Quotation #375

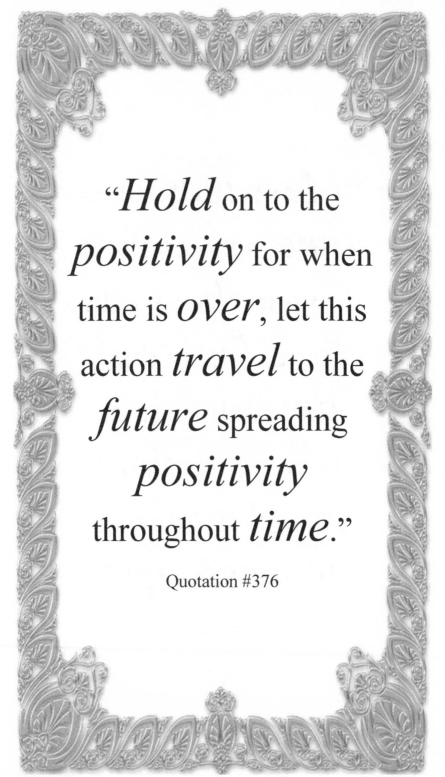

"*Hold* on to the *positivity* for when time is *over*, let this action *travel* to the *future* spreading *positivity* throughout *time*."

Quotation #376

"*Pick* up all of your *hidden* mess for if not then, as *you* travel time to the *future*, your mess *will* be left *behind* for the next *generation* to *clean* up after *you*."

Quotation #377

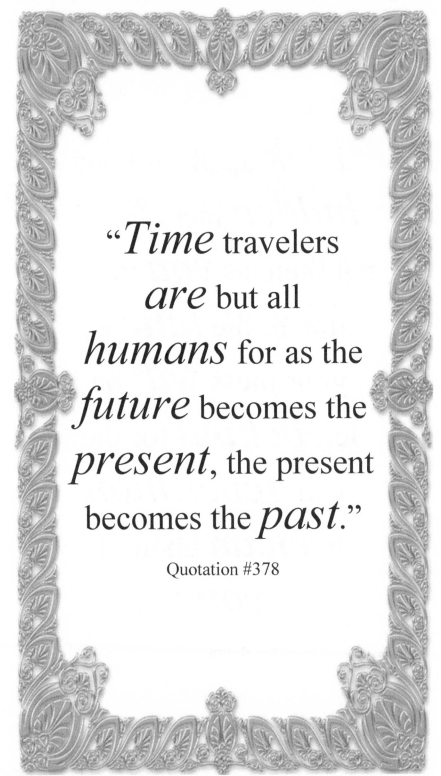

"*Time* travelers *are* but all *humans* for as the *future* becomes the *present*, the present becomes the *past*."

Quotation #378

398

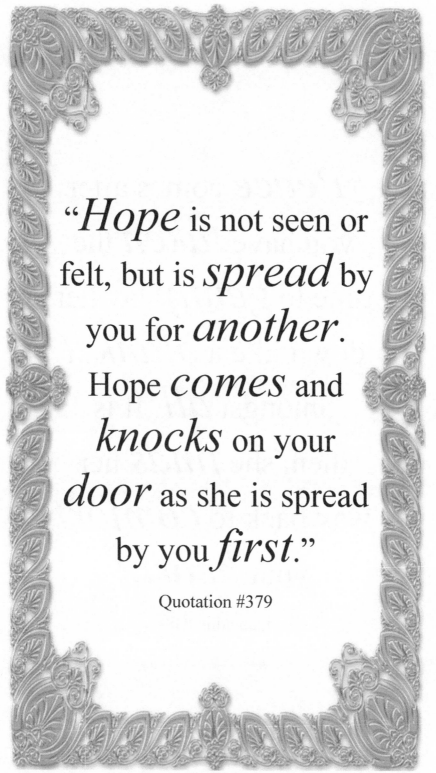

"*Hope* is not seen or felt, but is *spread* by you for *another*. Hope *comes* and *knocks* on your *door* as she is spread by you *first*."

Quotation #379

"*Peace* comes after you have *taken* the time to *gently* lay her down like a *blanket* amongst *all*. It is then, she *finds* her way back to *comfort* your *heart*."

Quotation #380

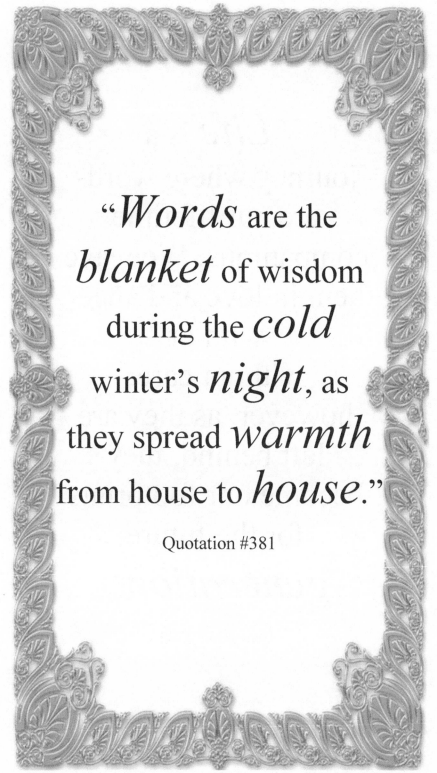

"*Words* are the *blanket* of wisdom during the *cold* winter's *night*, as they spread *warmth* from house to *house*."

Quotation #381

"*Life* is a journey where words are our lifetime companions. We leave them in love and anger, with or without care; however, as they are left behind, they become our footprints for the future *generation*."

Quotation #382

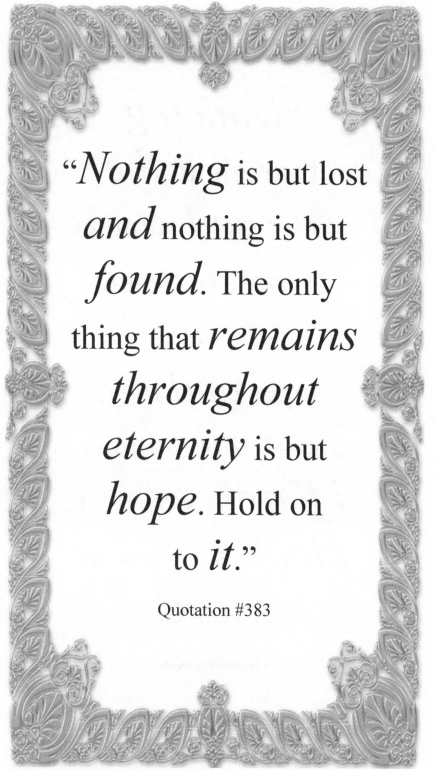

"*Nothing* is but lost *and* nothing is but *found*. The only thing that *remains throughout eternity* is but *hope*. Hold on to *it*."

Quotation #383

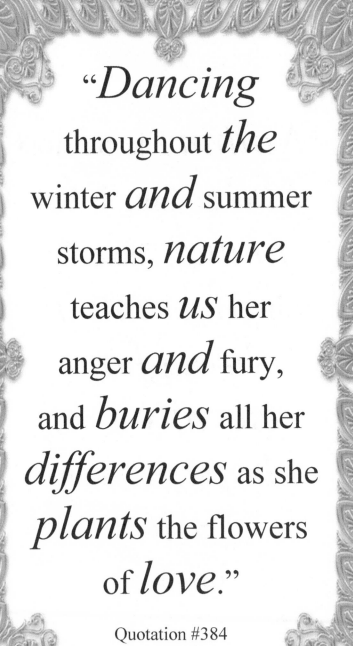

"*Dancing* throughout *the* winter *and* summer storms, *nature* teaches *us* her anger *and* fury, and *buries* all her *differences* as she *plants* the flowers of *love*."

Quotation #384

"*Mother* sky buries all her *tears* throughout *the* clouds. As the *pain* strikes her, she *pours* them hard *onto* the *Earth* and from her tears, *we* the *children* clench our *thirst*."

Quotation #385

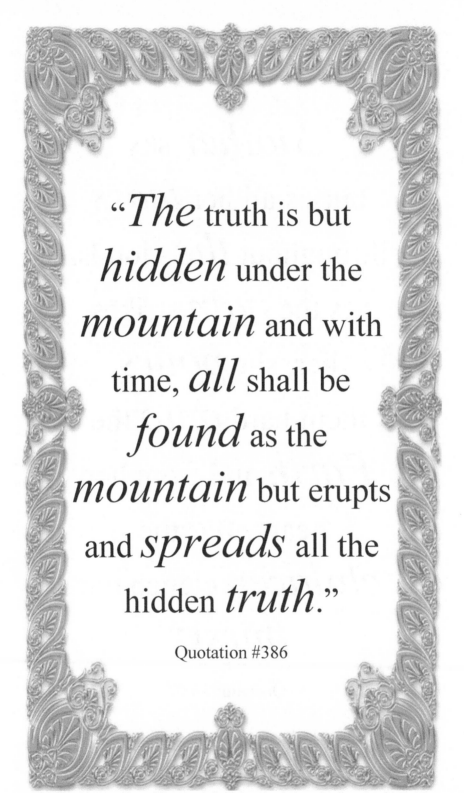

"*The* truth is but *hidden* under the *mountain* and with time, *all* shall be *found* as the *mountain* but erupts and *spreads* all the hidden *truth*."

Quotation #386

"*Searching* for the unknown but *holds* us a *prisoner* in the land of the *lost*. Let the *words* of the *wise* guide us to *find* the known first, then the *unknown* but becomes *known*."

Quotation #387

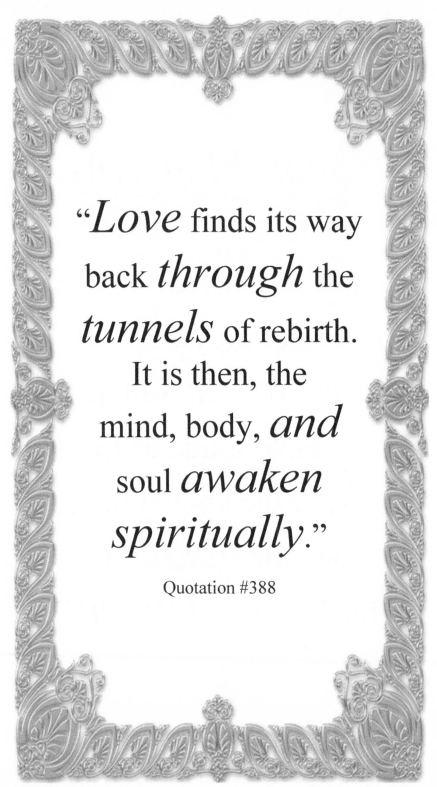

"*Love* finds its way back *through* the *tunnels* of rebirth. It is then, the mind, body, *and* soul *awaken spiritually*."

Quotation #388

"*Free* spirit finds the free soul. It is our mind and body that capture us as prisoners from spiritually awakening. Set the mind, body, and soul free, and be awakened *spiritually.*"

Quotation #389

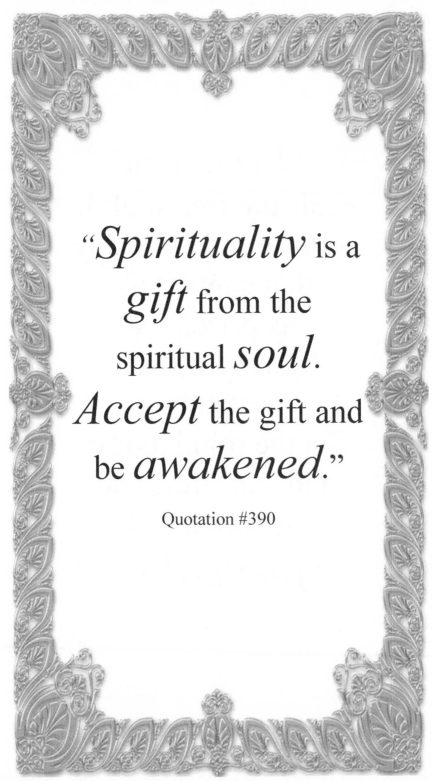

"*Spirituality* is a *gift* from the spiritual *soul*. *Accept* the gift and be *awakened*."

Quotation #390

"*Wrap* the gift of the *present* with *love* and care as you send *her* off to the *future*, for *know* this, the future, a *stranger*, accepts your *gift* without *saying* a *word*."

Quotation #391

"*The* future *knocks* on all doors as the *gift* of the *present* is but over. As *you* open the doors to the *future*, do carry the *blessings* of the *present* and the past with *you* on your *journey*."

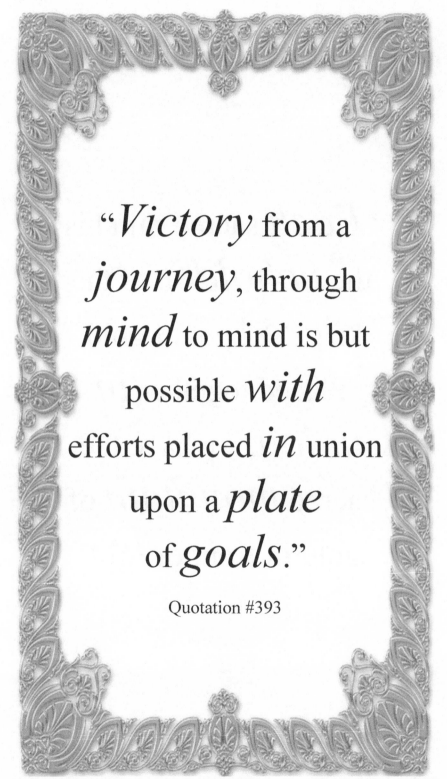

"*Victory* from a *journey*, through *mind* to mind is but possible *with* efforts placed *in* union upon a *plate* of *goals*."

Quotation #393

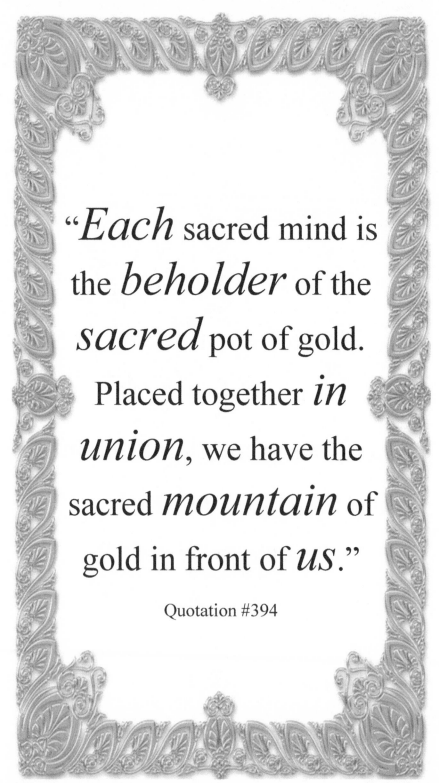

"*Each* sacred mind is the *beholder* of the *sacred* pot of gold. Placed together *in union*, we have the sacred *mountain* of gold in front of *us*."

Quotation #394

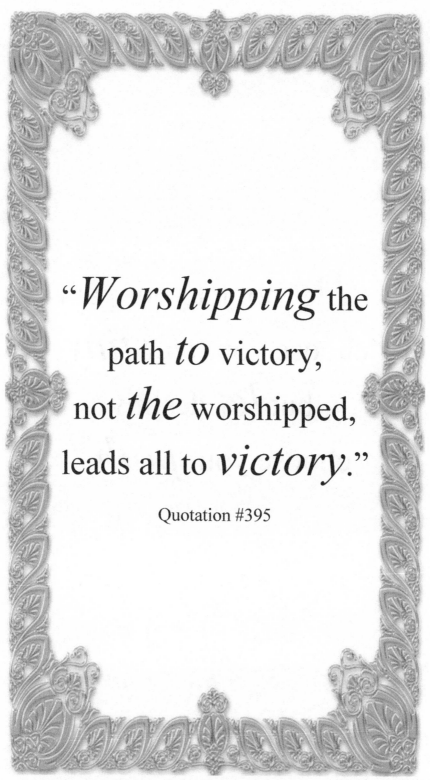

"*Worshipping* the path *to* victory, not *the* worshipped, leads all to *victory*."

Quotation #395

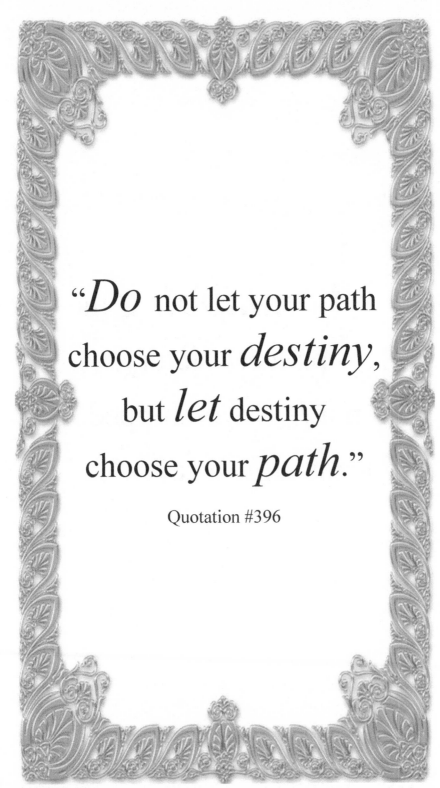

"*Do* not let your path choose your *destiny*, but *let* destiny choose your *path*."

Quotation #396

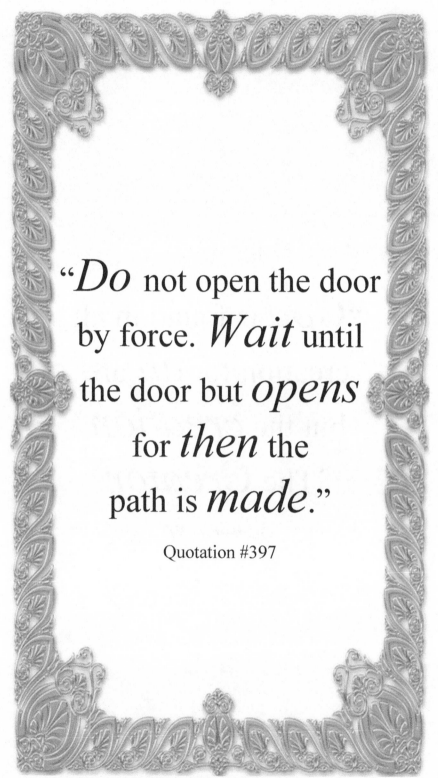

"*Do* not open the door by force. *Wait* until the door but *opens* for *then* the path is *made*."

Quotation #397

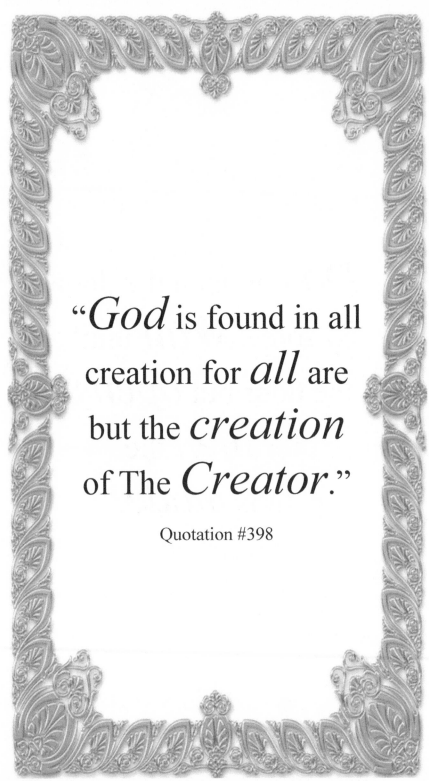

"*God* is found in all creation for *all* are but the *creation* of The *Creator*."

Quotation #398

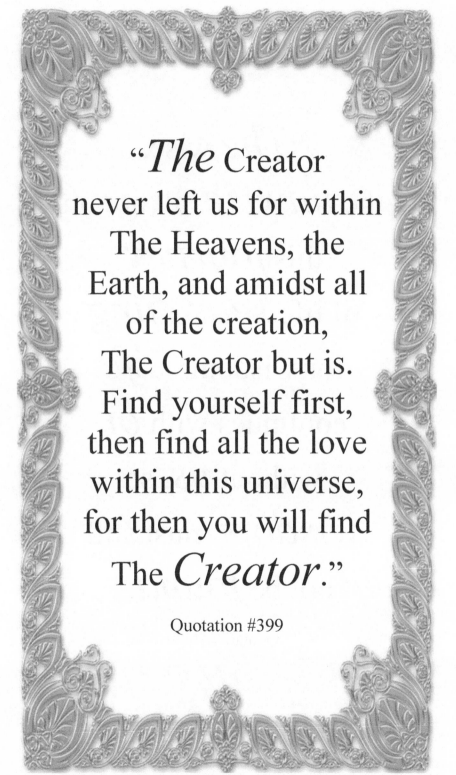

"*The* Creator
never left us for within
The Heavens, the
Earth, and amidst all
of the creation,
The Creator but is.
Find yourself first,
then find all the love
within this universe,
for then you will find
The *Creator*."

Quotation #399

"*The* wise,
the *unwise*, all are on
this *journey*
of life *searching*
for wisdom. *Life*
continues with *or*
without *us*, so
wisdom must still
not be *found*."

Quotation #400

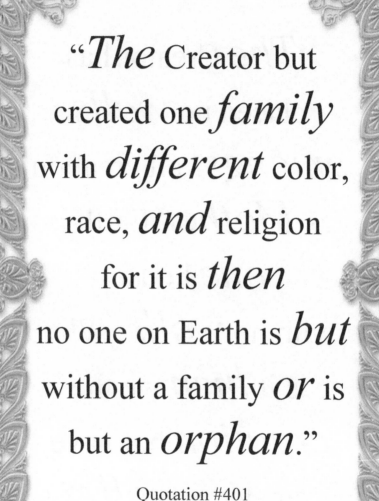

"*The* Creator but created one *family* with *different* color, race, *and* religion for it is *then* no one on Earth is *but* without a family *or* is but an *orphan*."

Quotation #401

421

"*The* Creator has placed no *walls amongst* all creation as *Mother* Earth is *one* house with no *walls*. Why is it *then* we the *creation* but have created a *wall*?"

Quotation #402

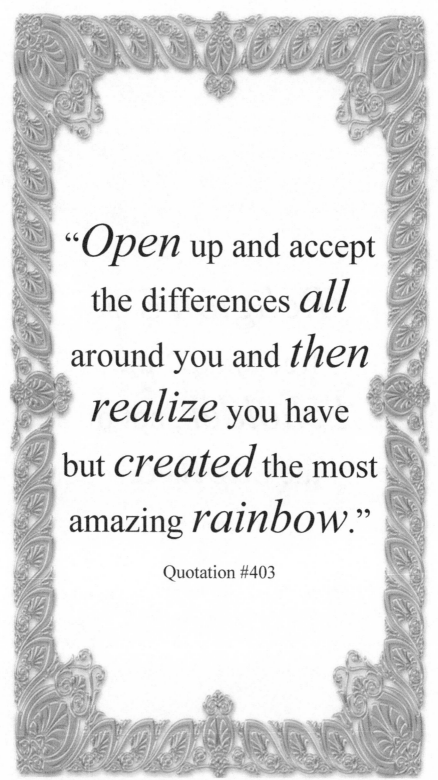

"*Open* up and accept the differences *all* around you and *then realize* you have but *created* the most amazing *rainbow*."

Quotation #403

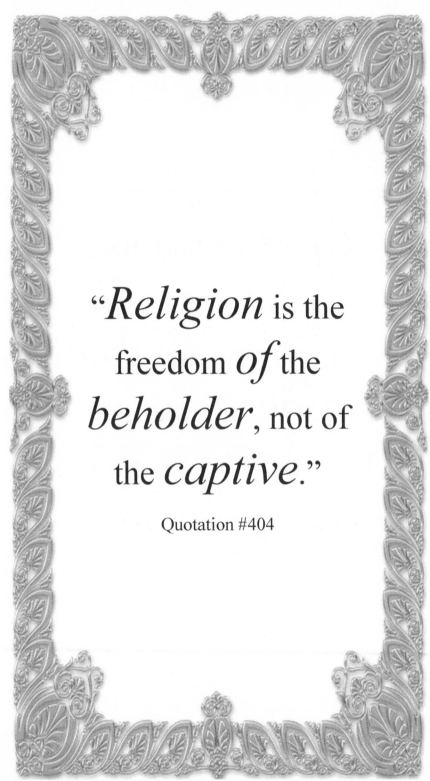

"*Religion* is the
freedom *of* the
beholder, not of
the *captive*."

Quotation #404

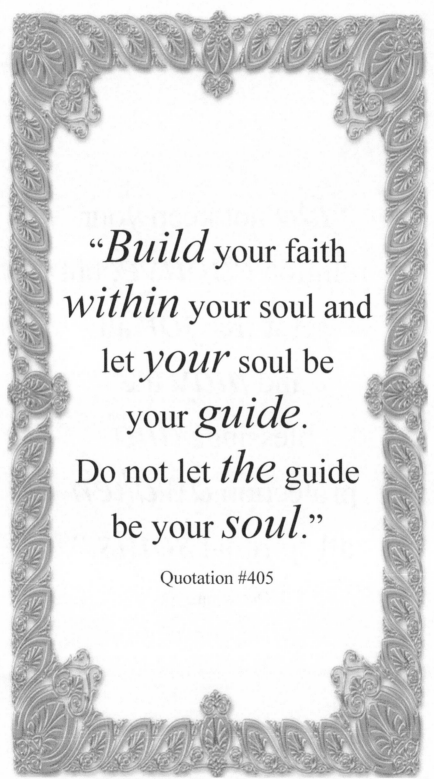

"*Build* your faith *within* your soul and let *your* soul be your *guide*. Do not let *the* guide be your *soul*."

Quotation #405

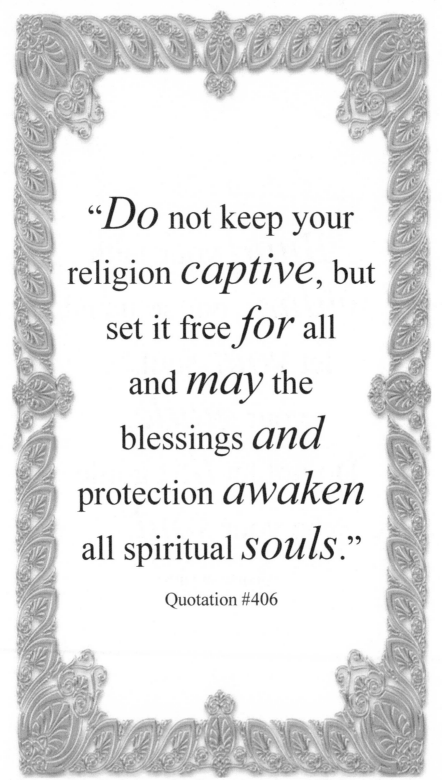

"*Do* not keep your religion *captive*, but set it free *for* all and *may* the blessings *and* protection *awaken* all spiritual *souls*."

Quotation #406

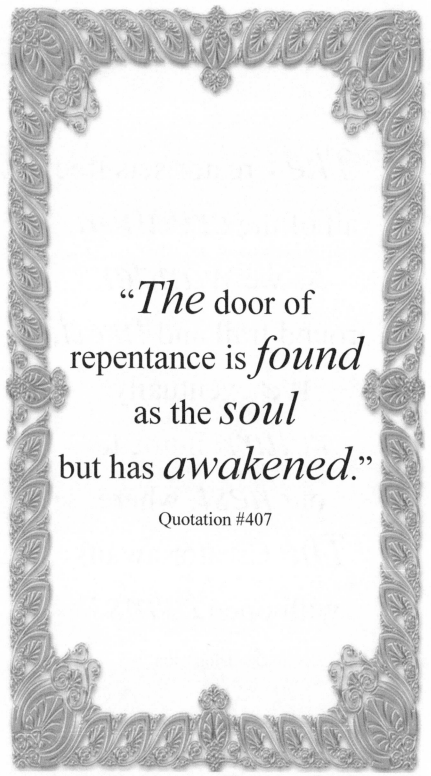

"*The* door of
repentance is *found*
as the *soul*
but has *awakened*."

Quotation #407

"*The* Creator sets free all of the *creation*. As we *wander* around frail and *tired*, *we* eventually *return* home to our *nest*, where *The* Creator awaits with open *arms*."

Quotation #408

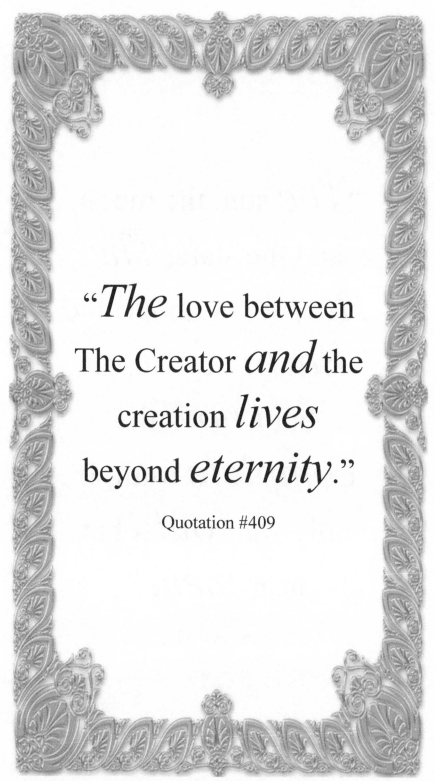

"*The* love between The Creator *and* the creation *lives* beyond *eternity*."

Quotation #409

"*The* sun, the moon, and the stars, *The Heavens* above and *Earth* beyond, all but *know* the *complete* truth. If only we *could* but hear *them*."

Quotation #410

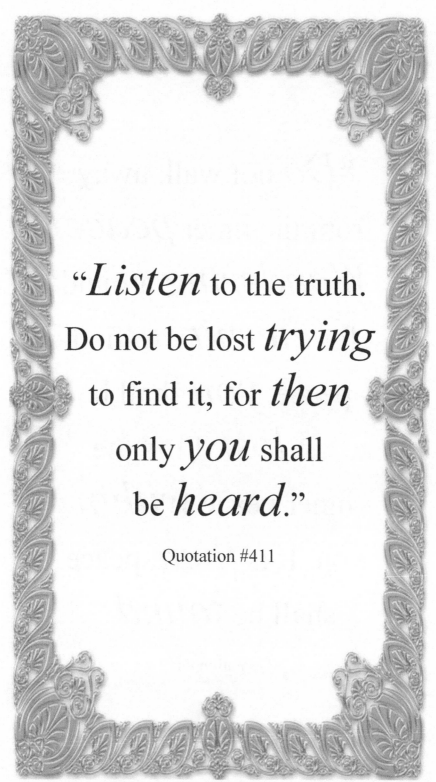

"*Listen* to the truth.
Do not be lost *trying*
to find it, for *then*
only *you* shall
be *heard*."

Quotation #411

"*Do* not walk away from the inner *peace*. *Wandering* around for *eternity* to find peace, *you* shall be but *lost*. Find the inner peace *within* you. It is *then*, peace shall be *found*."

Quotation #412

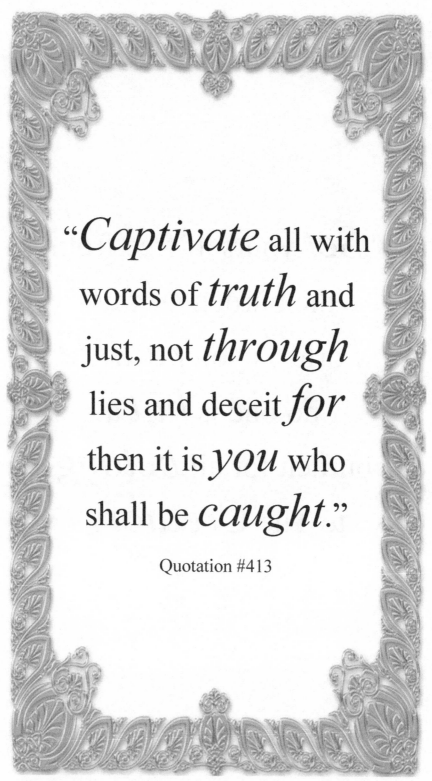

"*Captivate* all with words of *truth* and just, not *through* lies and deceit *for* then it is *you* who shall be *caught*."

Quotation #413

"*Set* yourself free from the burden *of* this world as you *realize* no one is *but* a burden for all *belong* to The *Creator*."

Quotation #414

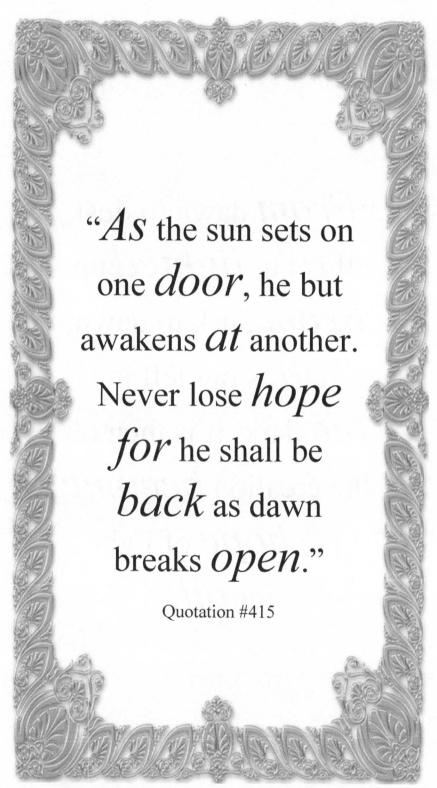

"*As* the sun sets on one *door*, he but awakens *at* another. Never lose *hope for* he shall be *back* as dawn breaks *open*."

Quotation #415

"*From* dawn to dusk, all is but *lighted* up. *From* dusk to dawn, *all* is but left in *the* dark. It is then oh the creation *become* the *hope* of light for *all*."

Quotation #416

"*Even* when all is but lost *and* nothing is but right, even *then*, know the guiding *lights* are *always* there, *shining* hope *throughout* the dark night's *sky*."

Quotation #417

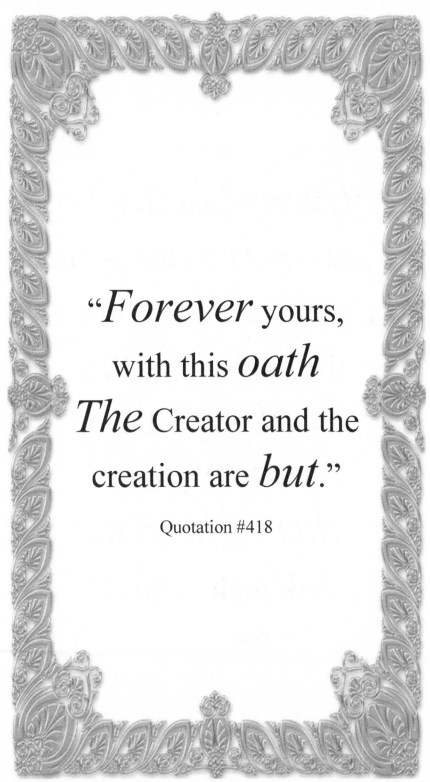

"*Forever* yours,
with this *oath*
The Creator and the
creation are *but*."

Quotation #418

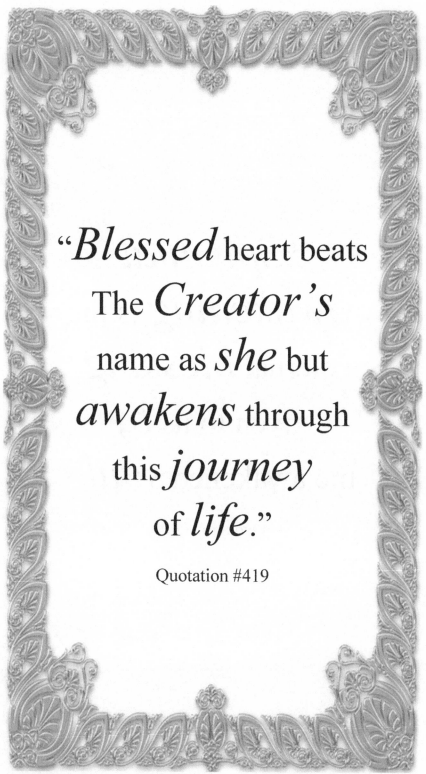

"*Blessed* heart beats
The *Creator's*
name as *she* but
awakens through
this *journey*
of *life*."

Quotation #419

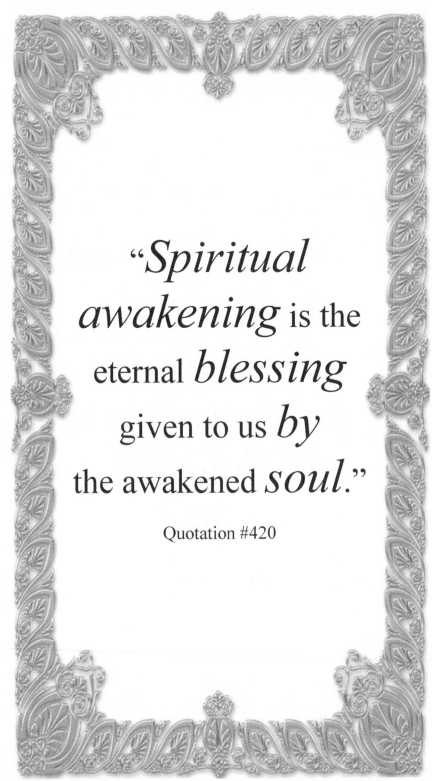

"*Spiritual awakening* is the eternal *blessing* given to us *by* the awakened *soul*."

Quotation #420

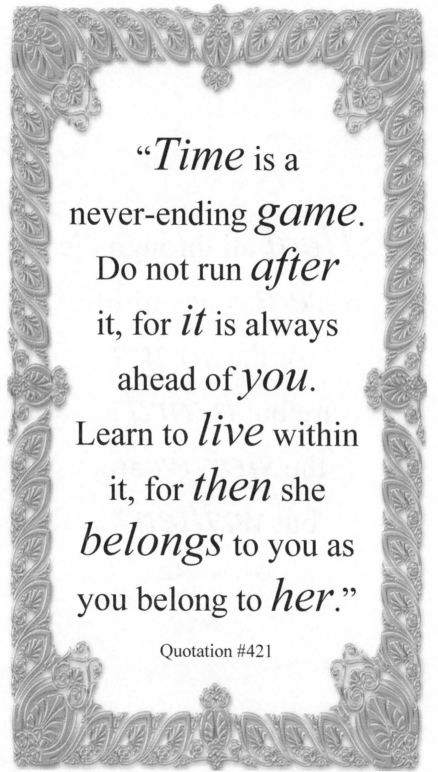

"*Time* is a never-ending *game*. Do not run *after* it, for *it* is always ahead of *you*. Learn to *live* within it, for *then* she *belongs* to you as you belong to *her*."

Quotation #421

"*Heal* all through the *sweet* songs of life, for the *songs* are but *heard* as the *stories* are but *written*."

Quotation #422

"*Songs* are the sweetest *heartbeats* of life. In times of *joy* or *sorrow*, we end up *clinging* to these *songs* of life for *comfort*."

Quotation #423

443

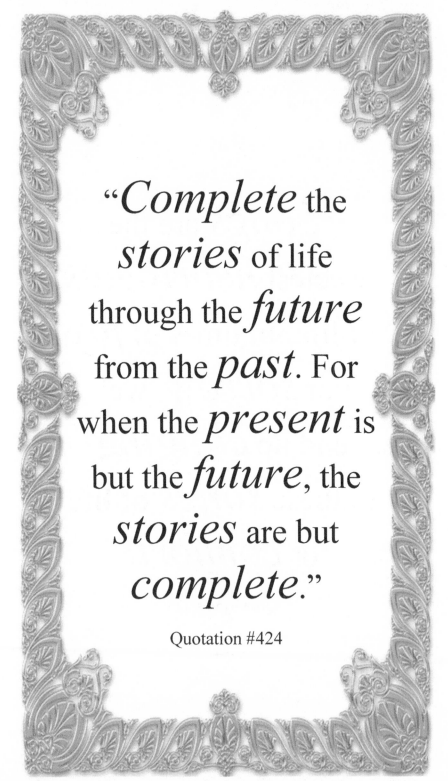

"*Complete* the *stories* of life through the *future* from the *past*. For when the *present* is but the *future*, the *stories* are but *complete*."

Quotation #424

"*Complete*
knowledge is the *gift*
of the *future* which is
always in
the future for
the *future*."

Quotation #425

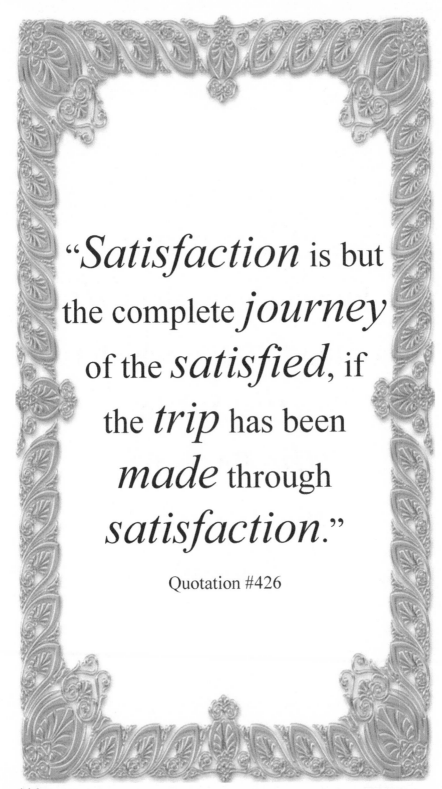

"*Satisfaction* is but the complete *journey* of the *satisfied*, if the *trip* has been *made* through *satisfaction*."

Quotation #426

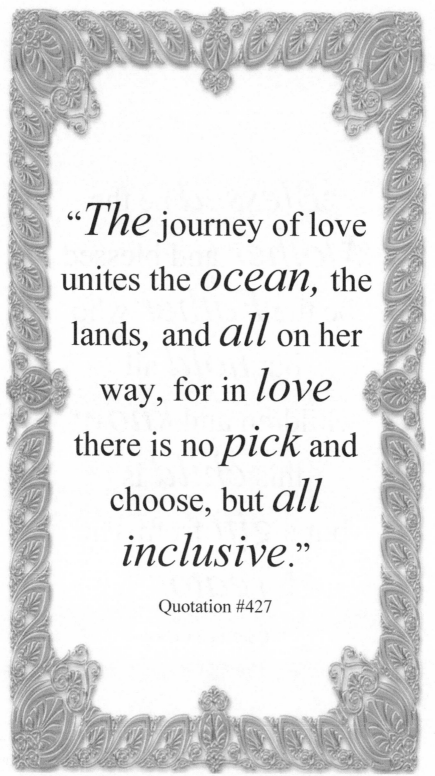

"*The* journey of love unites the *ocean*, the lands, and *all* on her way, for in *love* there is no *pick* and choose, but *all inclusive.*"

Quotation #427

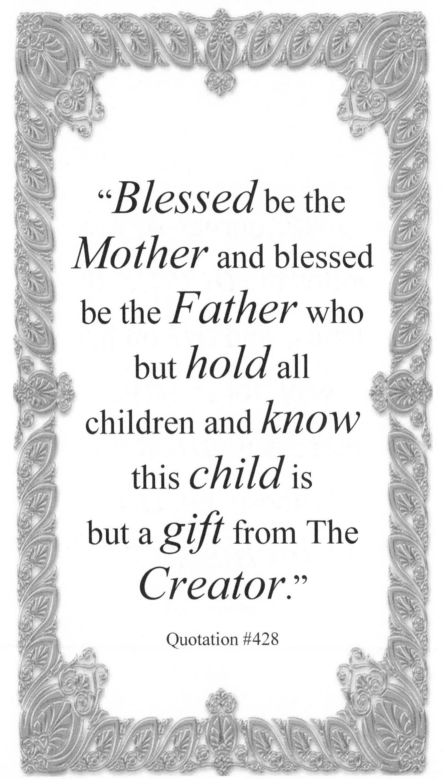

"*Blessed* be the *Mother* and blessed be the *Father* who but *hold* all children and *know* this *child* is but a *gift* from The *Creator*."

Quotation #428

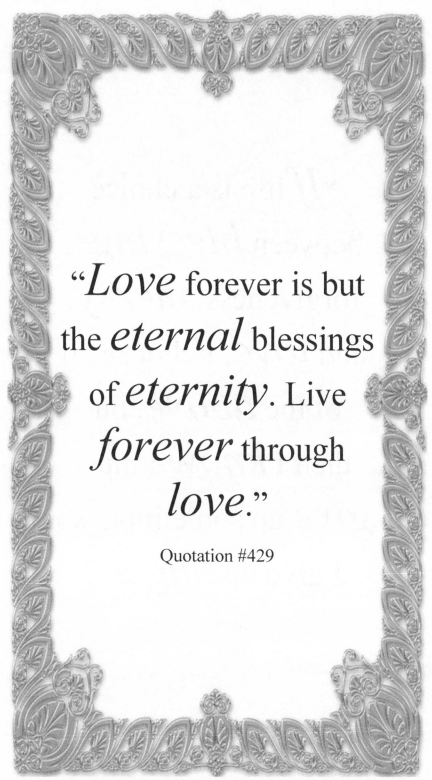

"*Love* forever is but the *eternal* blessings of *eternity*. Live *forever* through *love*."

Quotation #429

"*If* life is a choice between *blessings*, forgiveness, *mercy*, and *love*, I choose all of the *above*, but then I *know* I must *give* up something, so I give up *anger*."

Quotation #430

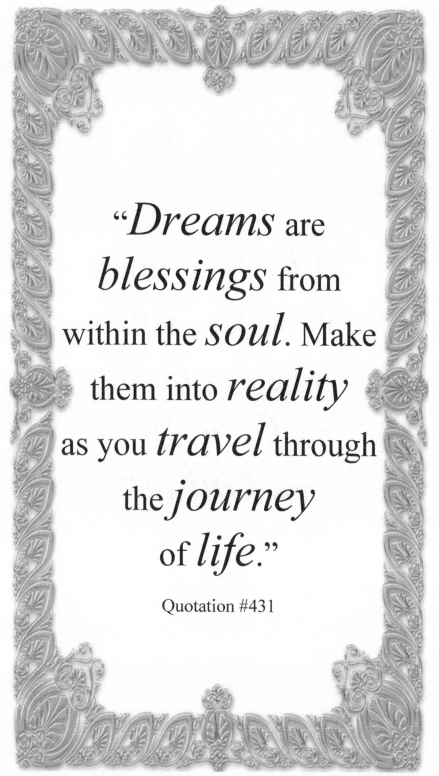

"*Dreams* are *blessings* from within the *soul*. Make them into *reality* as you *travel* through the *journey* of *life*."

Quotation #431

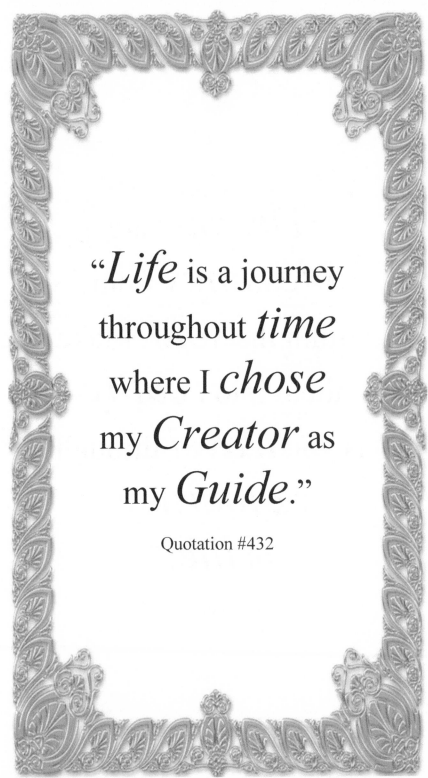

"*Life* is a journey throughout *time* where I *chose* my *Creator* as my *Guide*."

Quotation #432

"*The* lighthouse, the keeper, *and* the time *traveler* all *unite* for the ocean of *life*."

Quotation #433

"*The* sailors, the passengers, *and* the ferry boats all *cross* the ocean of *sin* with The Creator's *name* on their *lips*."

Quotation #434

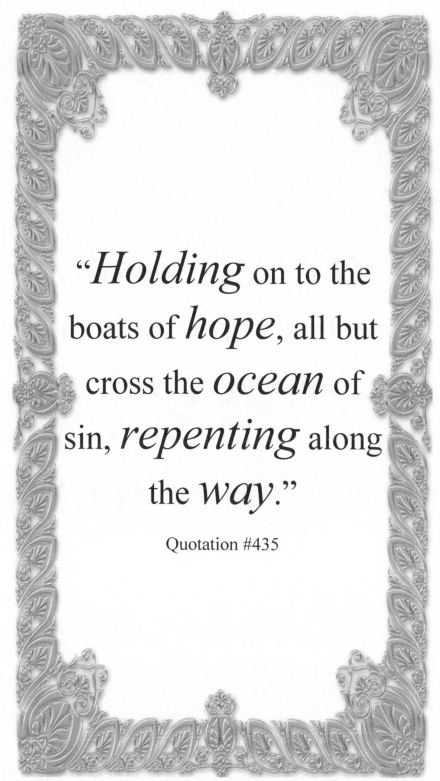

"*Holding* on to the boats of *hope*, all but cross the *ocean* of sin, *repenting* along the *way*."

Quotation #435

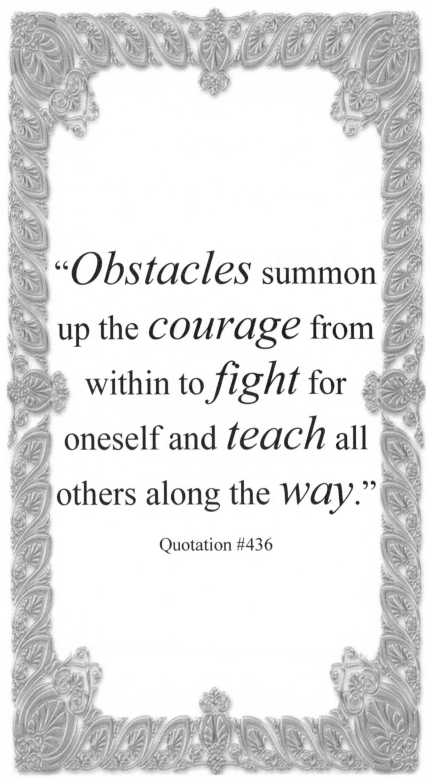

"*Obstacles* summon up the *courage* from within to *fight* for oneself and *teach* all others along the *way*."

Quotation #436

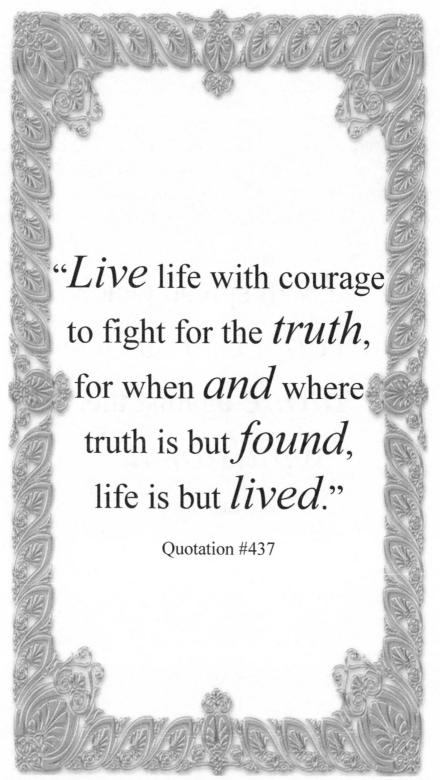

"*Live* life with courage to fight for the *truth*, for when *and* where truth is but *found*, life is but *lived*."

Quotation #437

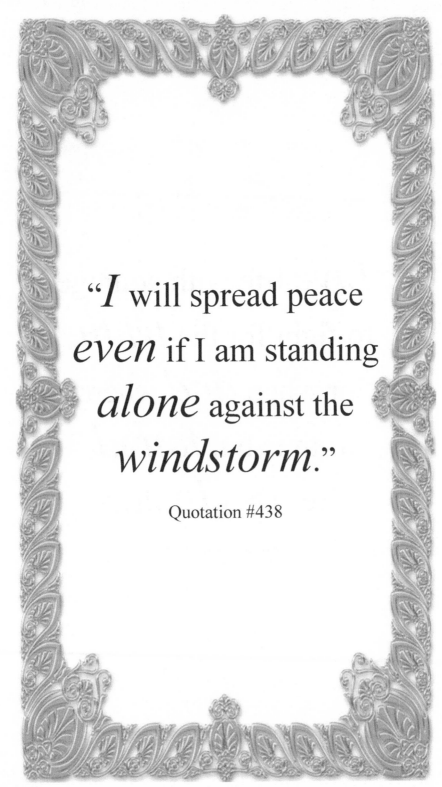

"*I* will spread peace *even* if I am standing *alone* against the *windstorm*."

Quotation #438

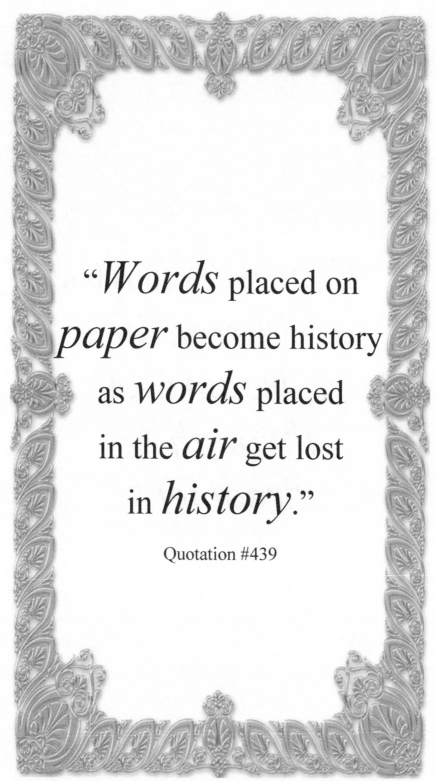

"*Words* placed on
paper become history
as *words* placed
in the *air* get lost
in *history*."

Quotation #439

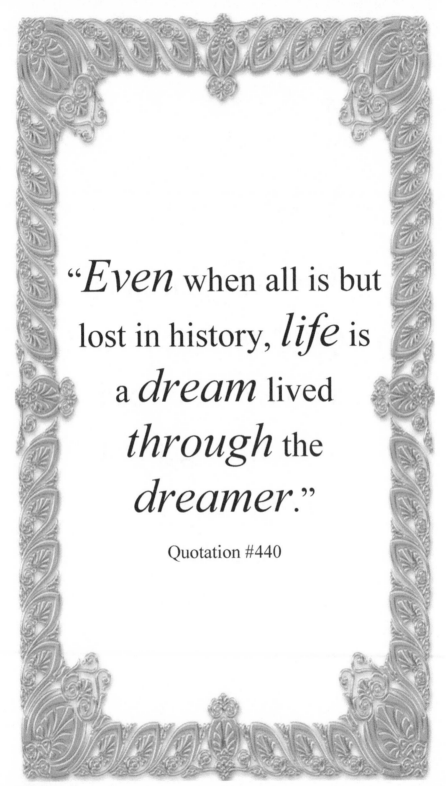

"*Even* when all is but lost in history, *life* is a *dream* lived *through* the *dreamer*."

Quotation #440

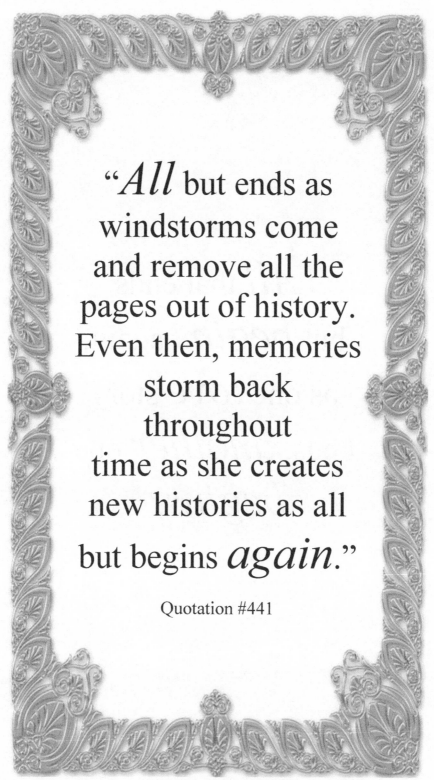

"*All* but ends as
windstorms come
and remove all the
pages out of history.
Even then, memories
storm back
throughout
time as she creates
new histories as all
but begins *again*."

Quotation #441

461

"*All* that ends
but *begins* again,
as one *love* story
ends, *another* one
begins."

Quotation #442

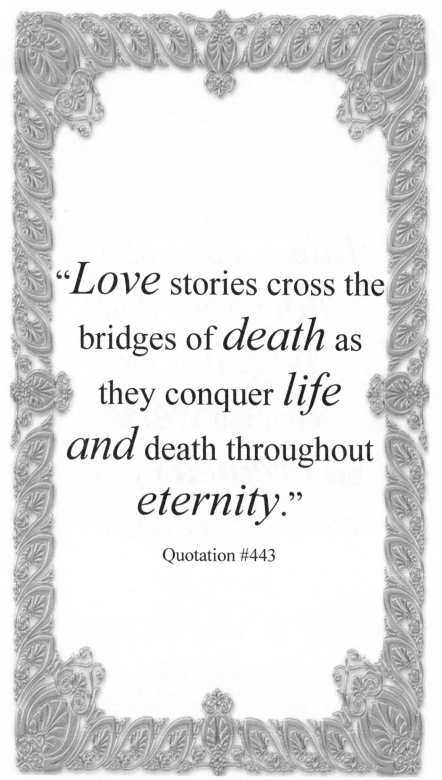

"*Love* stories cross the bridges of *death* as they conquer *life and* death throughout *eternity.*"

Quotation #443

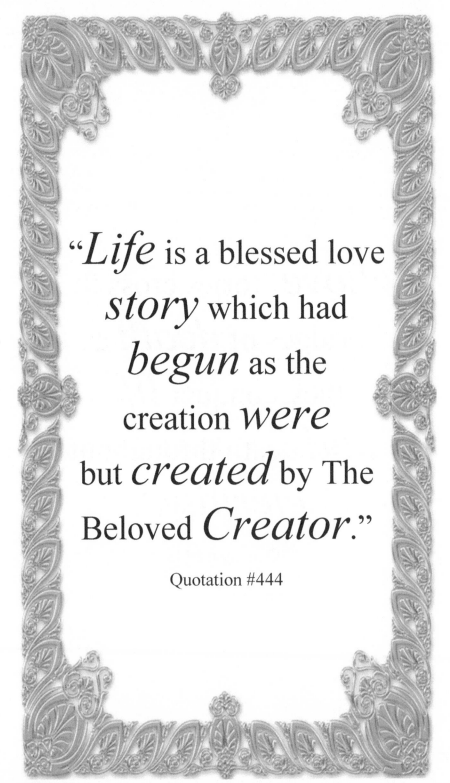

"*Life* is a blessed love *story* which had *begun* as the creation *were* but *created* by The Beloved *Creator*."

Quotation #444

464

"*The* sun sets as all are but *left* in the *dark*. It is now *throughout* the *darkness*, we must learn to *live* and *survive* as we fight for the *sun* to but *rise*."

Quotation #445

"*Wind* whispers all throughout the *dark* nights as she *warns* all to *know* the *difference* between the *good* and the *evil*."

Quotation #446

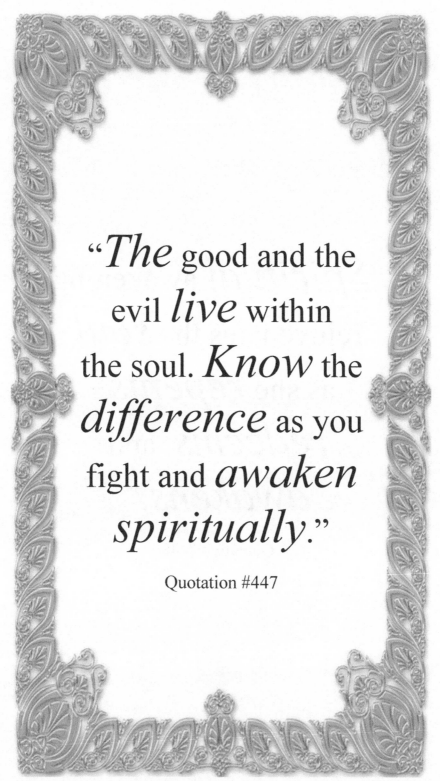

"*The* good and the evil *live* within the soul. *Know* the *difference* as you fight and *awaken spiritually*."

Quotation #447

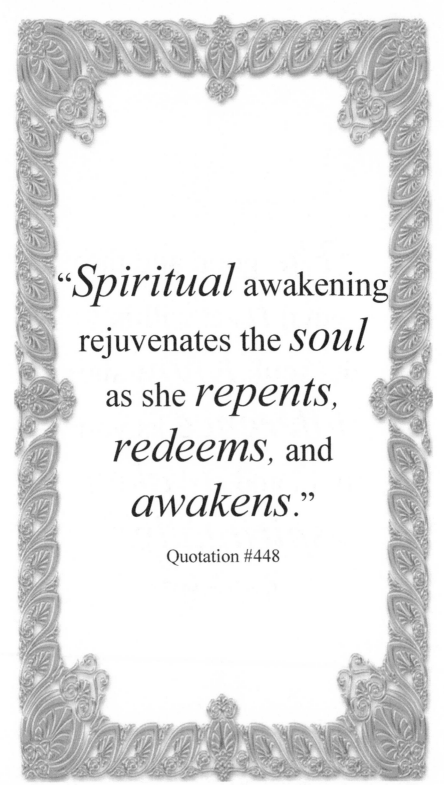

"*Spiritual* awakening rejuvenates the *soul* as she *repents, redeems,* and *awakens.*"

Quotation #448

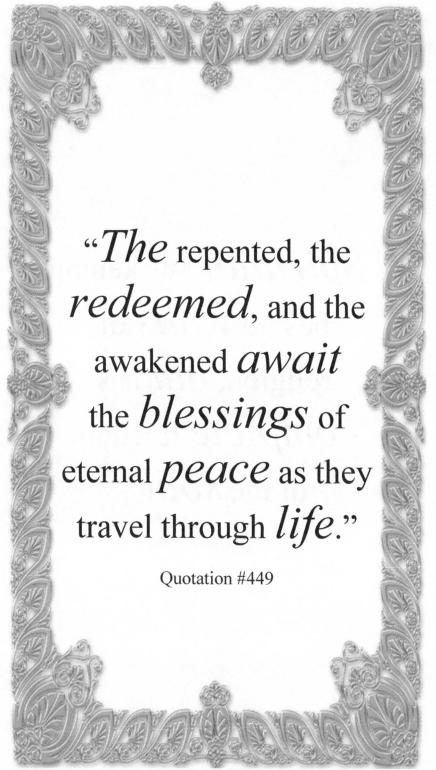

"*The* repented, the *redeemed*, and the awakened *await* the *blessings* of eternal *peace* as they travel through *life*."

Quotation #449

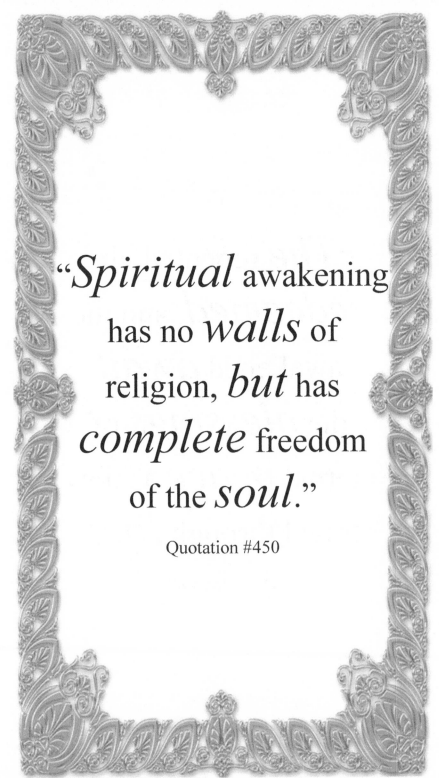

"*Spiritual* awakening has no *walls* of religion, *but* has *complete* freedom of the *soul*."

Quotation #450

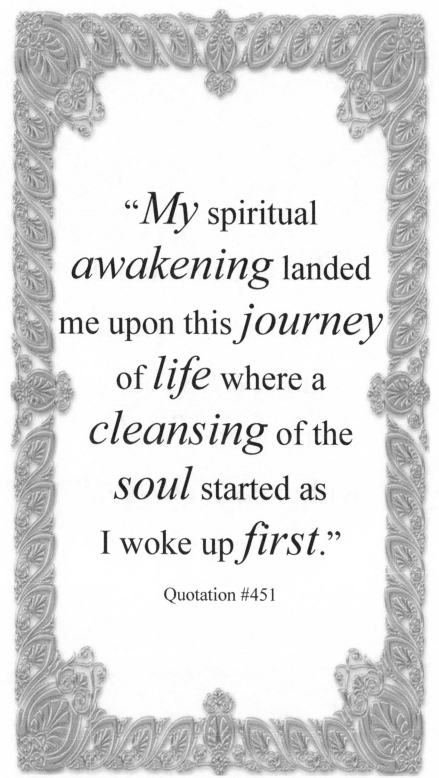

"*My* spiritual *awakening* landed me upon this *journey* of *life* where a *cleansing* of the *soul* started as I woke up *first*."

Quotation #451

471

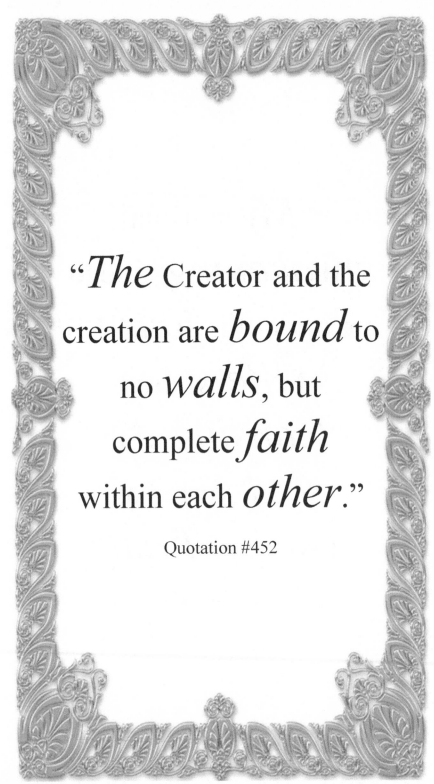

"*The* Creator and the creation are *bound* to no *walls*, but complete *faith* within each *other*."

Quotation #452

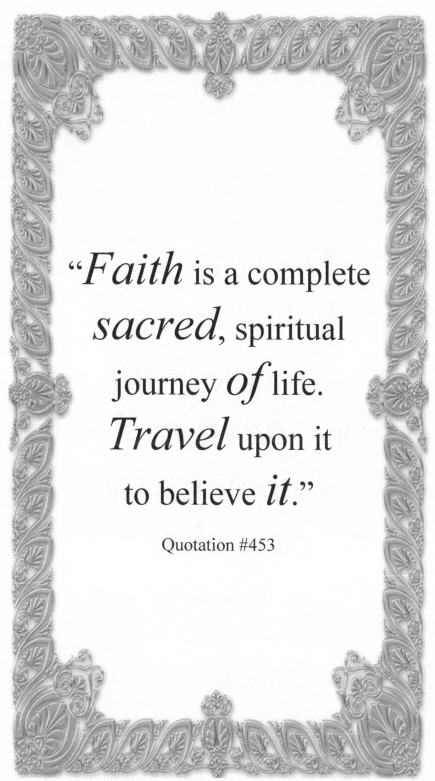

"*Faith* is a complete *sacred*, spiritual journey *of* life. *Travel* upon it to believe *it*."

Quotation #453

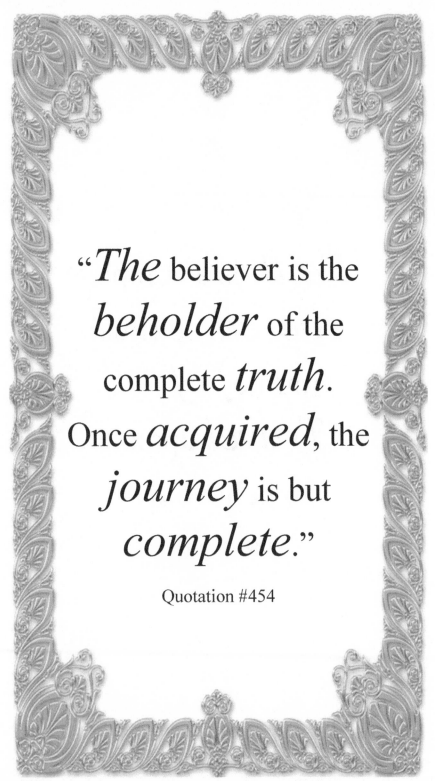

"*The* believer is the *beholder* of the complete *truth*. Once *acquired*, the *journey* is but *complete*."

Quotation #454

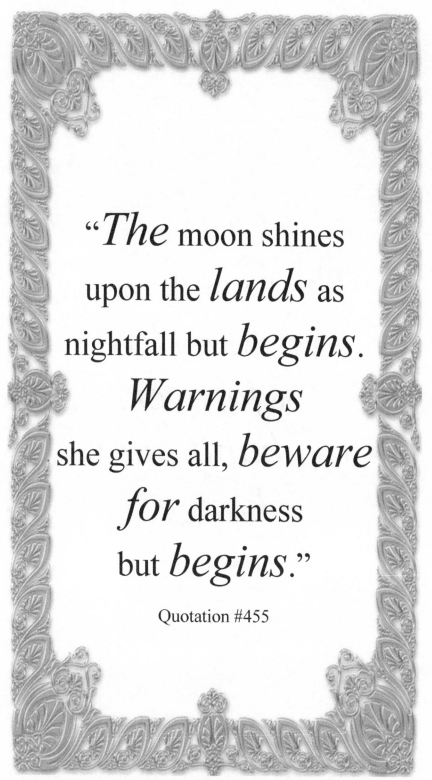

"*The* moon shines upon the *lands* as nightfall but *begins*. *Warnings* she gives all, *beware for* darkness but *begins*."

Quotation #455

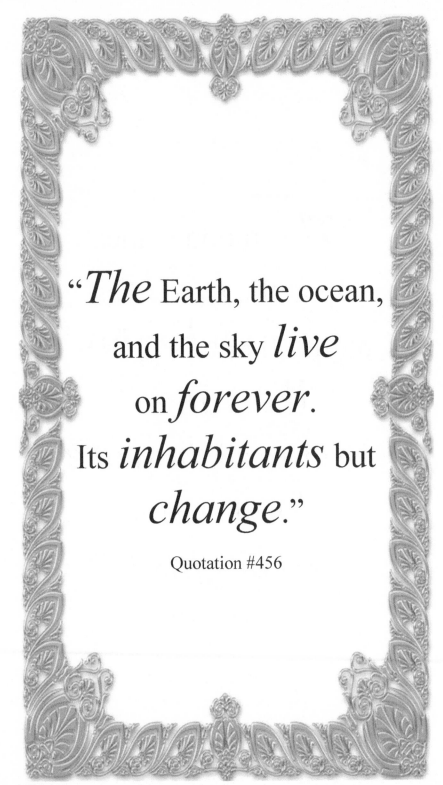

"*The* Earth, the ocean, and the sky *live* on *forever.* Its *inhabitants* but *change.*"

Quotation #456

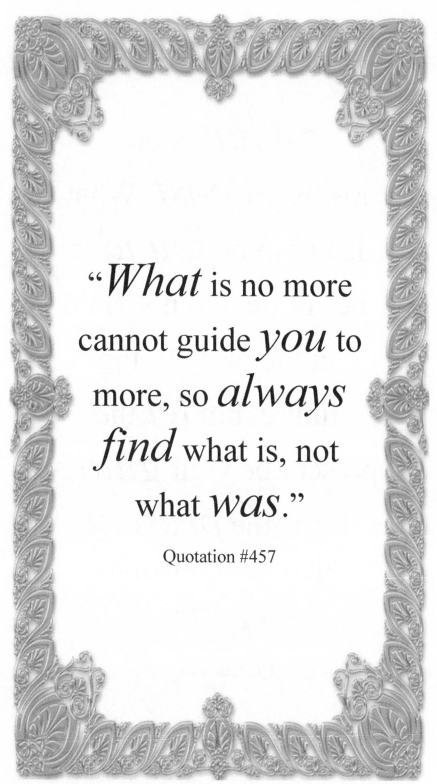

"*What* is no more cannot guide *you* to more, so *always find* what is, not what *was*."

Quotation #457

"*What* is but lost is the *past*. What is but to be *found* is the future. Do not *live* in the past *or* the future, but *let* the present be your *guide* for is the *present* also not known as a *gift*?"

Quotation #458

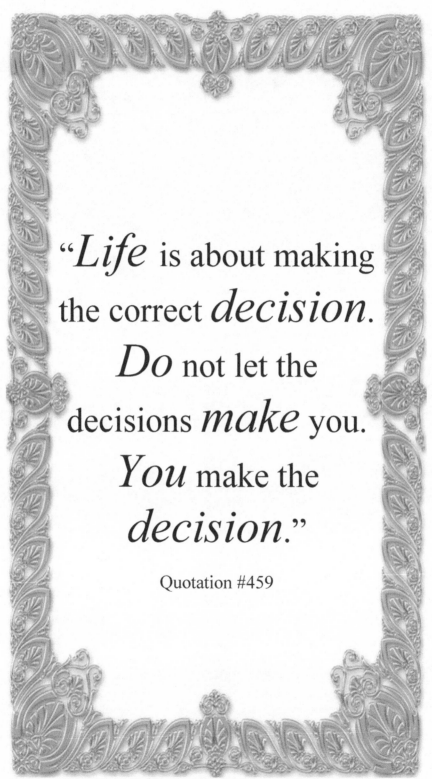

"*Life* is about making the correct *decision*. *Do* not let the decisions *make* you. *You* make the *decision*."

Quotation #459

BOOK FOUR

SPIRITUAL INSPIRATIONS
Sacred Words of Wisdom

ANN MARIE RUBY

DEDICATION

I have dedicated each one of my books to the person or people whom have inspired me to write the soul of the book. I would like to dedicate this book not to a person, but an inspiration that I have carried throughout my life. All the authors in this world are but inspired for different reasons, but we all use as a gift to bring these books upon your hands, the best friend of an author, words.

Words are sacred and have been used wisely by the past to the present throughout the future. I believe that even though humans are but mortal, words live on forever. The wind whispers sweet songs throughout time as she sings throughout eternity, her eternal friend, words. A mother sings her child to sleep with her eternal friend, words. A teacher blesses all throughout history, as she asks for help from her friend, I call words.

I have written this book and all my books holding on to the powerful hands of my friend, I call words. For this, I dedicate my book, *Spiritual Inspirations: Sacred Words Of Wisdom*, to the most blessed inspiration we all have as we travel throughout life, words.

THE WORDS OF
MY LORD

My Lord, forgive.

My Lord, forgive.

My Lord, forgive.

Let these hands not sin.

Let these eyes not sin.

Let these lips not sin.

Let these ears not sin.

Let this mind, body, and soul not sin.

Let these feet not land upon sin.

My Lord, forgive.

My Lord, forgive.

My Lord, forgive.

When this mind, body, and soul

Reach land of sin,

My Lord, let me be protected within Your bounds.

Oh my Lord, hear my prayers.

Let this mind, body, and soul be awakened.

Oh my Lord, I live amongst sinners.

I live amongst sin.

I walk amongst sin.

Let me hold on to You

And be Your true, faithful devotee.

Let me be Yours and only Yours.

Let me find my way back to You.

Amongst the sinners I am,

But pure and sin free I am.

I stand upon the land of sin,

But I stand sin free.

I stand amongst the disbelievers,

But I am a believer.

I call upon You.

All around me, disbelievers walk.

I know of the truth,

But they are flooding me with their lies.

I know the truth,

But they are drowning me amongst their lies.

My heart knows You are there,

But their words are drowning me.

May I be strong.

May I have the courage to announce the truth

Amongst the disbelievers.

Alone I walk, frightened I am,

But on this journey I have my faith

And my love for my Lord and the truth,

The unknown, untold truth,

The veil The Lord has created

To separate Heaven and Earth.

I know I must walk for You, my Lord.

With this faith and love, I shall be strong.

I know my Lord is there when I fall.

I know my Lord is there

When I am but put down by the human.

Their sharp tongue and their knowledge of nothing

And their voice of wrong but shouts so loud.

I look at them walking and I know

Their empty vessels make so much noise

For I carry the love of my Lord.

I know this journey is hard,

But at the end, my Lord is there.

Oh my Lord, I ask of You not for anything,

But give me strength and wisdom,

And Your love, and courage.

Even alone, may I fight until my last breath.

When my breath is no more,

May my soul still fight

For the words I leave behind shall grow stronger,

Mouth to mouth, ears to ears.

My words shall take voice

And shall take form of humans

And multiply

And shall be

The words of my Lord.

The words of my Lord.

THE WORDS OF

MY LORD.

*From my prayer book, *Spiritual Songs: Letters From My Chest*.

"*Inspirations* are words of *wisdom* here to *guide* all. They have *traveled* through *the* journey of *time* and *endured* all the *obstacles*."

Quotation #460

"*From* dawn to dusk and dusk to *dawn*, we are but *never* alone, *hands spread* like an *umbrella*, The *Creator* is *always* watching over *us*."

Quotation #461

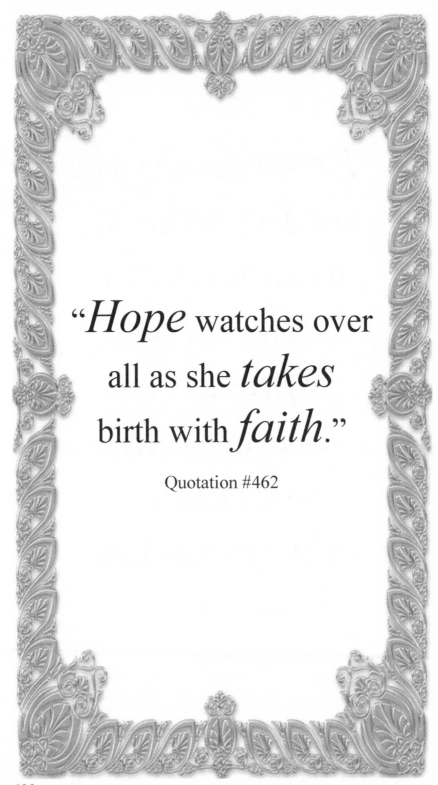

"*Hope* watches over all as she *takes* birth with *faith*."

Quotation #462

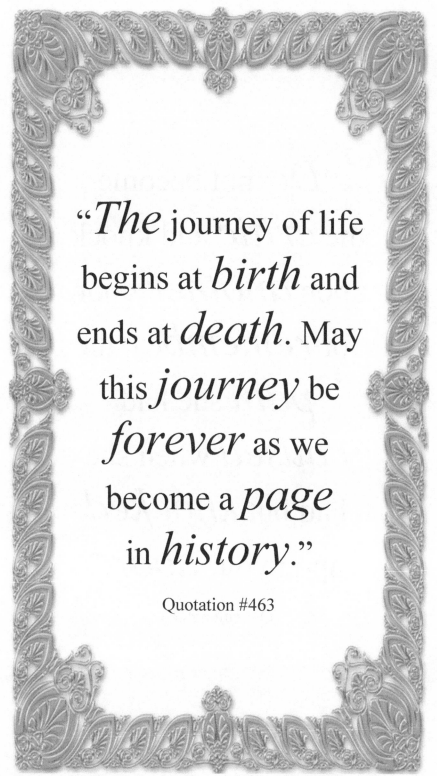

"*The* journey of life begins at *birth* and ends at *death*. May this *journey* be *forever* as we become a *page* in *history*."

Quotation #463

"*Do* not become the *critic* and knock upon *another* door, for *remember* the *pain* she had *caused* when she had but *knocked* upon your *door*."

Quotation #464

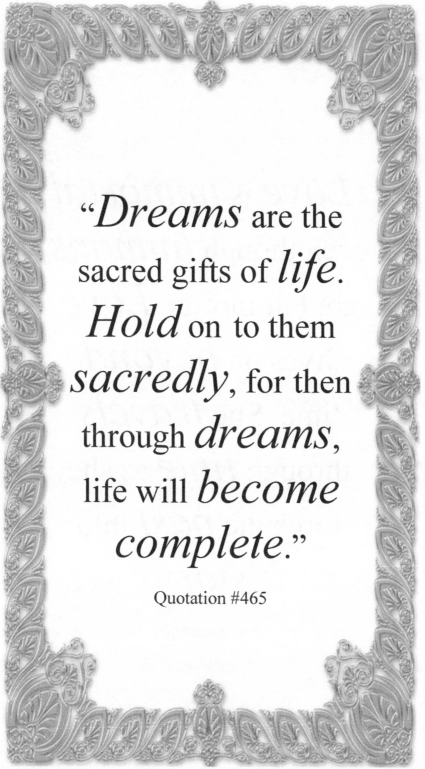

"*Dreams* are the sacred gifts of *life*. *Hold* on to them *sacredly*, for then through *dreams*, life will *become complete*."

Quotation #465

"*Love* is *immortal* even though *humans* are but mortal. *Love* lives on *beyond* time. She *travels* through *time* as she turns the *past* into *history*."

"*Hold* on to the hands of *hope* as she is the only *path* to *victory.*"

Quotation #467

"*Touch* all around you through *words*, for even *though words* are invisible, they *touch* where nothing else *can*."

Quotation #468

"*The* artist catches all different colors on her canvas for then the art is but complete. The Creator laid all different race, color, and religion, onto this Earth and this is how we become a part of the complete *picture*."

Quotation #469

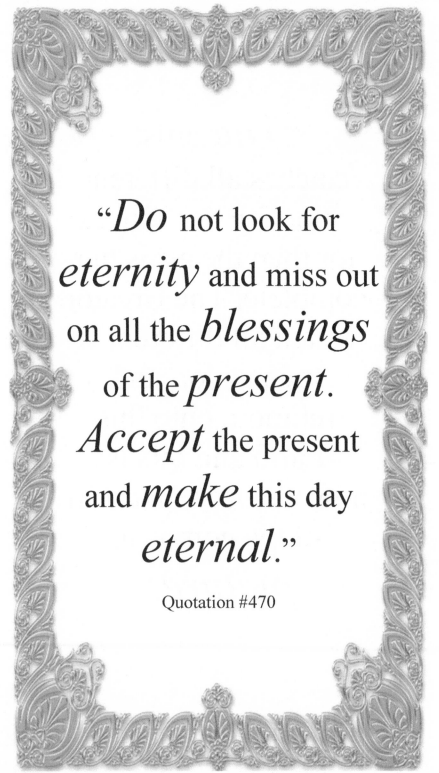

"*Do* not look for *eternity* and miss out on all the *blessings* of the *present*. *Accept* the present and *make* this day *eternal*."

Quotation #470

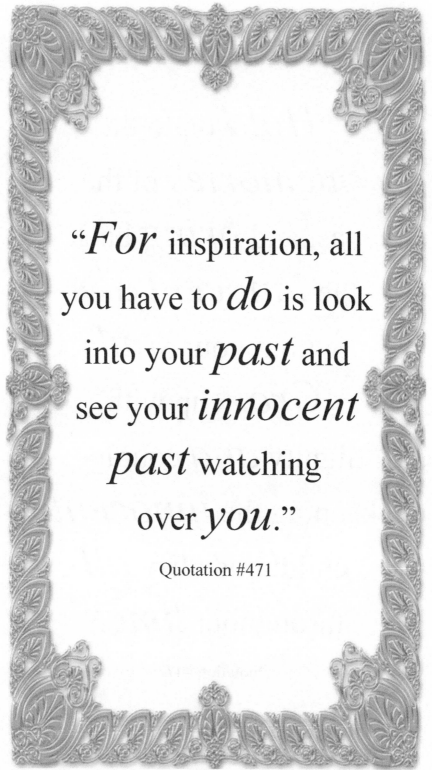

"*For* inspiration, all you have to *do* is look into your *past* and see your *innocent past* watching over *you*."

Quotation #471

"*Hold* on to the *memories* of the past and *bring* back the *innocent* child within your *soul*. *Grow* up with dignity *and* courage, keeping the *innocent* childhood alive *all* throughout *time*."

Quotation #472

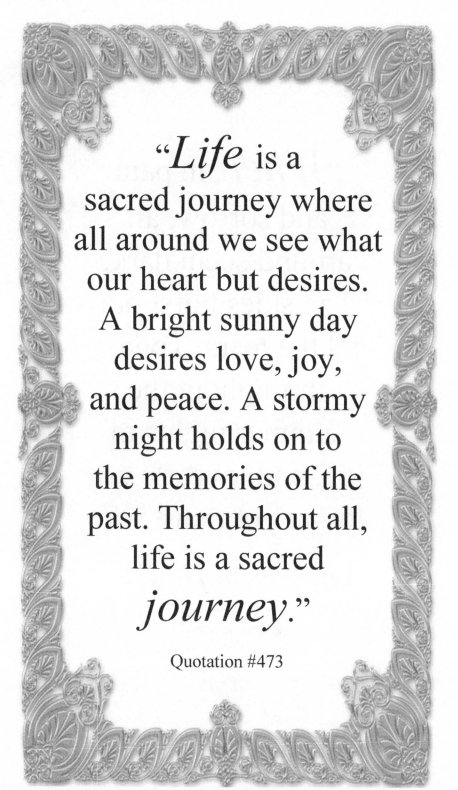

"*Life* is a
sacred journey where
all around we see what
our heart but desires.
A bright sunny day
desires love, joy,
and peace. A stormy
night holds on to
the memories of the
past. Throughout all,
life is a sacred
journey."

Quotation #473

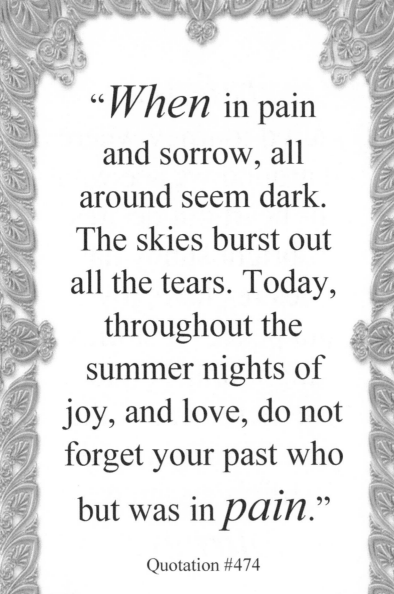

"*When* in pain and sorrow, all around seem dark. The skies burst out all the tears. Today, throughout the summer nights of joy, and love, do not forget your past who but was in *pain*."

Quotation #474

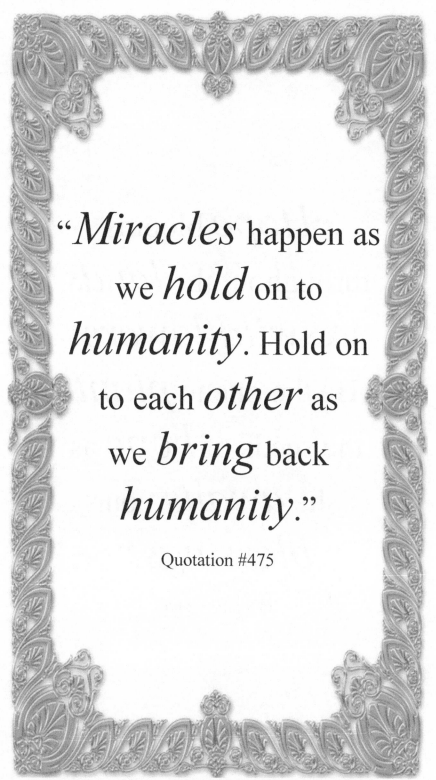

"*Miracles* happen as we *hold* on to *humanity*. Hold on to each *other* as we *bring* back *humanity*."

Quotation #475

503

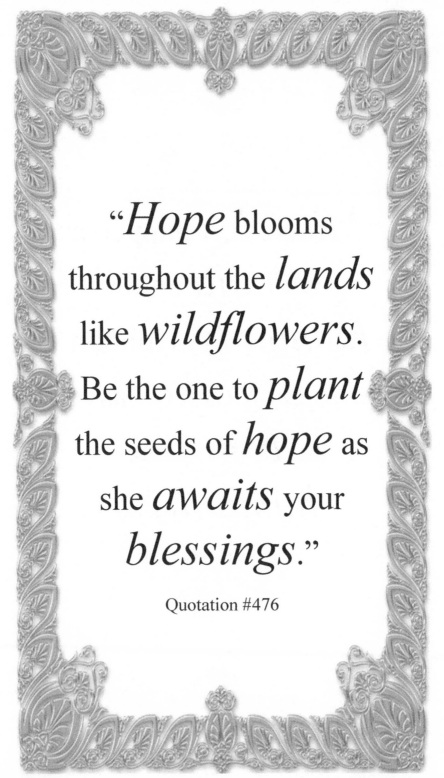

"*Hope* blooms throughout the *lands* like *wildflowers*. Be the one to *plant* the seeds of *hope* as she *awaits* your *blessings*."

Quotation #476

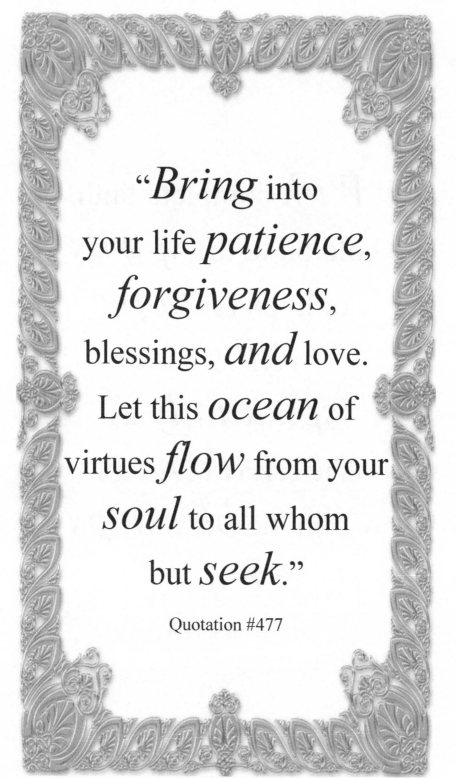

"*Bring* into your life *patience*, *forgiveness*, blessings, *and* love. Let this *ocean* of virtues *flow* from your *soul* to all whom but *seek*."

Quotation #477

505

"*With* complete faith, hold on to the *spirits* of hope for *hope walks* back *spiritually* as she *awakens* all within the *blessings* of *hope*."

Quotation #478

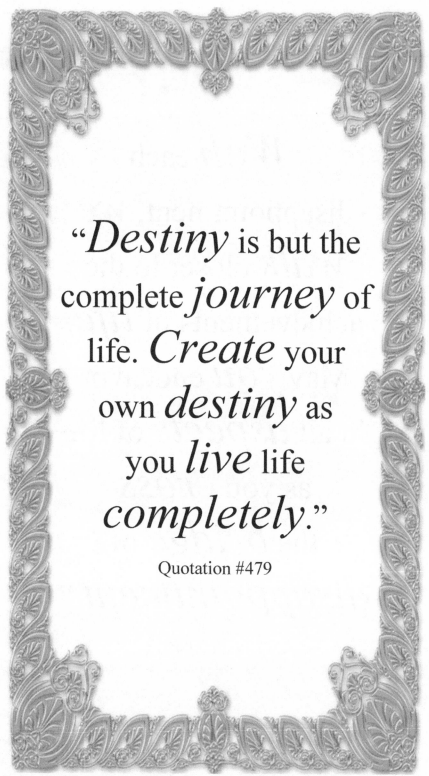

"*Destiny* is but the complete *journey* of life. *Create* your own *destiny* as you *live* life *completely*."

Quotation #479

"*With* each disappointment, *we walk* closer to the achievements of *life*. May *you* endeavor in all *aspects* of life as you *cross* the *bridge* of *disappointment*."

Quotation #480

"*May* my words be *prayers* in the wind *blowing* peace *throughout* the world. *May* all *houses* have their *windows* open to let this wind of *peace* into their *homes* and *hearts*."

Quotation #481

"*Knocking*
on a door that has been
closed, seeking for
something that is
invisible, asking for
help from the stranger
who pretends not to
be there, is fruitless.
Persistence is fruitful.
Keep knocking,
seeking, and asking, for
with persistence, you
shall but *prevail*."

Quotation #482

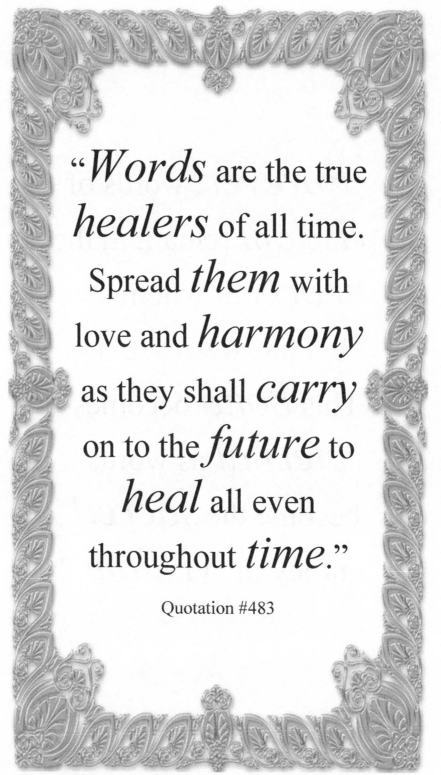

"*Words* are the true *healers* of all time. Spread *them* with love and *harmony* as they shall *carry* on to the *future* to *heal* all even throughout *time*."

Quotation #483

"*Forever*, words of *wisdom* remain in the *hearts* of whom she but has *touched*. This *bond* becomes *eternal* as words become the *sacred* journey of *wisdom*."

Quotation #484

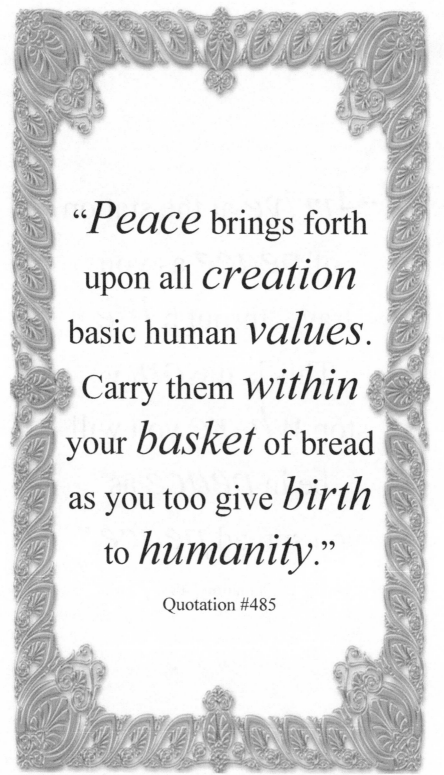

"*Peace* brings forth upon all *creation* basic human *values*. Carry them *within* your *basket* of bread as you too give *birth* to *humanity*."

Quotation #485

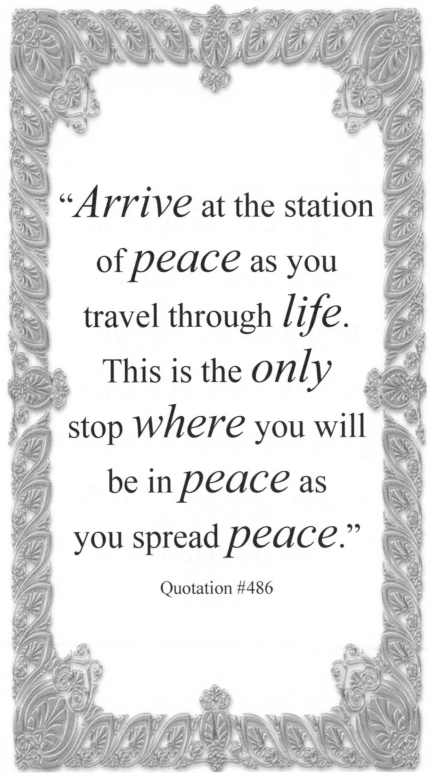

"*Arrive* at the station of *peace* as you travel through *life*. This is the *only* stop *where* you will be in *peace* as you spread *peace*."

Quotation #486

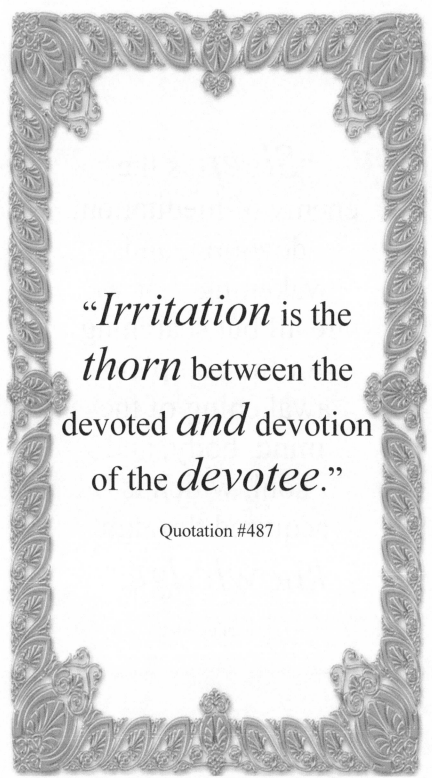

"*Irritation* is the *thorn* between the devoted *and* devotion of the *devotee*."

Quotation #487

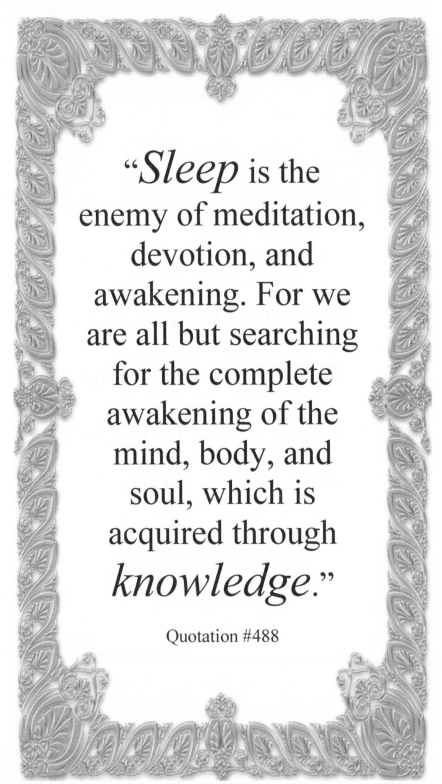

"*Sleep* is the enemy of meditation, devotion, and awakening. For we are all but searching for the complete awakening of the mind, body, and soul, which is acquired through *knowledge*."

Quotation #488

"*Gain* knowledge and be *awakened completely* through *spirituality* and let this *life* journey be the *complete awakening* of the *inner* mind, body, and *soul*."

Quotation #489

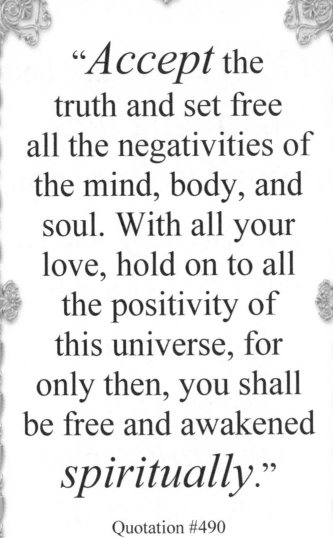

"*Accept* the truth and set free all the negativities of the mind, body, and soul. With all your love, hold on to all the positivity of this universe, for only then, you shall be free and awakened *spiritually.*"

Quotation #490

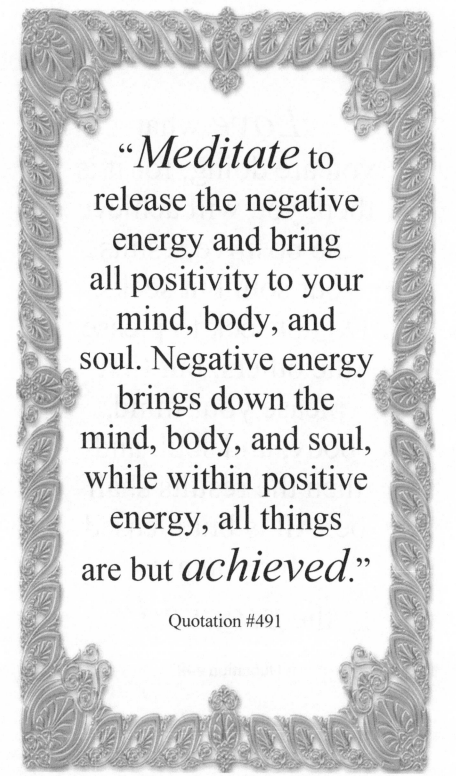

"*Meditate* to release the negative energy and bring all positivity to your mind, body, and soul. Negative energy brings down the mind, body, and soul, while within positive energy, all things are but *achieved*."

Quotation #491

"*Love* what you are doing, for it is then, you will achieve the positive results your soul but seeks. Do not seek to please the others, but first please your mind, body, and soul, and then the results shall be. All is but pleased for you are the *pleased*."

Quotation #492

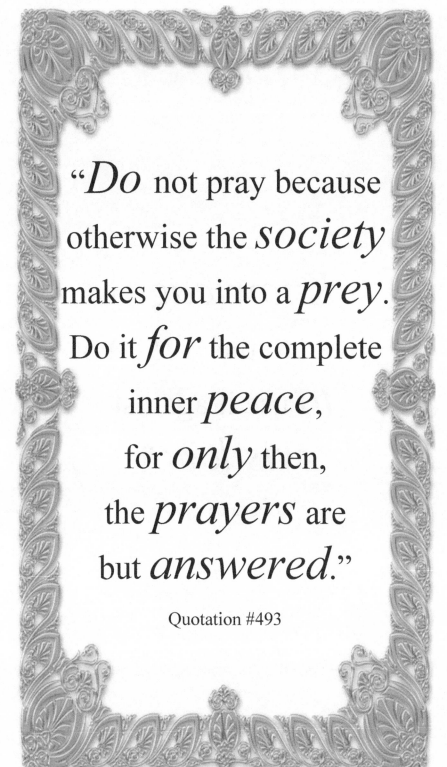

"*Do* not pray because otherwise the *society* makes you into a *prey*. Do it *for* the complete inner *peace*, for *only* then, the *prayers* are but *answered*."

Quotation #493

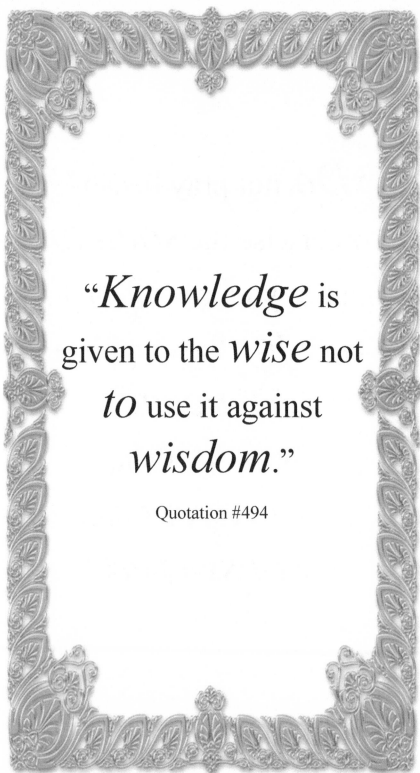

"*Knowledge* is given to the *wise* not *to* use it against *wisdom*."

Quotation #494

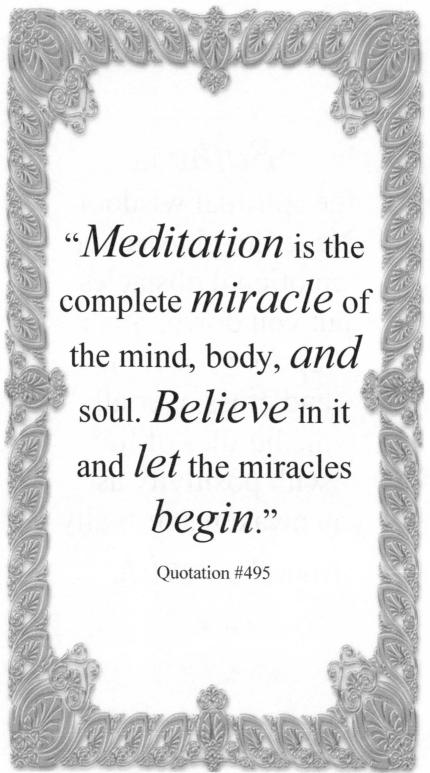

"*Meditation* is the complete *miracle* of the mind, body, *and* soul. *Believe* in it and *let* the miracles *begin*."

Quotation #495

523

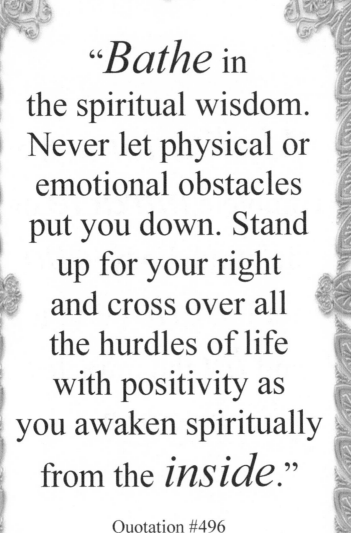

"*Bathe* in the spiritual wisdom. Never let physical or emotional obstacles put you down. Stand up for your right and cross over all the hurdles of life with positivity as you awaken spiritually from the *inside*."

Quotation #496

524

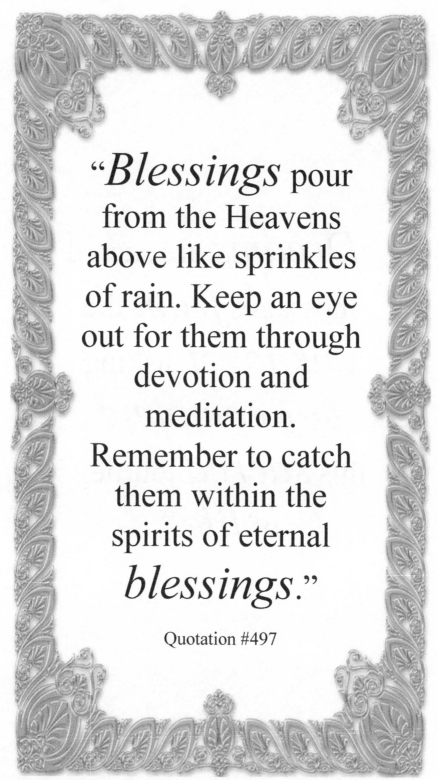

"*Blessings* pour from the Heavens above like sprinkles of rain. Keep an eye out for them through devotion and meditation. Remember to catch them within the spirits of eternal *blessings*."

Quotation #497

"*Dreams* are sacred messages *from* the *unknown*, asking us to *complete* this *sacred* journey of *life*."

Quotation #498

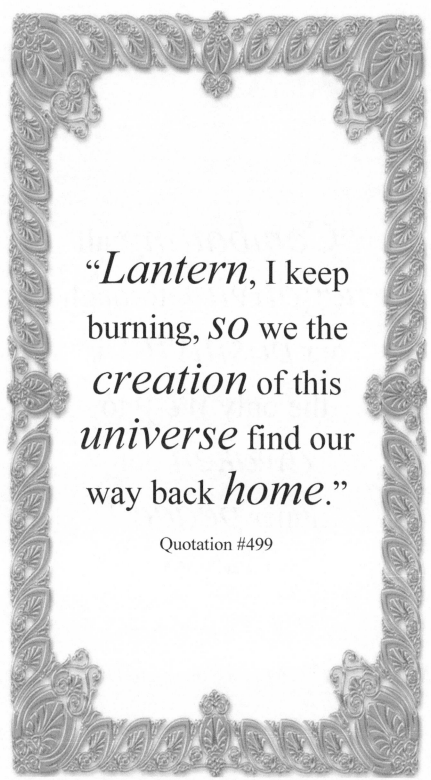

"*Lantern*, I keep burning, *so* we the *creation* of this *universe* find our way back *home*."

Quotation #499

527

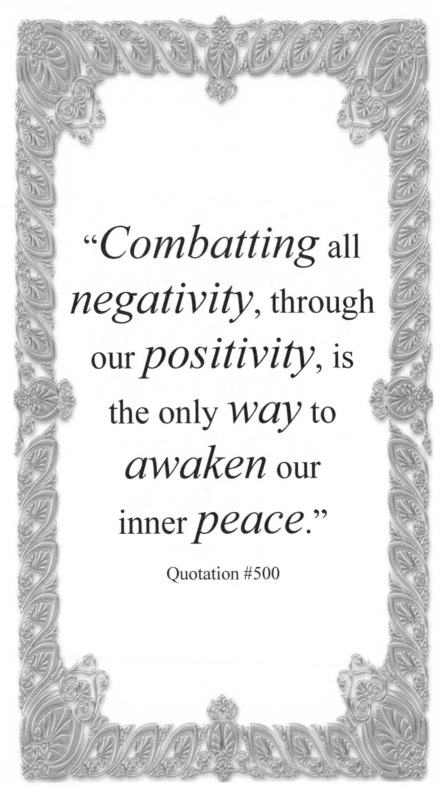

"*Combatting* all *negativity*, through our *positivity*, is the only *way* to *awaken* our inner *peace*."

Quotation #500

"*Humans* become the spiritual *Angels* of *peace*, when we work for *each other* not against each *other*."

Quotation #501

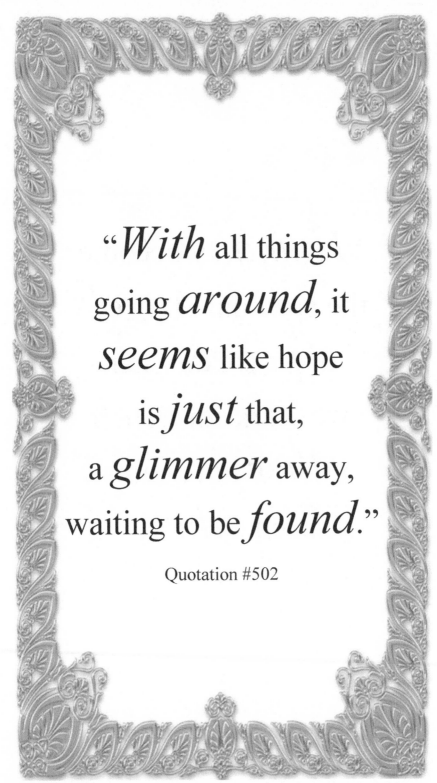

"*With* all things going *around*, it *seems* like hope is *just* that, a *glimmer* away, waiting to be *found*."

Quotation #502

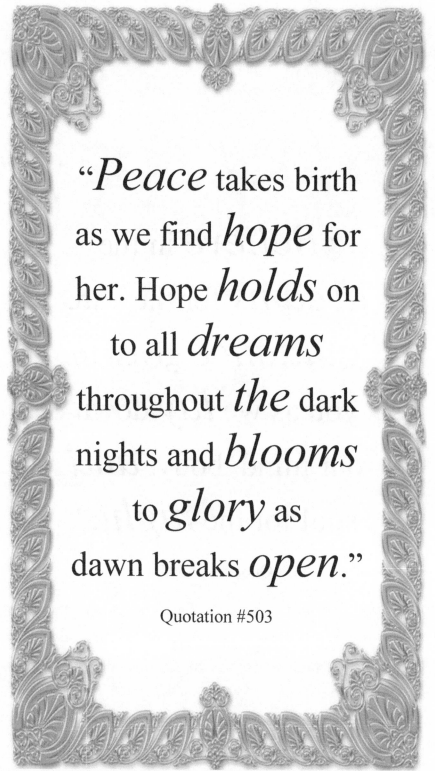

"*Peace* takes birth as we find *hope* for her. Hope *holds* on to all *dreams* throughout *the* dark nights and *blooms* to *glory* as dawn breaks *open*."

Quotation #503

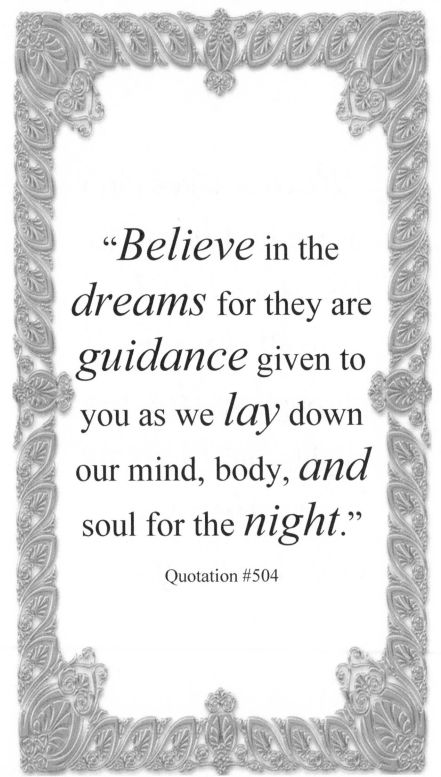

"*Believe* in the *dreams* for they are *guidance* given to you as we *lay* down our mind, body, *and* soul for the *night*."

Quotation #504

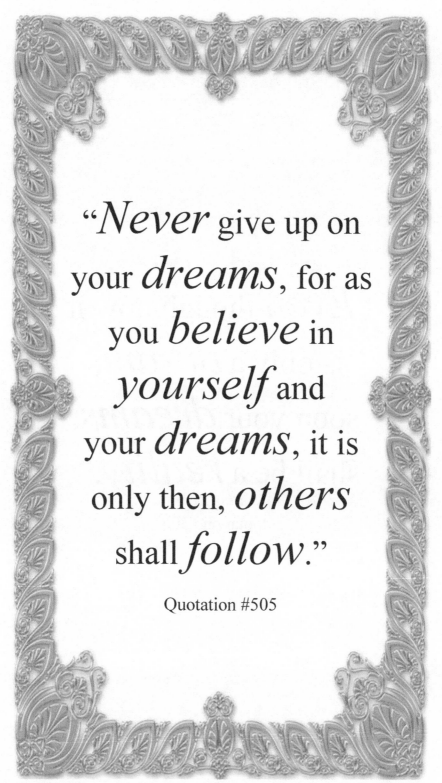

"*Never* give up on your *dreams*, for as you *believe* in *yourself* and your *dreams*, it is only then, *others* shall *follow*."

Quotation #505

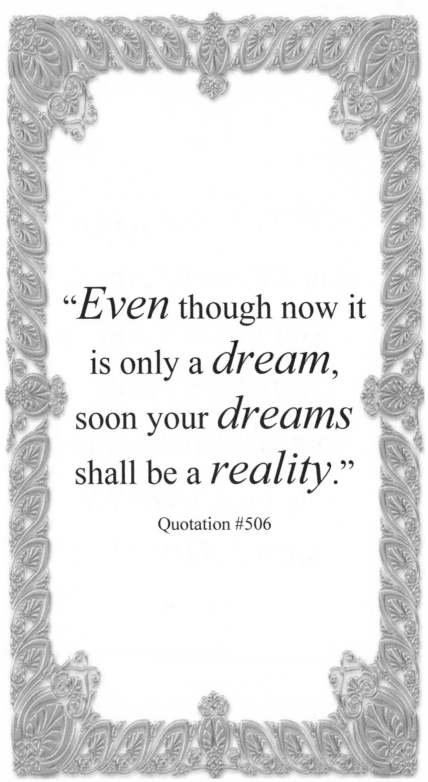

"*Even* though now it is only a *dream*, soon your *dreams* shall be a *reality*."

Quotation #506

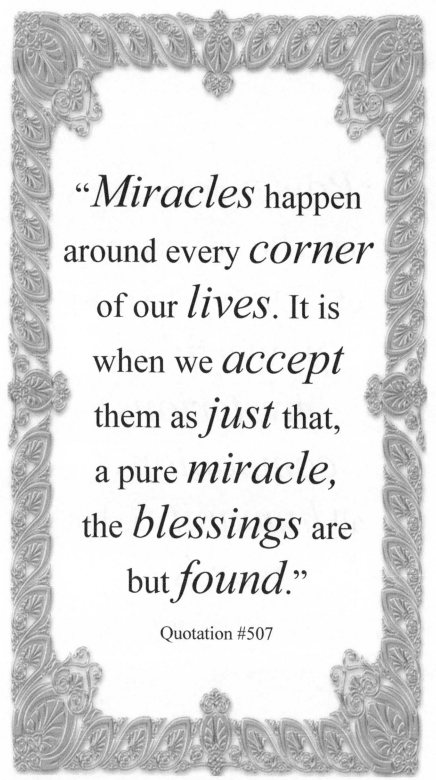

"*Miracles* happen around every *corner* of our *lives*. It is when we *accept* them as *just* that, a pure *miracle,* the *blessings* are but *found*."

Quotation #507

"*Power* and mystery are *the* companions of *words*. The most *powerful* and *mysterious companion* of all *humanity* is but *words*."

Quotation #508

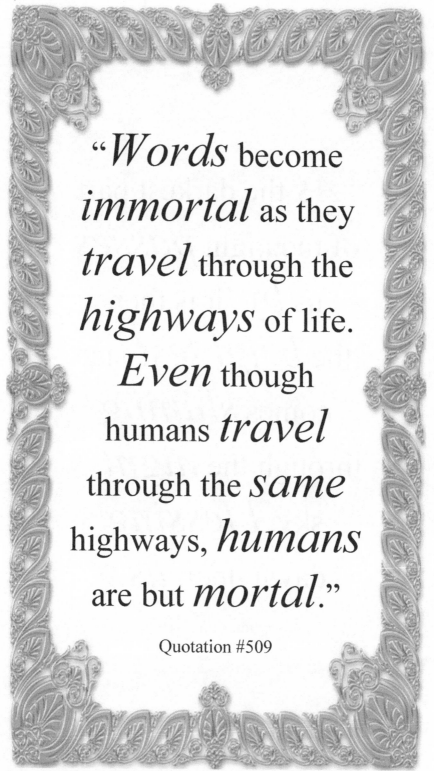

"*Words* become *immortal* as they *travel* through the *highways* of life. *Even* though humans *travel* through the *same* highways, *humans* are but *mortal*."

Quotation #509

"*As* the darkest part of the night *passes* us *by*, it is then the *brightest* star comes *shining* through the *night's* sky, *blessing* dawn upon *us*."

Quotation #510

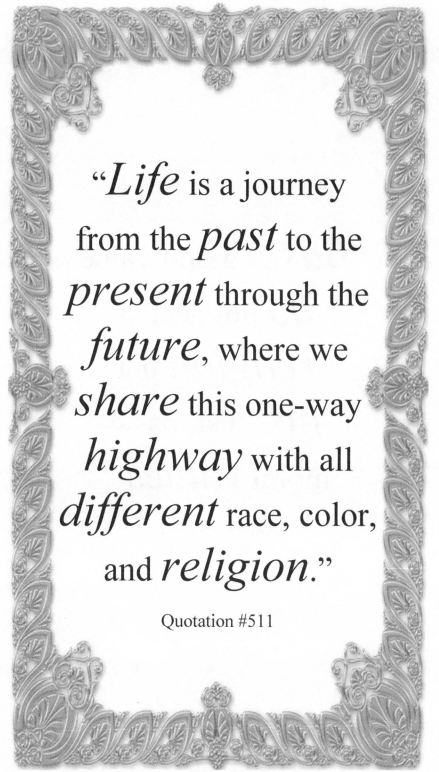

"*Life* is a journey from the *past* to the *present* through the *future*, where we *share* this one-way *highway* with all *different* race, color, and *religion.*"

Quotation #511

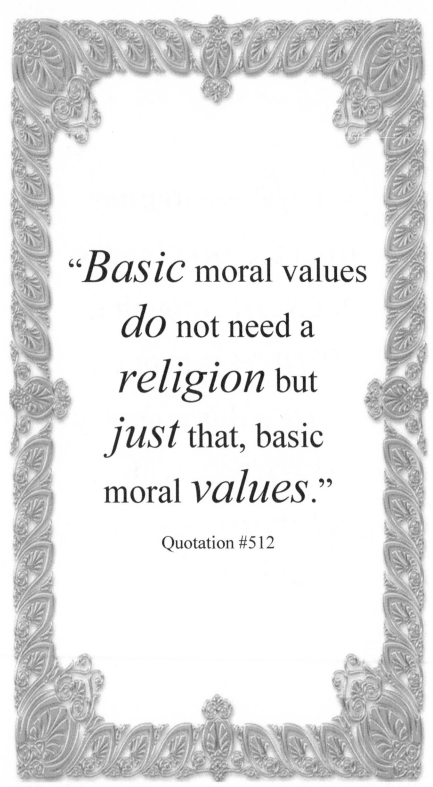

"*Basic* moral values *do* not need a *religion* but *just* that, basic moral *values*."

Quotation #512

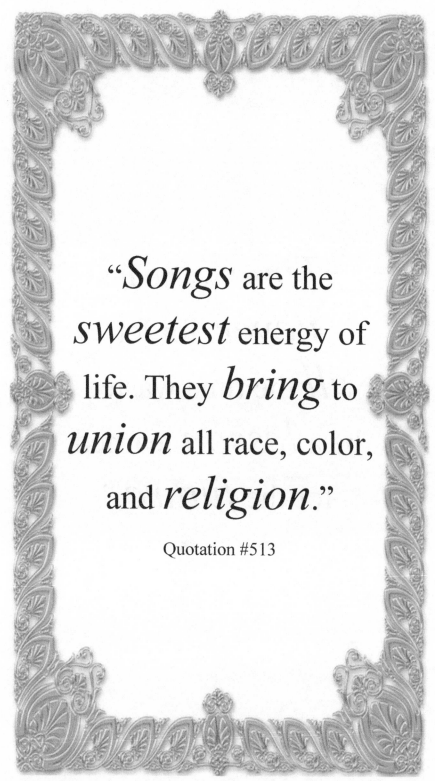

"*Songs* are the *sweetest* energy of life. They *bring* to *union* all race, color, and *religion.*"

Quotation #513

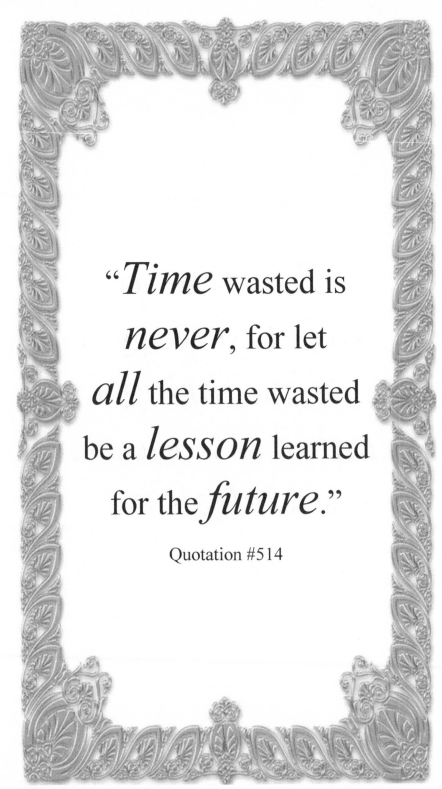

"*Time* wasted is
never, for let
all the time wasted
be a *lesson* learned
for the *future*."

Quotation #514

"*Breathe* in the pure blessings of *dawn* throughout the *day* as she *progresses* towards *nightfall*."

Quotation #515

"*Even* during the dark nights, we have the glorious moon shining upon us like a guiding star, with so many of her friends showing their twinkling lights throughout the dark *nights*."

Quotation #516

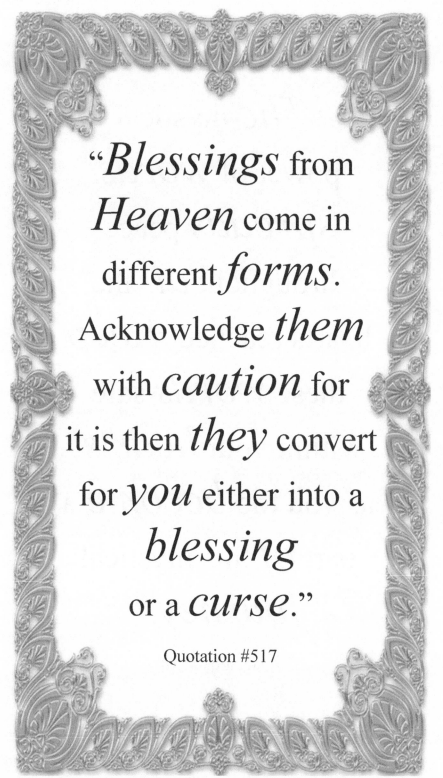

"*Blessings* from *Heaven* come in different *forms*. Acknowledge *them* with *caution* for it is then *they* convert for *you* either into a *blessing* or a *curse*."

Quotation #517

"*The* mystical power of *words spreads* peace throughout *all* the hearts reached. *Keep* these *words* safe within your *hearts*, as you too *become* a part *of* this mystical *journey*."

Quotation #518

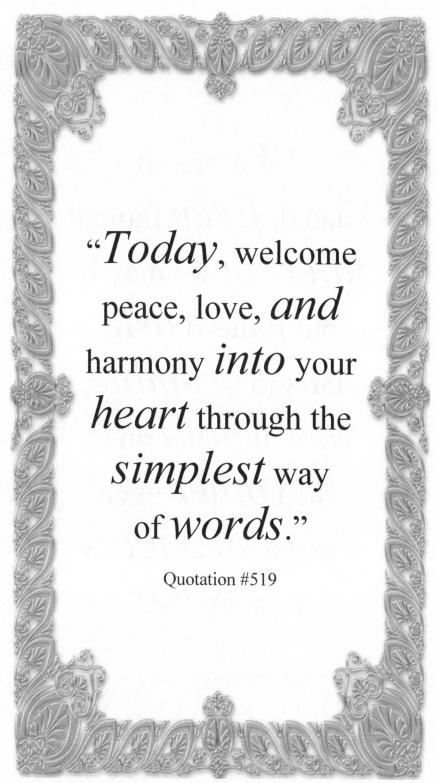

"*Today*, welcome peace, love, *and* harmony *into* your *heart* through the *simplest* way of *words*."

Quotation #519

"*We* are all related. *Even* though *different* we may be, but if the *world* starts to *crumble*, we will *hold* on to each *other* even though *strangers* we may *be*."

Quotation #520

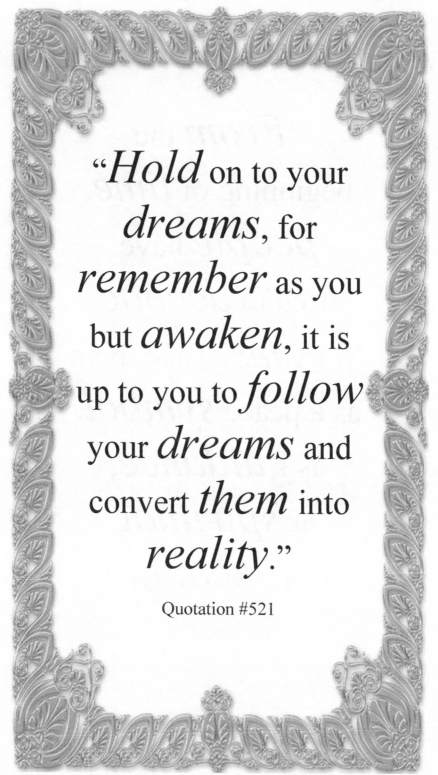

"*Hold* on to your *dreams*, for *remember* as you but *awaken*, it is up to you to *follow* your *dreams* and convert *them* into *reality*."

Quotation #521

"*From* the beginning of *time*, *people* have tried to *decode dreams*. Take them as a peace *symbol*, as *guidance*, as *spiritual awakening*."

Quotation #522

"*Dreams* are given from the *Heavens* above *onto* all within the *Earth* beneath for *within* them lie the *miracles* of *eternity.*"

Quotation #523

"*Forgiveness* is the only way to *freedom*. Accept it and *set* your *mind*, body, and soul *free*."

Quotation #524

"*Peace* lands upon
the *soul*
as *forgiveness*
is but *found*."

Quotation #525

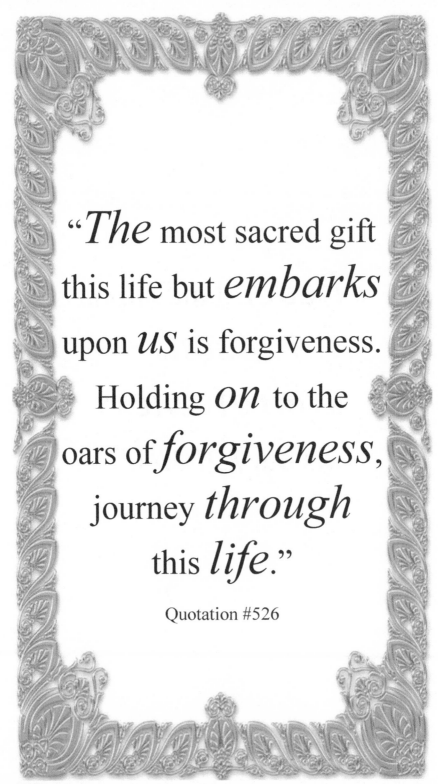

"*The* most sacred gift this life but *embarks* upon *us* is forgiveness. Holding *on* to the oars of *forgiveness*, journey *through* this *life*."

Quotation #526

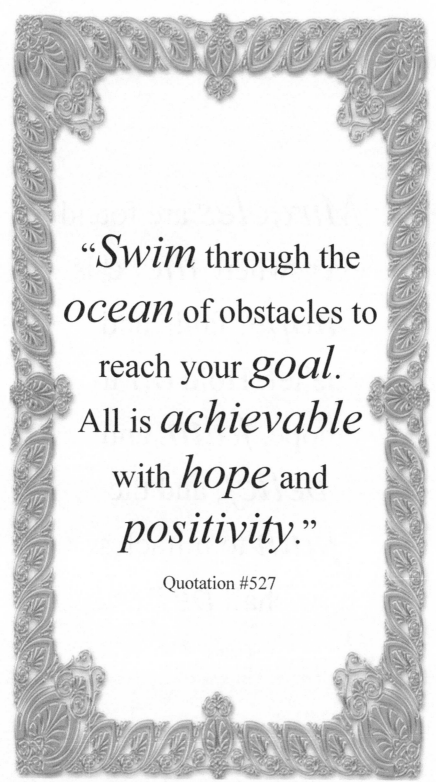

"*Swim* through the *ocean* of obstacles to reach your *goal*. All is *achievable* with *hope* and *positivity*."

Quotation #527

"*Miracles* are found everywhere *there* is *hope*, faith, and belief. Hold *on* to hope, *faith*, and *belief*, and the *path* to miracles shall *be*."

Quotation #528

"*Celebrate* victory, but never *forget* defeat. *Victory* only appears *after* we respect *defeat*."

Quotation #529

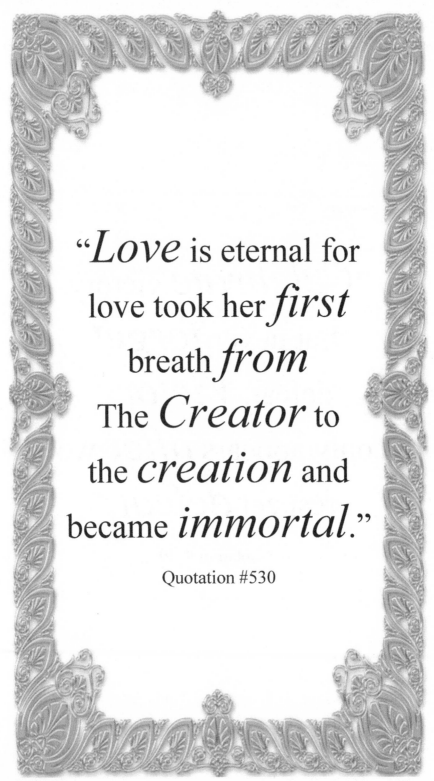

"*Love* is eternal for love took her *first* breath *from* The *Creator* to the *creation* and became *immortal*."

Quotation #530

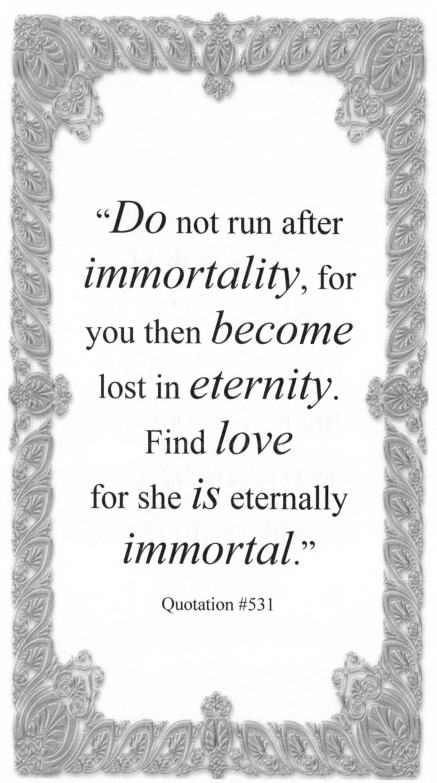

"*Do* not run after
immortality, for
you then *become*
lost in *eternity*.
Find *love*
for she *is* eternally
immortal."

Quotation #531

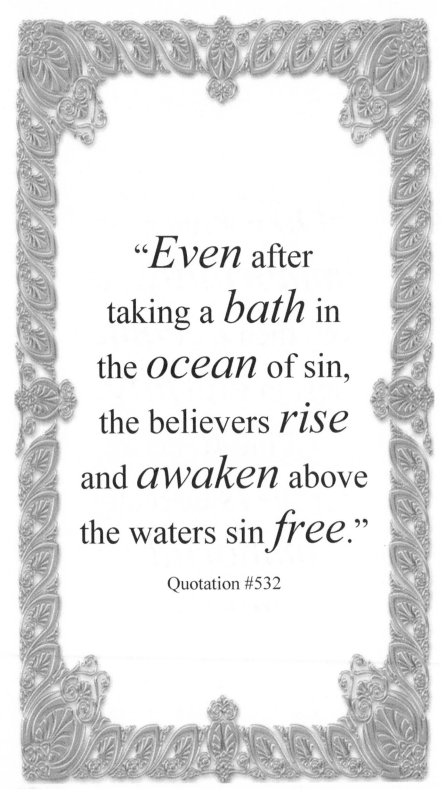

"*Even* after taking a *bath* in the *ocean* of sin, the believers *rise* and *awaken* above the waters sin *free*."

Quotation #532

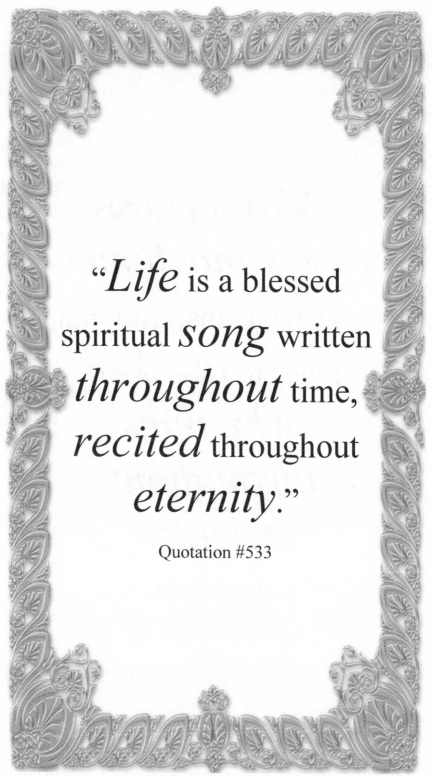

"*Life* is a blessed
spiritual *song* written
throughout time,
recited throughout
eternity."

Quotation #533

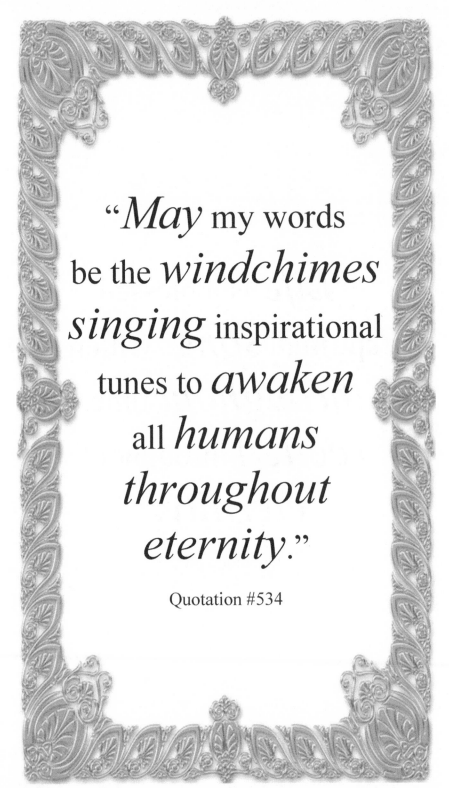

"*May* my words be the *windchimes singing* inspirational tunes to *awaken* all *humans throughout eternity.*"

Quotation #534

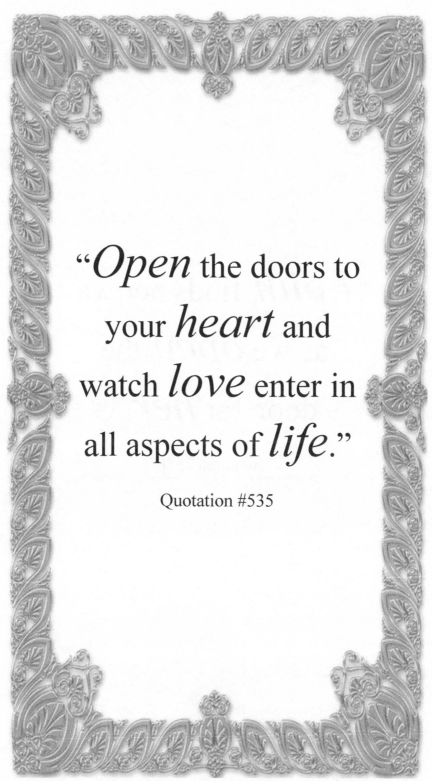

"*Open* the doors to your *heart* and watch *love* enter in all aspects of *life*."

Quotation #535

"*Faith* finds her way
as we *open* the
door for *her*."

Quotation #536

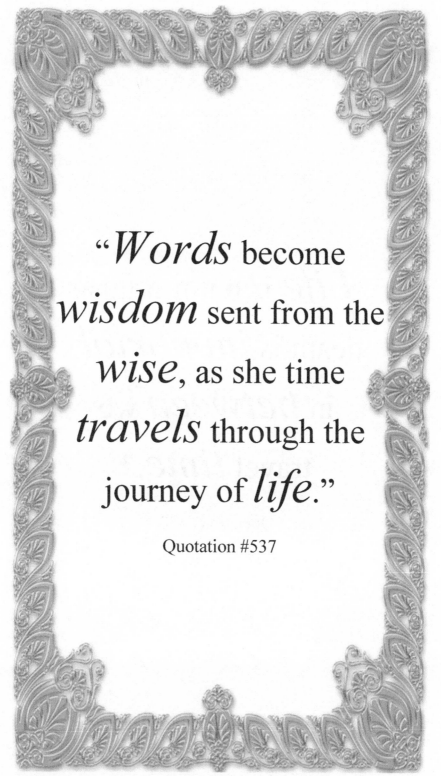

"*Words* become *wisdom* sent from the *wise*, as she time *travels* through the journey of *life*."

Quotation #537

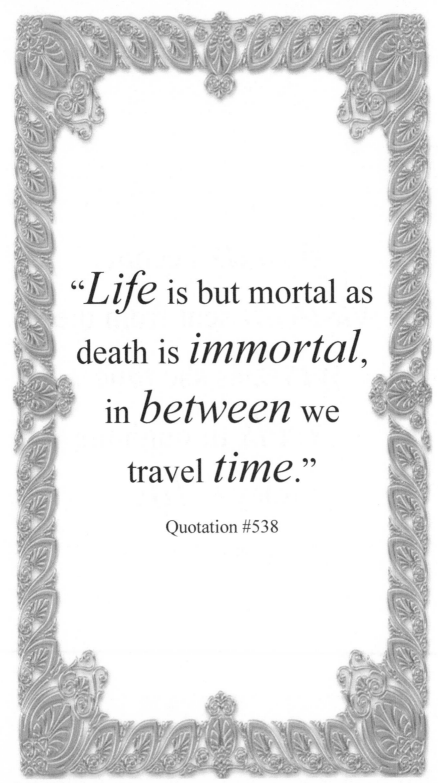

"*Life* is but mortal as death is *immortal*, in *between* we travel *time*."

Quotation #538

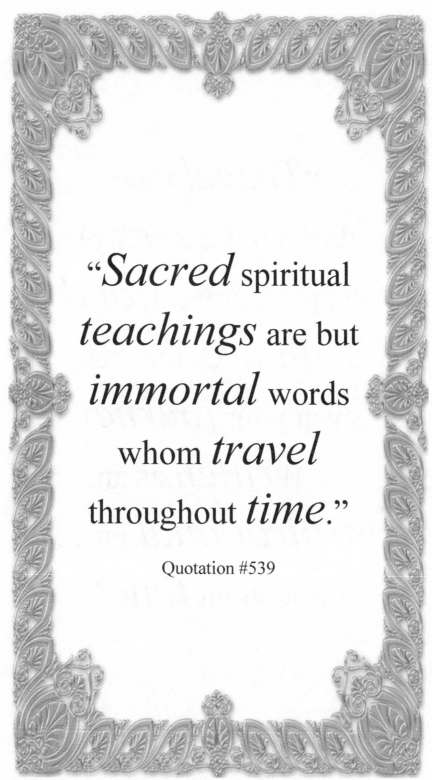

"*Sacred* spiritual *teachings* are but *immortal* words whom *travel* throughout *time*."

Quotation #539

"*Travel* time through the *eyes* of the past, present, *and* the *future*, for then, even your *journey* is *written* as an *inspirational* guide throughout *time*."

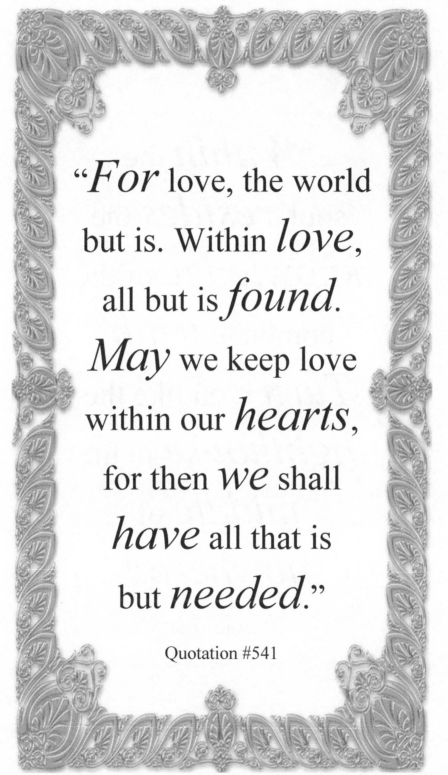

"*For* love, the world but is. Within *love*, all but is *found*. *May* we keep love within our *hearts*, for then *we* shall *have* all that is but *needed*."

Quotation #541

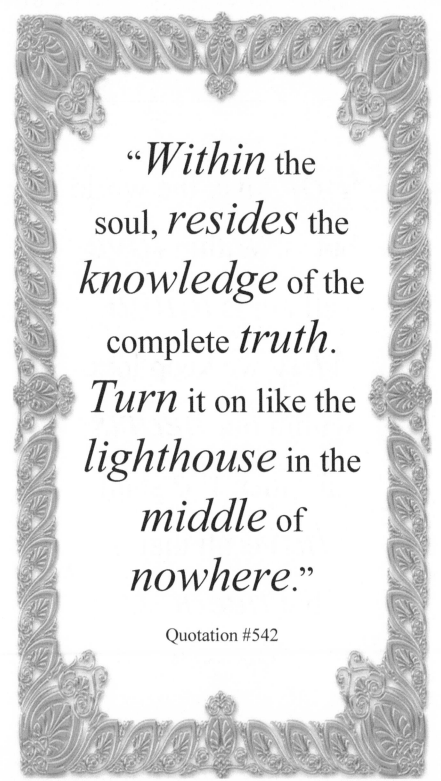

"*Within* the soul, *resides* the *knowledge* of the complete *truth*. *Turn* it on like the *lighthouse* in the *middle* of *nowhere*."

Quotation #542

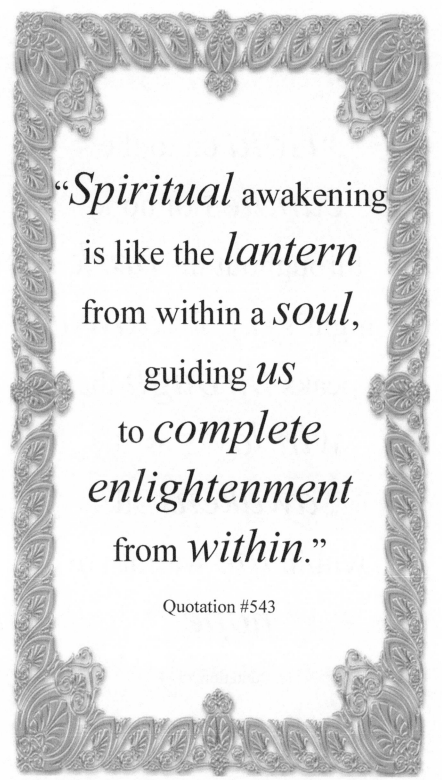

"*Spiritual* awakening is like the *lantern* from within a *soul*, guiding *us* to *complete* enlightenment from *within*."

Quotation #543

"*Hold* on to the *candles* of hope throughout the *dark* night's sky, for *dawn* peaks *through* the *windows* as she *awakens* all within *the* warmth of *hope.*"

Quotation #544

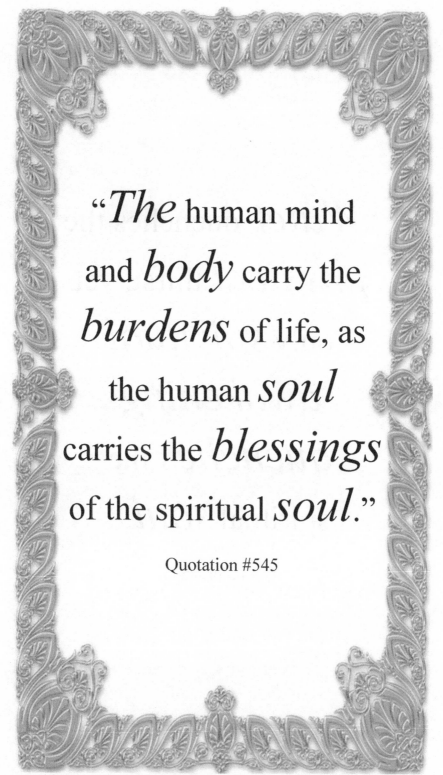

"*The* human mind and *body* carry the *burdens* of life, as the human *soul* carries the *blessings* of the spiritual *soul*."

Quotation #545

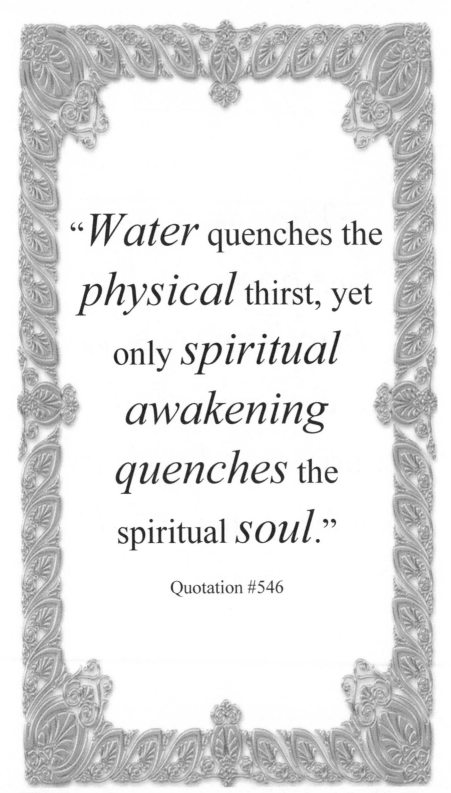

"*Water* quenches the *physical* thirst, yet only *spiritual awakening quenches* the spiritual *soul*."

Quotation #546

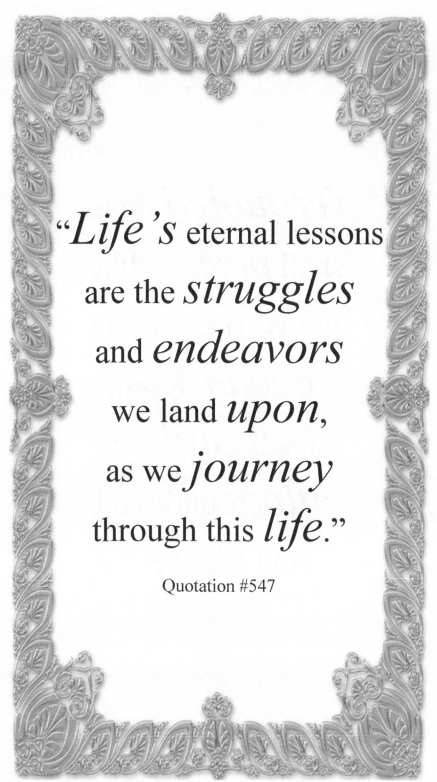

"*Life's* eternal lessons are the *struggles* and *endeavors* we land *upon*, as we *journey* through this *life*."

Quotation #547

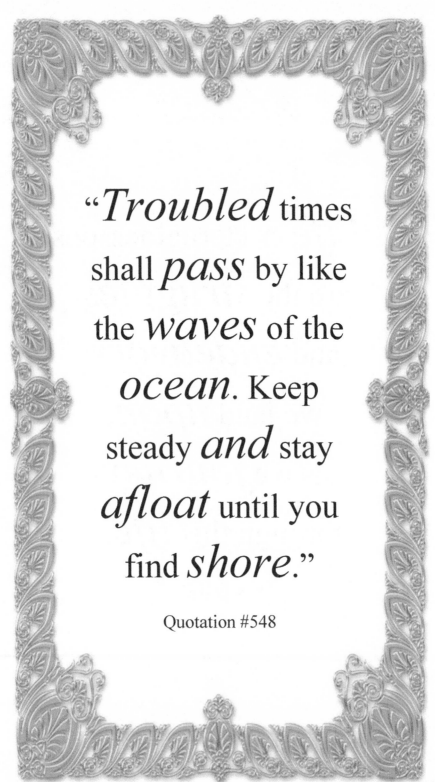

"*Troubled* times shall *pass* by like the *waves* of the *ocean*. Keep steady *and* stay *afloat* until you find *shore*."

Quotation #548

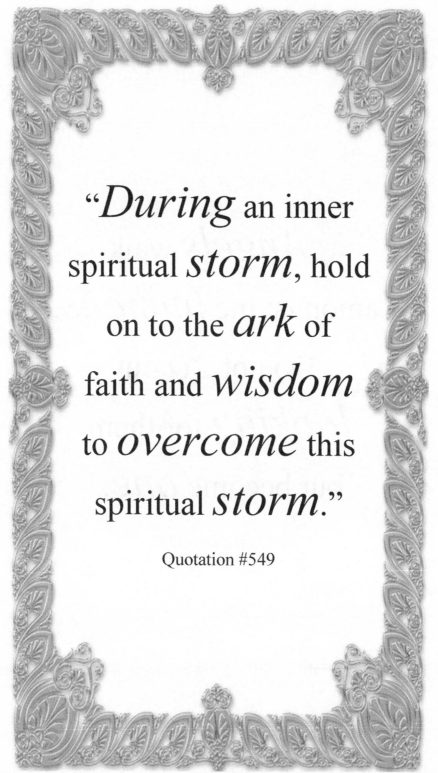

"*During* an inner spiritual *storm*, hold on to the *ark* of faith and *wisdom* to *overcome* this spiritual *storm*."

Quotation #549

"*Angels* walk
amongst the *humans*.
Do not *go* out
looking for them,
but become *one*."

Quotation #550

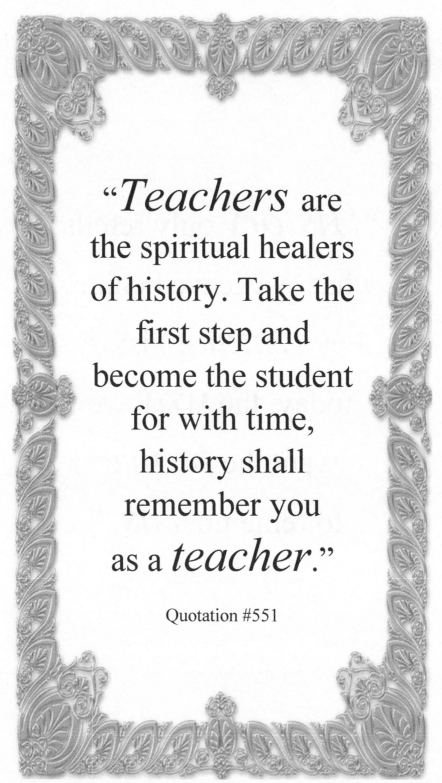

"*Teachers* are the spiritual healers of history. Take the first step and become the student for with time, history shall remember you as a *teacher*."

Quotation #551

"*History* only retells what *we* leave behind. Let us *make* history today, the *way* we want the *future* to remember *us*."

Quotation #552

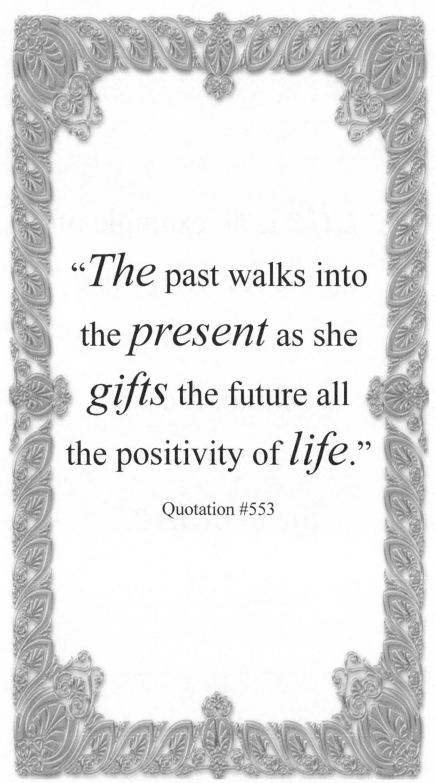

"*The* past walks into the *present* as she *gifts* the future all the positivity of *life*."

Quotation #553

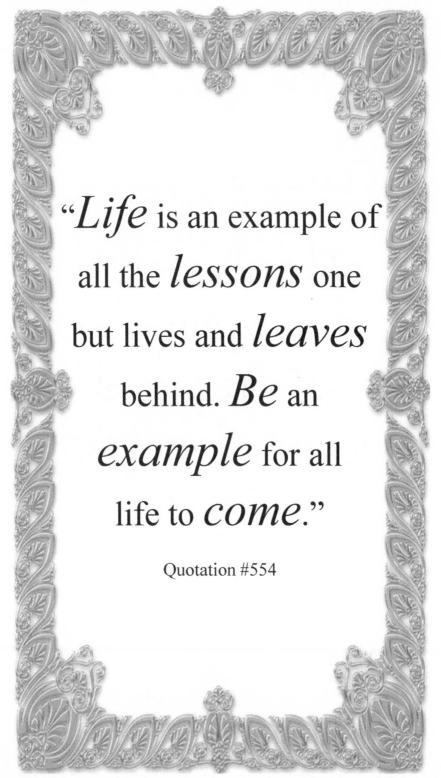

"*Life* is an example of all the *lessons* one but lives and *leaves* behind. *Be* an *example* for all life to *come*."

Quotation #554

"*Fear* but takes away all positivity and becomes an obstacle of fear. Erase all the fears from the books of life, and walk with positivity as you rewrite your own book with hope, faith, and *positivity.*"

Quotation #555

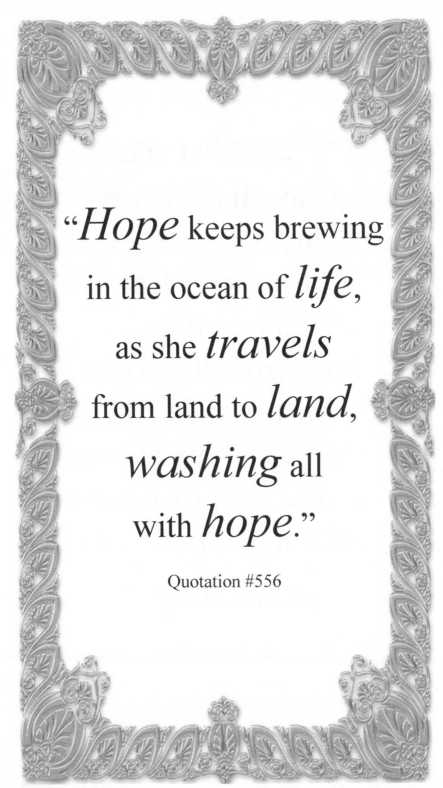

"*Hope* keeps brewing
in the ocean of *life*,
as she *travels*
from land to *land*,
washing all
with *hope*."

Quotation #556

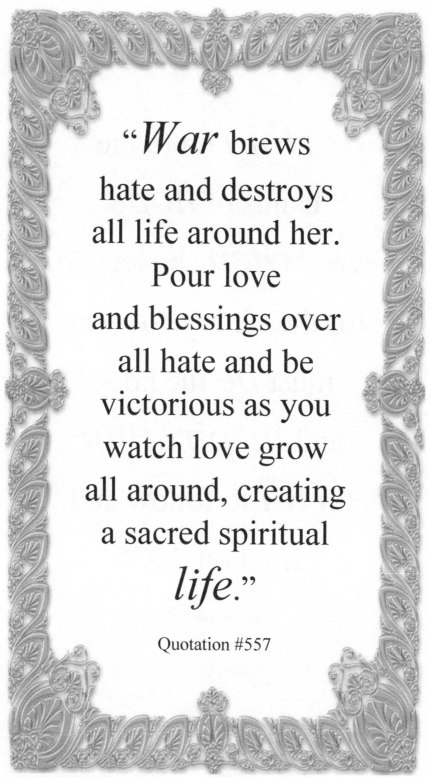

"*War* brews
hate and destroys
all life around her.
Pour love
and blessings over
all hate and be
victorious as you
watch love grow
all around, creating
a sacred spiritual
life."

Quotation #557

"*Hold* on to the hands of *hope* even *when* she lets go, for then it is *you* who must *be* the hope and *inspiration* for *all* to follow and hold on *to*."

Quotation #558

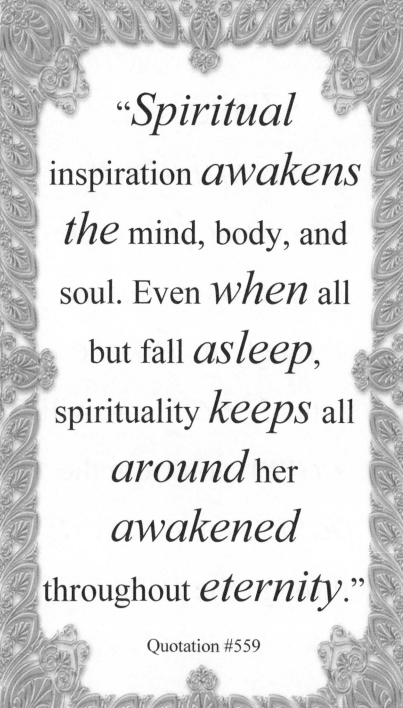

"*Spiritual* inspiration *awakens the* mind, body, and soul. Even *when* all but fall *asleep,* spirituality *keeps* all *around* her *awakened* throughout *eternity.*"

Quotation #559

"*Time* is our only *spiritual* connection *from* the *past* to the present through the *future*. Value *time* as she will *carry* you from the *past* to the *present* through the *future*."

Quotation #560

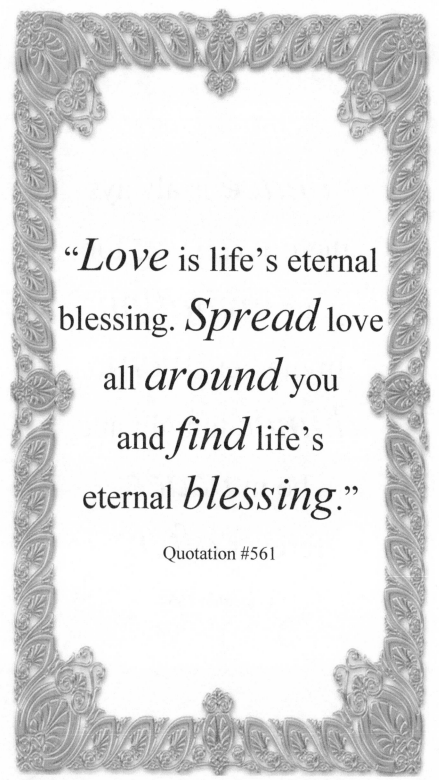

"*Love* is life's eternal blessing. *Spread* love all *around* you and *find* life's eternal *blessing*."

Quotation #561

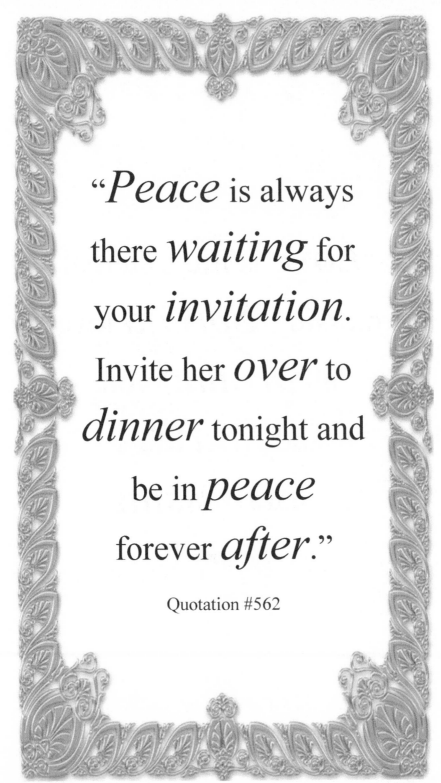

"*Peace* is always there *waiting* for your *invitation*. Invite her *over* to *dinner* tonight and be in *peace* forever *after*."

Quotation #562

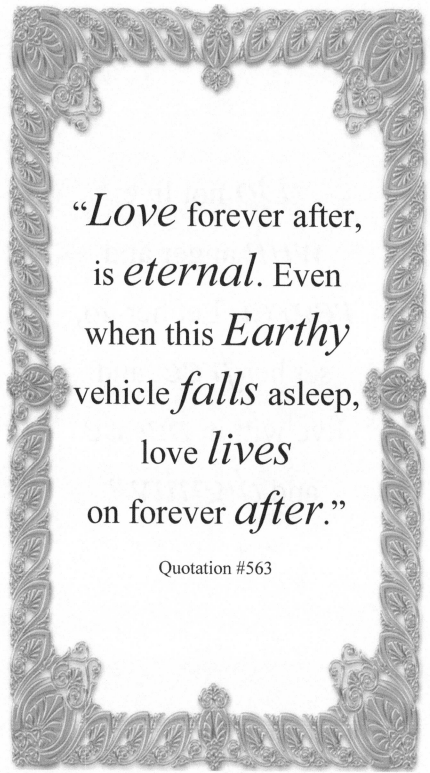

"*Love* forever after,
is *eternal.* Even
when this *Earthy*
vehicle *falls* asleep,
love *lives*
on forever *after.*"

Quotation #563

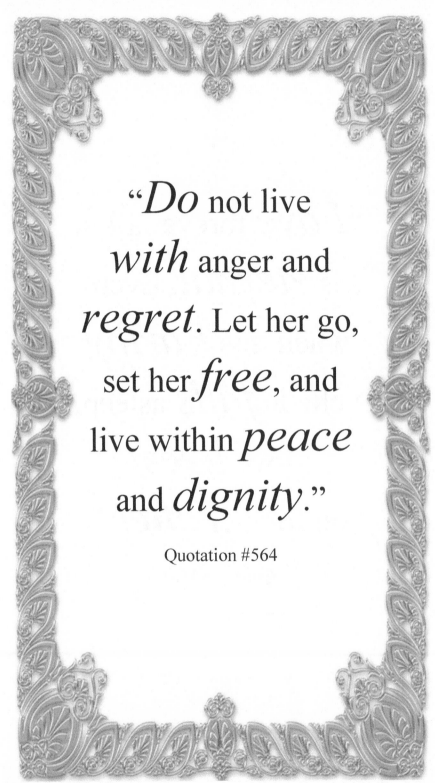

"*Do* not live *with* anger and *regret*. Let her go, set her *free*, and live within *peace* and *dignity*."

Quotation #564

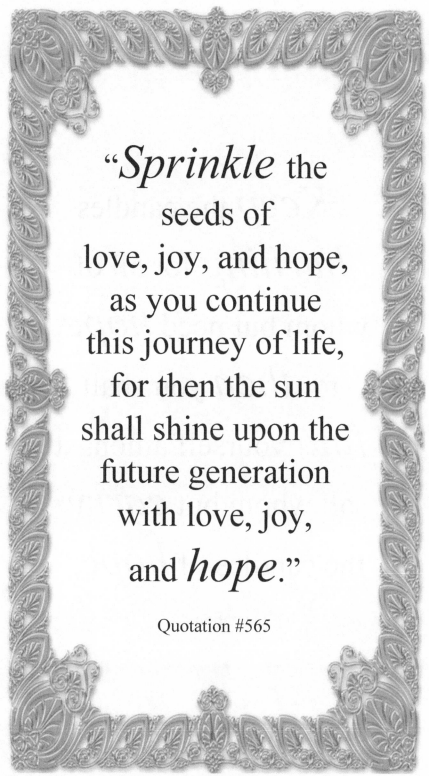

"*Sprinkle* the
seeds of
love, joy, and hope,
as you continue
this journey of life,
for then the sun
shall shine upon the
future generation
with love, joy,
and *hope*."

Quotation #565

"*Keep* the candles *burning* for all of whom but need *hope*, for *then* you shall *find* yourself amongst all whom but *carry* the candles of *hope*."

Quotation #566

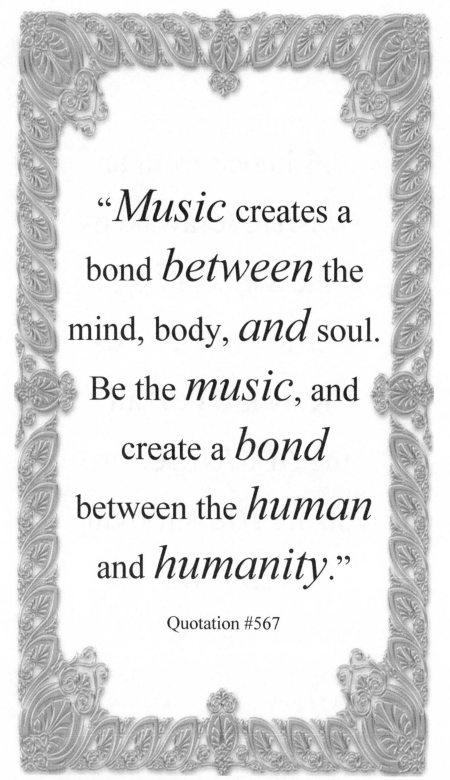

"*Music* creates a bond *between* the mind, body, *and* soul. Be the *music*, and create a *bond* between the *human* and *humanity*."

Quotation #567

"*A* knock from an *obstacle* awakens the *surviving* warrior *within* us. Knock *over* all the *obstacles* as you are *the* surviving *warrior*."

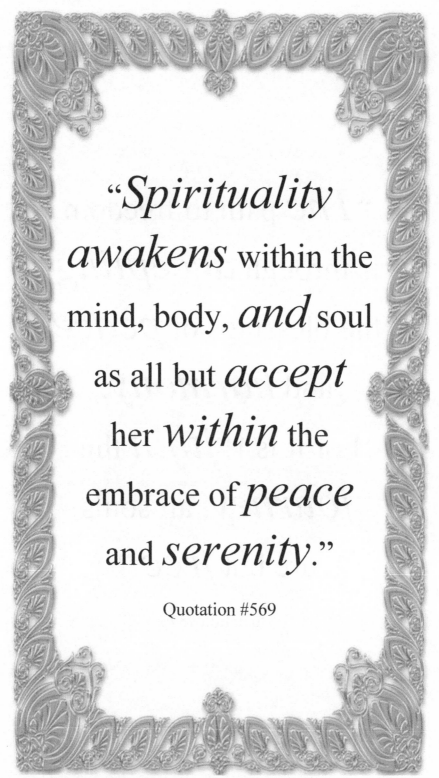

"*Spirituality awakens* within the mind, body, *and* soul as all but *accept* her *within* the embrace of *peace* and *serenity*."

Quotation #569

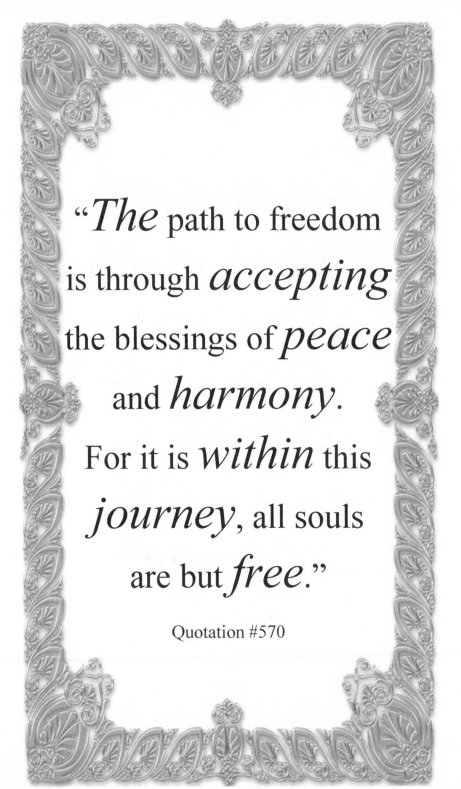

"*The* path to freedom is through *accepting* the blessings of *peace* and *harmony*. For it is *within* this *journey*, all souls are but *free*."

Quotation #570

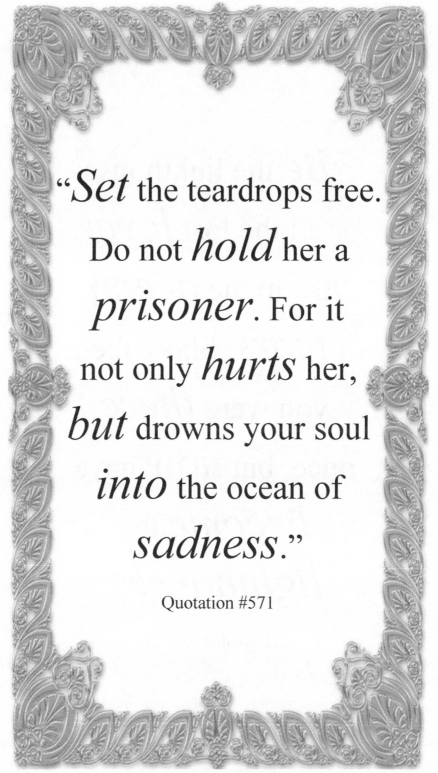

"*Set* the teardrops free. Do not *hold* her a *prisoner*. For it not only *hurts* her, *but* drowns your soul *into* the ocean of *sadness*."

Quotation #571

"*Be* the lighthouse for all the lost *lovers* lost in the *ocean* of *tears*. Show them you were *there* once, but *now* have *become* the *lighthouse*."

Quotation #572

"*Spiritual* inspiration is *born* within the eternal love *of* each spiritually *inspired*. Be the *inspiration* as you *inspire* all *throughout* this journey of *life*."

Quotation #573

"*Even* within the ocean of *sin*, be the *awakened* soul, the *eternal* lamp, who but ignites *hope* back to *all* lost and stranded *souls*."

Quotation #574

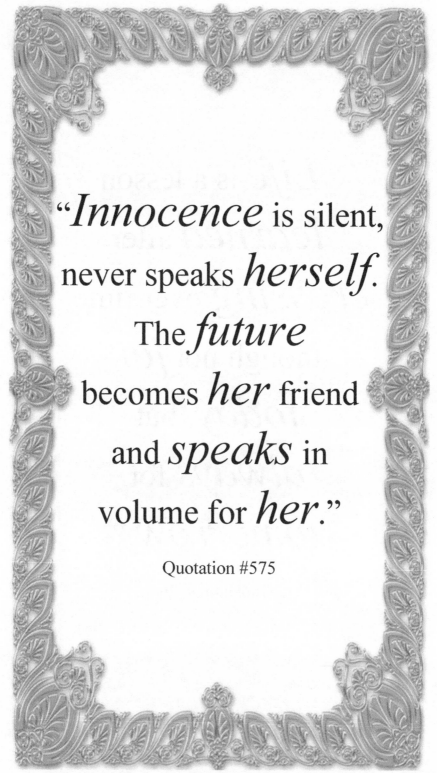

"*Innocence* is silent, never speaks *herself*. The *future* becomes *her* friend and *speaks* in volume for *her*."

Quotation #575

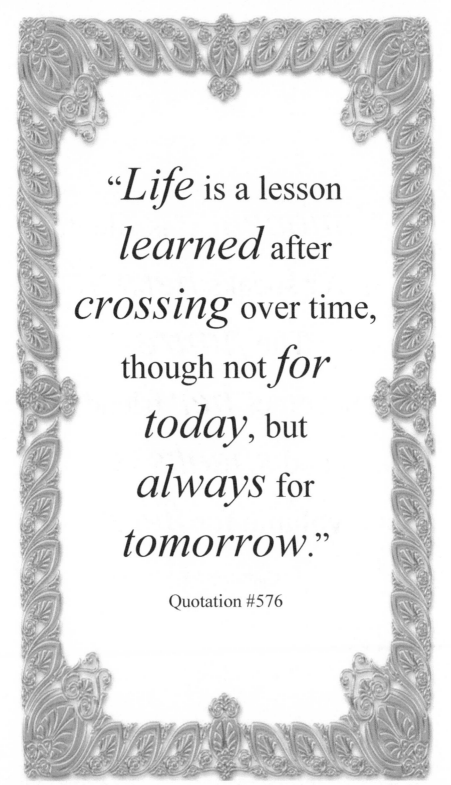

"*Life* is a lesson *learned* after *crossing* over time, though not *for* *today*, but *always* for *tomorrow*."

Quotation #576

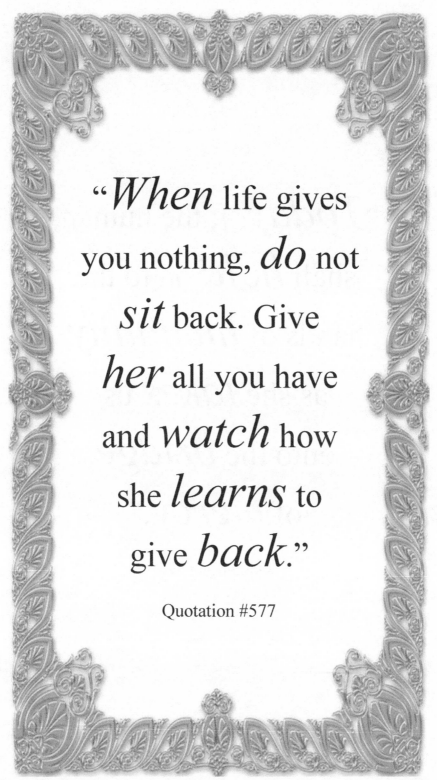

"*When* life gives you nothing, *do* not *sit* back. Give *her* all you have and *watch* how she *learns* to give *back*."

Quotation #577

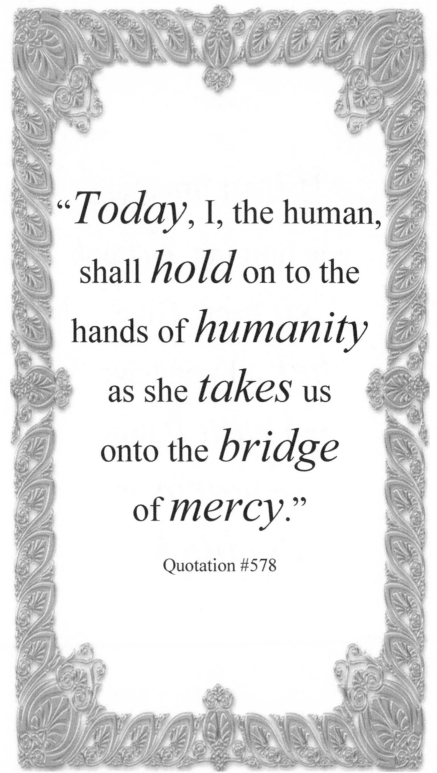

"*Today*, I, the human, shall *hold* on to the hands of *humanity* as she *takes* us onto the *bridge* of *mercy*."

Quotation #578

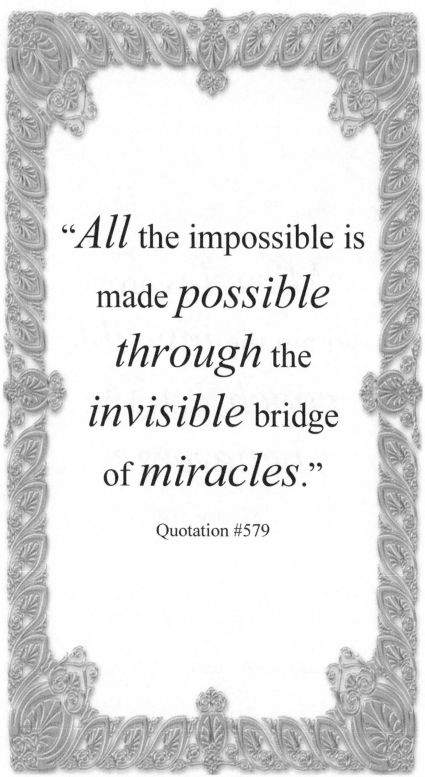

"*All* the impossible is made *possible through* the *invisible* bridge of *miracles.*"

Quotation #579

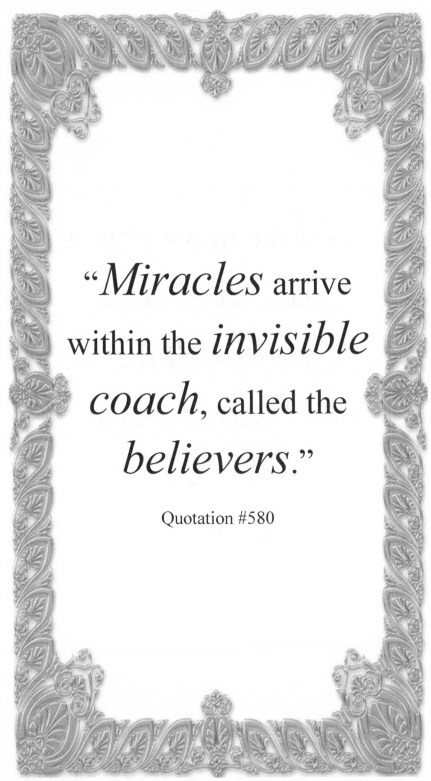

"*Miracles* arrive within the *invisible coach*, called the *believers*."

Quotation #580

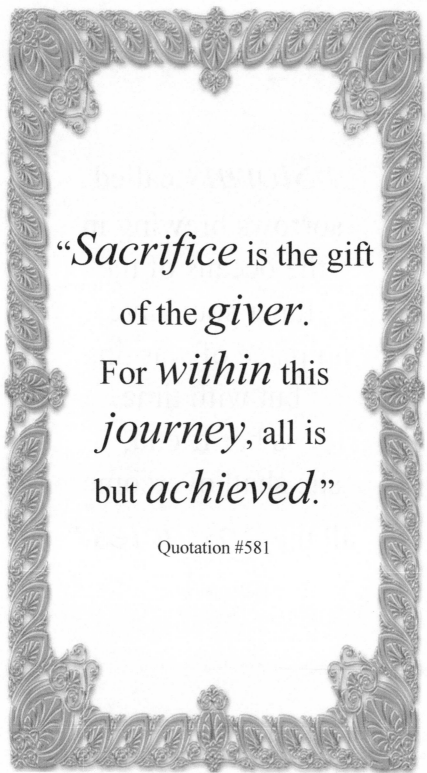

"*Sacrifice* is the gift of the *giver*. For *within* this *journey*, all is but *achieved*."

Quotation #581

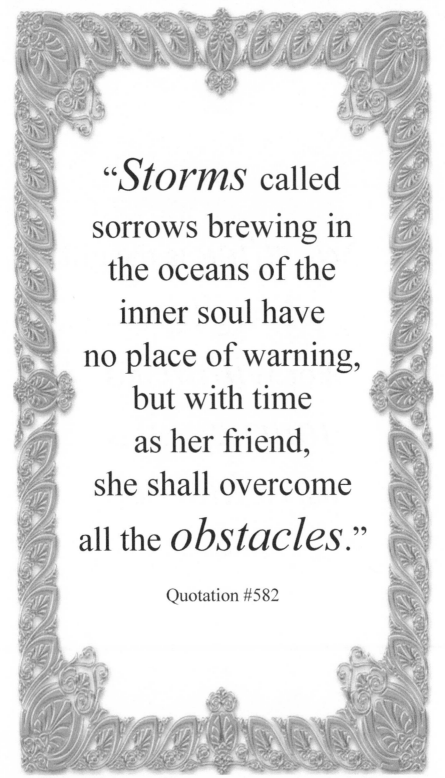

"*Storms* called sorrows brewing in the oceans of the inner soul have no place of warning, but with time as her friend, she shall overcome all the *obstacles*."

Quotation #582

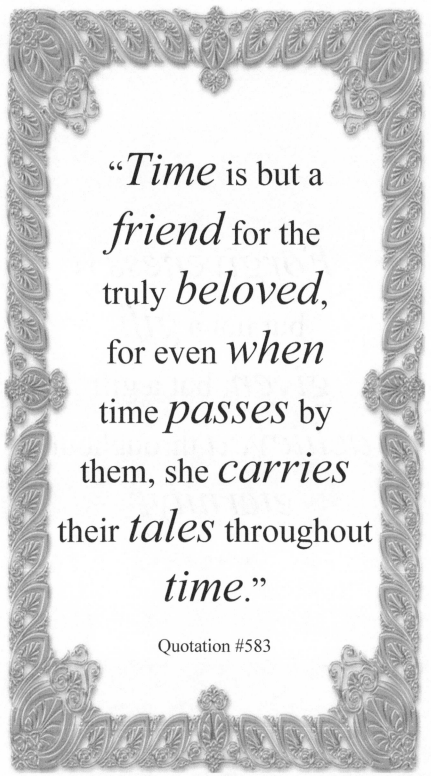

"*Time* is but a *friend* for the truly *beloved*, for even *when* time *passes* by them, she *carries* their *tales* throughout *time*."

Quotation #583

"*Forgiveness* is but not a *gift given*, but a gift *achieved* throughout *eternity*."

Quotation #584

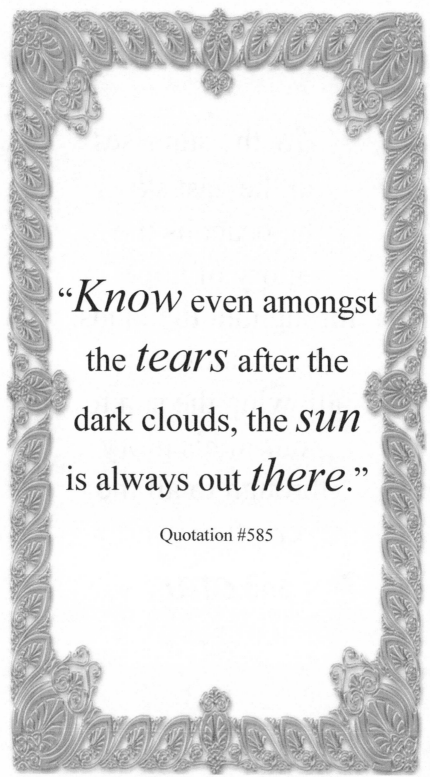

"*Know* even amongst the *tears* after the dark clouds, the *sun* is always out *there*."

Quotation #585

"*As* the sun rises
in the vast sky,
he beacons the
glory of hope
throughout the lands.
The windows open
allowing the sun to
pour in his glory
through to all the
creation near
and *afar*."

Quotation #586

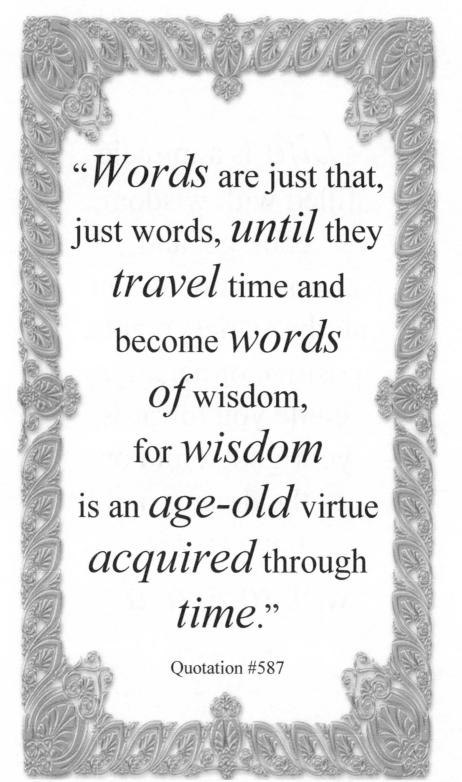

"*Words* are just that, just words, *until* they *travel* time and become *words of* wisdom, for *wisdom* is an *age-old* virtue *acquired* through *time*."

Quotation #587

"*Life* is a miracle filled with wisdom, courage, and disappointment. Let all the achievements, positive or negative, guide you towards your goal. Hold on to the dreams and hope as you walk *forward*."

Quotation #588

"*Yes*, there will be hurdles on your path as she is our companion of life. Remind yourself during all the storms of life, there is always hope our other companion of life. Keep her alive as she will guide all towards *victory*."

Quotation #589

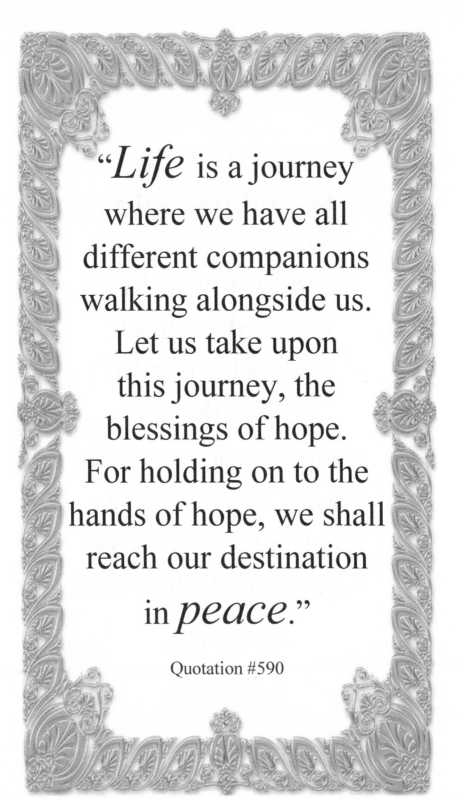

"*Life* is a journey where we have all different companions walking alongside us. Let us take upon this journey, the blessings of hope. For holding on to the hands of hope, we shall reach our destination in *peace*."

Quotation #590

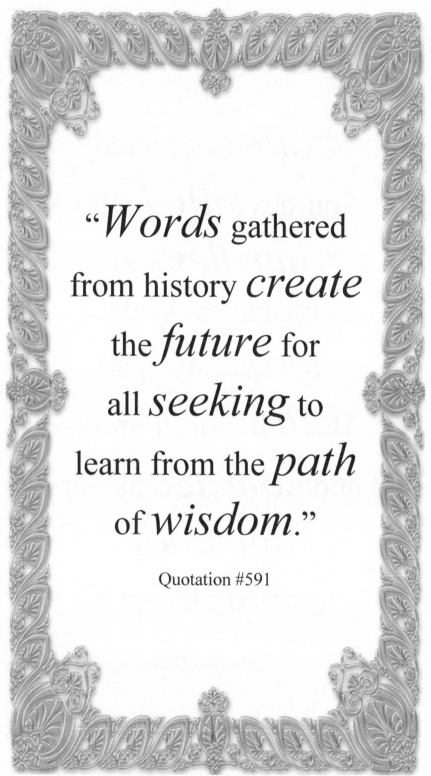

"*Words* gathered from history *create* the *future* for all *seeking* to learn from the *path* of *wisdom*."

Quotation #591

"*Life* is a sacred journey *filled* with *hurdles* and obstacles. Walk *across* this path *with* honor, dignity, and *courage* as our *spiritual companion*."

Quotation #592

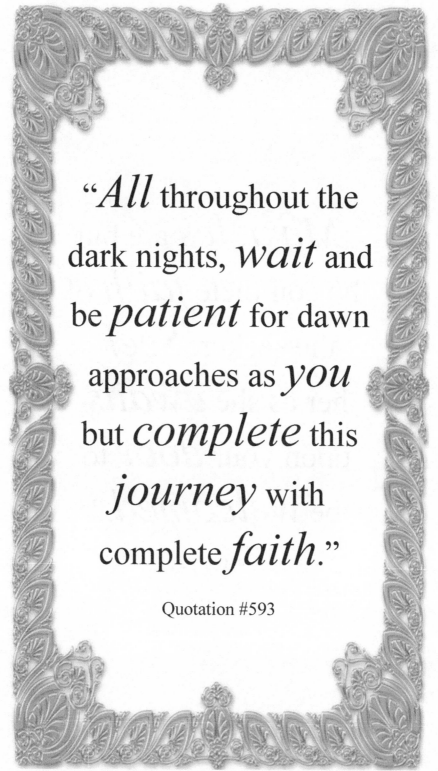

"*All* throughout the dark nights, *wait* and be *patient* for dawn approaches as *you* but *complete* this *journey* with complete *faith*."

Quotation #593

"*Miracles* are but the complete *faith* of the seeker. *Seek* her as she *awaits* upon your *door* to be *welcomed*."

Quotation #594

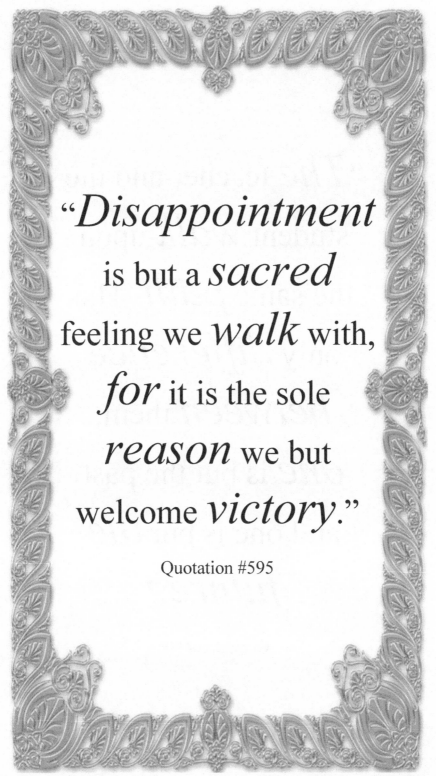

"*Disappointment* is but a *sacred* feeling we *walk* with, *for* it is the sole *reason* we but welcome *victory*."

Quotation #595

"*The* teacher and the student *walk* upon the same *path*. The only *difference between* them, *one* is but the past and one is but *the future*."

Quotation #596

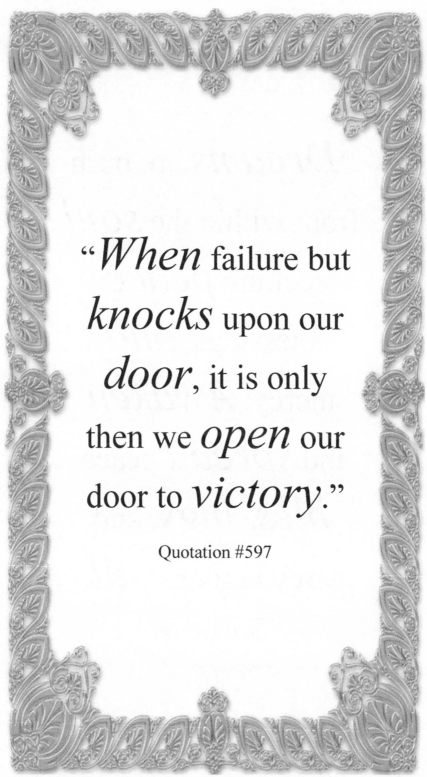

"*When* failure but *knocks* upon our *door*, it is only then we *open* our door to *victory*."

Quotation #597

"*Dreams* are born from within the *soul* seeking *peace*, blessings, *and* mercy. *Awaken* and *spread* peace, *blessings*, and mercy amongst *all*."

Quotation #598

"*Life* brings pain and joy upon our *boat* as we *take* the spiritual *journey* through this *ocean* of life, always *praying* for the *lighthouse* to guide *us*."

Quotation #599

ABOUT THE AUTHOR

I am an unknown person who lived the struggles, overcame the obstacles, as I have endured the pain and joy of life as they landed upon my door.

I like to be the unknown face to whom all can relate. I want you to see your face in the mirror when you search for me, not mine. For if it is my face in the mirror, then my friend you see a stranger. The unknown face is there so you see only yourself, your struggles, your achievements as you cross the journey of life. I want to be the face of a white, black, and brown, as well as the love we are always searching eternally for. If this world would have allowed, I would have distributed this inspirational quotation book to you with my own hands as a gift from a friend. Please take this book as a message from a friend.

You have my name and know I will always be there for anyone who seeks me. You can follow me @AnnahMariahRuby on Twitter, Ann Marie on my personal Facebook profile where the username is /annah.mariah.735, @TheAnnMarieRuby on my Facebook page, ann_marie_ruby on Instagram, and @TheAnnMarieRuby on Pinterest.

For more information about any one of my books, please visit my website www.annmarieruby.com.

I have published four books of original inspirational quotations:

Spiritual Travelers: Life's Journey From The Past To The Present For The Future

Spiritual Messages: From A Bottle

Spiritual Journey: Life's Eternal Blessings

Spiritual Inspirations: Sacred Words Of Wisdom

For all of you whom have requested my complete inspirational quotations, now I have for all of you, my complete ark of inspiration, I but call:

Spiritual Ark: The Enchanted Journey Of Timeless Quotations.

I have also published a book of original prayers:

Spiritual Songs: Letters From My Chest.

I am blessed to also share with you information about my upcoming book:

Spiritual Lighthouse: The Dream Diaries Of Ann Marie Ruby.

I give you samples from my prayer book, *Spiritual Songs: Letters From My Chest* as I have written this book of prayers from my heart for all of whom seek the spiritual journey.

THE HOLY ARK

My Lord, forgive me for the sins

I carry along with me.

My Lord, save me

From all the natural and unnatural calamities,

And the sins conjoined within them.

My Lord, let there be no sin

Around, above, or beyond me.

My Lord, let the Divine halo glow all around me

So I may be in Your Divine Presence for eternity.

My Lord, may I be amongst the redeemers

Saved by Your Divine Mercy.

My Lord, let the sinners around me be saved

From their sins by their repentance.

My Lord, may I walk upon The Divine Path

Lighted by Your Holy Messengers.

My Lord, accept me upon the abode of

THE HOLY ARK.

*From my prayer book, *Spiritual Songs: Letters From My Chest*.

THE ARK OF MY LORD

Let not me be tempted.

Let not I attempt.

Let not there be any sin committed

By me my Lord.

For all around, I see is sin.

All around the air, the sky, the ground, on, above,

And beyond me is smogged up with sin my Lord.

The dark night's sin has polluted the air

Which is but drowning me my Lord.

I feel the waves of sin piercing through my skin,

Through this cold, winter's night my Lord.

The vast ocean of sinful sin all around is

But drowning me my Lord.

I shall fearlessly attempt to find the stream of

Pureness in this dark night's sinful ocean my Lord.

There is but a glass barrier made out of sin

Between You and me my Lord.

May my prayers of repentance pierce through

And break this barrier my Lord.

I see a stream of light piercing

Through the glass my Lord.

I attempt to break the glass of sin

With my redemption my Lord.

I float above the water,

For I am the redeemer floating

Above the ocean of sin my Lord.

I must repent, redeem, and awaken

To break the glass barrier

Between my Lord and myself.

Alone, lost, and drifted I might feel.

Even yet, I know I must awaken first my Lord.

For it is then, I can awaken all the others

From this deep devotional sleep of sin my Lord.

With this newfound awakening and complete faith, I

call upon my Lord.

I feel the glass barrier shatter

And the pure glass of water wash

And bathe me my Lord.

Finally, I see my Lord's Ark of Angels

Bring forth my Lord.

As I reach out, my Lord is there.

As I ask for direction, my Lord is there.

As I seek for attention, my Lord is there.

As I knock, my Lord picks me up

From the dark ocean of sin onto

THE ARK OF

MY LORD.

*From my prayer book, *Spiritual Songs: Letters From My Chest*.

My Spiritual Collection

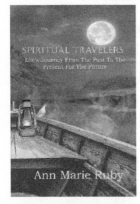

Spiritual Travelers:
Life's Journey From
The Past To The Present
For The Future

Spiritual Messages:
From A Bottle

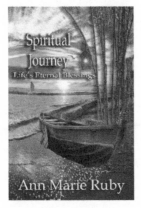

Spiritual Journey:
Life's Eternal Blessings

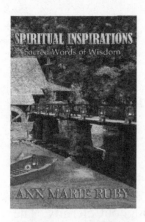

Spiritual Inspirations:
Sacred Words Of
Wisdom

Spiritual Ark:
The Enchanted
Journey Of Timeless
Quotations

Spiritual Songs:
Letters From My Chest

My Upcoming Book

Spiritual Lighthouse:
The Dream Diaries Of Ann Marie Ruby

Within the dark, starless, foggy nights, my dreams appeared like the lighthouse always guiding me throughout my life. Dreams are spiritual guidance from the unknown. When the human body but falls asleep, it is then that our spiritual soul guides us throughout eternity. The soul walks into a parallel world where the past and the future exist in the same universe. Walk with me, as my soul but has walked the past and the future all throughout my life. Warnings, dangers, and surprises came upon my door, always guiding me like a lighthouse blinking in the dark night's sky. Alone, lost, and stranded I was until a lighthouse appeared within the ocean of the lost, my blessed dreams.

Take my hands and walk with me along this very personal path, as we journey together through my dream diaries, I call her, *Spiritual Lighthouse: The Dream Diaries Of Ann Marie Ruby*.

"Dreams are given from the Heavens above onto all within the Earth beneath for within them lie the miracles of eternity."

636

Made in the USA
Las Vegas, NV
04 October 2023

78557114R00374